D1646174

LONGMAN LITERATURE SHAKESPEARE

Hamlet

William Shakespeare

Editors: Julia Markus and Paul Jordan

New Longman Shakespeare Series

Contents

Introduction

Shakespeare's life and times

Shakespeare was born into a time of change. Important discoveries about the world were changing people's whole way of life, their thoughts and their beliefs. The fact that we know very little of Shakespeare's particular life story does not mean that we cannot step into his world.

What do we know about Shakespeare?

Imagine for a minute you are Shakespeare, born in 1564, the son of a businessman who is making his way in Stratford-upon-Avon. When you are thirteen, Francis Drake sets off on a dangerous sea voyage around the world, to prove that it is round, not flat, and to bring back riches. The trades people who pass in and out of your town bring with them stories of other countries, each with their own unique culture and language. You learn in school of ancient heroic myths taught through Latin and Greek, and often, to bring these stories alive, travelling theatres pass through the town acting, singing, performing, and bringing with them tales of London. But, at the age of fourteen your own world shifts a little under your feet; your father has got into serious debt, you find yourself having to grow up rather fast.

This is an unremarkable life so far – the death of your sisters is not an uncommon occurrence at this time, and even when you marry at eighteen, your bride already pregnant at the ceremony, you are not the first to live through life in this way. After your daughter, your wife gives birth to twins, a girl and a boy, one of whom dies when he is eleven. But before this, for some reason only you know, perhaps to do with some poaching you are involved in or because your marriage to a woman eight years older than you is having difficulties, you travel to London. There you eventually join the theatre, first as an actor and then as a writer. You write for the theatres in the inn yards, then for Queen Elizabeth in court, and when she dies, for King James I. As well as this you write for the large theatres which are being built in London: the Rose, the Globe, Blackfriars and the Swan. You die a rich man.

What did Shakespeare find in London?

When Shakespeare first travelled to London he found a city full of all that was best and'worst in this new era of discovery. There was trade in expensive and fashionable items, a bubbling street life with street-theatre, pedlars of every sort, sellers of songs and poems. Industry was flourishing in textiles, mining, the manufacture of glass, iron and sugar. The place to be known was the court of Queen Elizabeth. She was unmarried and drew many admirers even in her old age, maintaining a dazzling social world with her at its centre. There were writers and poets, grasping what they could of the new world, building on the literature of other countries, charting the lingering death of medieval life and the chaotic birth of something new.

By contrast, Shakespeare also found poverty, death and disease. The plague, spread by rats, found an easy home in these narrow streets, often spilling over with dirt and sewage: it killed 15,000 people in London in 1592 alone. It was an overcrowded city: the increased demand for wool for trade brought about the enclosure of land in the countryside, and this, coupled with bad harvests, brought the peasants, thrown off their land and made poor, into London to seek wealth.

What was England like in Shakespeare's day?

England was a proud nation. Elizabeth would not tolerate rivals and destroyed her enemies. In 1587 she had Mary Queen of Scots executed for treason, and in 1588 her navy defeated a huge armada of ships from Spain. Both acts were prompted by religion. In maintaining the Protestant Church of England her father, King Henry VIII, had established, Elizabeth stood out against a strong Catholic Europe. Within the Protestant religion too, there were divisions, producing extreme groups such as the Puritans who believed that much of the Elizabethan social scene was sinful, the theatres being one of their clearest targets for disapproval. Her power was threatened for other reasons too. In 1594 her doctor was executed for attempting to poison her, and in 1601 one of her favourites, the Earl of Essex, led an unsuccessful revolt against her.

When Elizabeth died in 1603 and James I succeeded her, he brought a change. He was a Scottish king, and traditionally Scotland and England had had an uneasy relationship. He was interested in witchcraft and he supported the arts, but not in the same way as Elizabeth had. He too met with treason, in the shape of Guy Fawkes and his followers, who in 1605 attempted to blow up The Houses of Parliament. If Shakespeare needed examples of life at its extremes, he had them all around him, and his closeness to the court meant he understood them more than most.

What other changes did Shakespeare see?

Towards the end of Shakespeare's life, in Italy, a man Shakespeare's age invented the telescope and looked at the stars. His radical discoveries caused him to be thrown out of the Catholic Church. For fifteen centuries people had believed in a picture of the universe as held in crystal spheres with order and beauty, and everything centring around the earth. In this belief the sun, moon and stars were the heavens; they ruled human fate, they were distant and magical. Galileo proved this was not so. So, the world was no longer flat and the earth was not the centre of the universe. It must have felt as if nothing was to be trusted any more.

What do Shakespeare's plays show us about Elizabethan life?

Even without history books much of Shakespeare's life can be seen in his plays. They are written by one who knows of the tragedy of sudden death, and illness, and of the splendour of the life of the court in contrast to urban and rural poverty. He knows the ancient myths of the Greeks and Romans, the history of change in his own country, and, perhaps from reading the translations carried by merchants to London, he knows the literature of Spain and Italy.

His plays also contain all the hustle and bustle of normal life at the time. We see the court fool, the aristocracy, royalty, merchants and the servant classes. We hear of bear-baiting, fortune-telling, entertaining, drinking, dancing and singing. As new changes happen they are brought into the plays, in the form of maps, clocks, or the latest fashions. Shakespeare wrote to perform, and his plays were performed to bring financial reward. He studied his audience closely and produced what they wanted. Sometimes, as with the focus on witchcraft in **Macbeth** written for King James I, this was the celebration of something which fascinated them; sometimes, as with the character of Shylock in **The Merchant of Venice**, it was the mockery of something they despised.

What do Shakespeare's plays tell us about life now?

You can read Shakespeare's plays to find out about Elizabethan life, but in them you will also see reflected back at you the unchanging aspects of humanity. It is as if in all that changed around him, Shakespeare looked for the things that would *not* change — like love, power, honour, friendship and loyalty — and put them to the test. In each he found strength and weakness.

We see *love*:

- which is one-sided,
- between young lovers,
- in old age,
- between members of one family,
- lost and found again.

We see *power*:

- used and abused,
- in those who seek it,
- in those who protect it with loyalty,
- in the just and merciful rule of wise leaders,
- in the hands of unscrupulous tyrants.

We see *honour*:

- in noble men and women,
- lost through foolishness,
- stolen away through trickery and disloyalty.

We see *friendship*:

- between men and men, women and women, men and women,
- between masters and servants,
- put to the test of jealousy, grief and misunderstanding.

These are just some examples of how Shakespeare explored in his plays what it was to be human. He lived for fifty-two years and wrote thirty-seven plays, as well as a great number of poems. Just in terms of output this is a remarkable achievement. What is even more remarkable is the way in which he provides a window for his audiences into all that is truly human, and it is this quality that often touches us today.

What are Comedies, Tragedies and Histories?

When Shakespeare died, his players brought together the works he had written, and had them published. Before this some of the plays had only really existed as actors' scripts written for their parts alone. Many plays in Shakespeare's day and before were not written down at all, but spoken, and kept in people's memories from generation to generation. So, making accurate copies of Shakespeare's plays was not easy and there is still much dispute over how close to the original scripts our current editions are. Ever since they were first published people have tried to make sense of them.

Sometimes they are described under three headings: Comedy, Tragedy and History. The dates on the chart that follows refer to the dates of the first recorded performances or, if this is not known, the date of first publication. They may have been performed earlier but history has left us no record; dating the plays exactly is therefore difficult.

COMEDY	HISTORY	TRAGEDY
	King John (1590)	
	Henry VI, Part I (1592)	
Comedy of Errors (1594) *The Taming of the Shrew* (1594) *Two Gentlemen of Verona* (1594)		*Titus Andronicus* (1594)
The Merry Wives of Windsor (1597)	*Richard II* (1597) *Richard III* (1597)	*Romeo and Juliet* (1597)
The Merchant of Venice (1598) *Love's Labour's Lost* (1598)	*Henry IV, Part II* (1598)	
As You Like it (1600) *A Midsummer Night's Dream* (1600) *Much Ado About Nothing* (1600) *Twelfth Night* (1600)	*Henry V* (1600) *Henry VI, Part II* (1600) *Henry VI, Part III* (1600)	
Troilus and Cressida (1601)		
		Hamlet (1602)
Measure for Measure (1604) *All's Well That Ends Well* (1604)	*Henry IV, Part I* (1604)	*Othello* (1604)

COMEDY	HISTORY	TRAGEDY
		Julius Caesar (1605)
		Macbeth (1606) King Lear (1606)
		Antony and Cleopatra (1608) Timons of Athens (1608) Coriolanus (1608)
Pericles (1609)		
Cymbeline (1611) The Winter's Tale (1611)		
The Tempest (1612)	Henry VIII (1612)	

Comedy = a play which maintains a thread of joy throughout and ends happily for most of its characters.

Tragedy = a play in which characters must struggle with circumstances and in which most meet death and despair.

History = a play focusing on a real event or series of events which actually happened in the past.

These three headings can be misleading. Many of the comedies have great sadness in them, and there is humour in most of the tragedies, some of which at least point to happier events in the future. Some of the tragedies, like **Hamlet** and **Julius Caesar**, make history their starting point.

We do not know exactly when each play was written but from what we know of when they were performed we can see that Shakespeare began by writing poetry, then histories and comedies. He wrote most of his tragedies in the last ten years of his life, and in his final writings wrote stories full of near-tragic problems which, by the end of the plays, he resolved. Sometimes these final plays (**Pericles**, **Cymbeline, The Winter's Tale** and **The Tempest**) are called Comedies, sometimes they are called Romances or simply The Late Plays.

Where were Shakespeare's plays performed?

Plays in Shakespeare's day were performed in several places, not just in specially designed theatres.

Inn Yard Theatres: Players performed in the open courtyards of Elizabethan inns. These were places where people could drink, eat and stay the night. They were popular places to make a break in a journey and to change or rest horses. Some inns built a permanent platform in the yard, and the audience could stand in the yard itself, or under shelter in the galleries which overlooked the yard. The audiences were lively and used to the active entertainment of bear-baiting, cock-fighting, wrestling and juggling. Plays performed here needed to be action-packed and appealing to a wide audience. In 1574 new regulations were made to control performances in response to the number of fights which regularly broke out in the audience.

Private House Theatres: The rich lords of Elizabethan times would pay travelling theatre companies to play in the large rooms of their own private houses for the benefit of their friends. There was no stage and the audience were all seated. Torches and candles were used to create artificial lighting. Costumes played an important part in creating atmosphere but there were no sets.

Public Hall Theatres: Some town councils would allow performances of plays in their grand halls and council buildings. As well as this, ceremonial halls such as the Queen's courts in Whitehall were frequently used in this way, as were halls at Hampton Court, Richmond and Greenwich Palace. For these performances, designed for a larger audience than those given in private houses, scaffolding would be arranged for tiered seating which would surround a central acting area. Audiences were limited to those with a high social standing.

Public Theatres: Unlike Public Hall theatres, these theatres were built for the purpose of presenting plays. At the end of the sixteenth century there were about 200,000 people living in London, and eleven public theatres showing performances. Of these, about half a dozen were so large that they seated about 2,000 people. The audiences, who were drawn from all sections of society, paid to see performances which began at 2 p.m. The audience sat in covered galleries or stood in an open courtyard which also contained the stage. Whilst the theatres were within the City of London they were subject to its laws. They could not perform during times of worship, and they were closed during outbreaks of the plague. Theatres were often the scenes of fighting and because of the trouble this caused, in 1596 performances of plays were forbidden within the city boundaries. Thus, people started building theatres outside the city on the south side of the River Thames.

What were the performances like?

To some extent this depended on the play being performed and the audience watching. A play performed before the court of the queen or king would need to be one that did not offend the ruler. Plays performed in the inn yard or the public theatres needed to have a wide appeal and several distractions such as dancing and music to keep the audience's attention.

Wherever they performed, the players had to create the illusion that the whole world could be seen inside their play. They had no sets, except in some cases tapestries which were hung up to show changes in scenery, but they did have bright costumes in which to perform. Scenes of battle or shipwreck were suggested by words rather than special effects, though we do know that they used burning torches, as it was due to a fire caused by one of these that the first Globe Theatre burnt down during a performance in 1613.

Actors joined together in companies, who would perform several different plays, and be sponsored by the nobility. Shakespeare became a key member of the Lord Chamberlain's company which Queen Elizabeth sponsored, and which went on to be called The King's Men when James I became king.

There were no women on the Elizabethan stage. Most female characters would be played by boys whose voices had not yet broken, or if it was an old character, by men in the company. Actors carried a reputation for being immoral and ungodly people, and were therefore thought unsuitable company for women. The men of Shakespeare's company became famous for playing particular types of characters such as the fool, the lover or the villain. Shakespeare probably created many of his parts with particular actors in mind.

Where can I find out more about Shakespeare?

Shakespeare is perhaps the world's most famous playwright and there is no shortage of books written about him. In your library or bookshop you will find books which look at:

- Shakespeare's life;
- the history of England under the reign of Queen Elizabeth I and James I;
- European history, art and literature of the sixteenth and seventeenth century;
- discoveries made throughout the world during Elizabethan times;
- characters, themes and ideas in Shakespeare's writing.

In Stratford-upon-Avon you can visit his birthplace, and much of the town consists of buildings which would have stood in Shakespeare's day. In addition to this there are many museums and exhibitions which tell more about Shakespeare's life and work.

Some theatrical companies today, such as the Royal Shakespeare Company, devote themselves to performing Shakespeare's plays in London, Stratford, and on tour around the country. They are always seeking new ways to bring the plays to life. However, perhaps the best way to find out more about Shakespeare is to study his plays by reading and acting them yourself. Shakespeare wrote about what he knew, and the key to discovering how his mind and emotions worked is to look at what he wrote.

Shakespeare's language

Speaking Shakespeare

This is probably not the first play by Shakespeare that you have studied, and so you may already have encountered the richness and complexity of his language. It may seem an obvious point, but Shakespeare didn't write books: he wrote plays to be performed by actors in front of audiences, so *hearing* the words of the play is very important. However, speaking the lines can be difficult at first, for several reasons:

- The plays were written about four hundred years ago, and the English language has changed considerably since then. Some words Shakespeare uses in **Hamlet**, like 'espials', 'fardels' or 'berattle' have dropped out of the language altogether. Others have changed their meaning: for instance when the Ghost says he was 'disappointed' when he was killed, you might think this is a curious understatement until you realise that in Shakespeare's day the word meant 'unprepared' rather than the present meaning. The notes opposite the text will help you with these difficulties.

- Much of **Hamlet** is written in verse, which is of course not a medium of everyday speech.

- The language is dense with imagery: simile, metaphor and personification are in constant use.

- Partly because of the imagery, the language is often tightly packed with meaning. It can take several sentences of modern English to 'unpack' just a phrase or two of Shakespeare's language.

The best way to start building your confidence as a reader is to practise. If you are studying the play as a group, you will probably be reading all or most of it aloud. Below are some tips for effective reading. It might be an idea to practise reading aloud in pairs before you get engrossed in the story.

- Pause at commas, colons and semi-colons.
- Take a breath at the full stops at the end of sentences.
- Don't pause at the end of lines unless the punctuation tells you to.
- Try to follow the meaning of the words, placing emphasis on appropriate words in order to get the meaning across.
- Read at a normal speaking pace, not quicker or slower.
- Don't worry about making mistakes. Everyone does!

'I've heard that before somewhere . . .'

Hamlet is probably the best-known play of England's best-known playwright, so it is not surprising that many of its lines have entered the English language. If you look 'more in sorrow than anger', suspect 'foul play', tread the 'primrose path' or behave as if 'to the manner born', you are quoting from *Hamlet*. So are you if you advise someone 'neither a borrower nor a lender be', or that 'brevity is the soul of wit', or 'to thine own self be true'. You can't 'speak daggers' or 'be cruel only to be kind' or 'protest too much' without quoting *Hamlet*, and where would thriller writers be without 'murder most foul'? Hamlet was the first to tell us that every 'dog will have his day', and to suffer 'heartache'.

Prose and blank verse

Every play by Shakespeare is written partly in *prose* (ordinary written language) and partly in *verse,* which may or may not rhyme. If it does not rhyme, it is called *blank verse*.

Most of *Hamlet* is in blank verse. The verse-form of most of the verse in the play, as in all of Shakespeare's plays, is known as *iambic pentameters.* A pentameter is a line of verse with five stressed syllables, and an iambic pentameter is one where each stressed syllable is preceded by one that is unstressed, making a total of ten syllables in the line.

Stress may be an unfamiliar concept to you when discussing language. The name 'William Shakespeare' consists of four syllables, alternately stressed and unstressed. The rhythm of an iambic pentameter sounds very natural in everyday speech, and you probably speak several iambic pentameters in the course of a day without knowing it in saying things like 'I'll have some chips and burgers for my lunch', or 'Oh dear! My English homework's overdue'. An example of a pair of perfectly regular iambic pentameters in **Hamlet**, which also incidentally rhyme, comes at the end of Act 1, scene 5, lines 206–7:

> The time is out of joint. O cursed spite,
> That ever I was born to set it right!

The word 'cursed' is pronounced with two syllables, as 'curse-ed', so using ' to show a stressed syllable and – to show an unstressed syllable, the stress patterns of the lines look like this:

> The time is out of joint. O cursed spite,

> That ever I was born to set it right!

The verse in **Hamlet**, however, is rarely this regular for long. Shakespeare uses the basic pattern very freely. The famous line:

> To be, or not to be – that is the question

has eleven syllables, and its five stresses should probably come like this:

> To be, or not to be – that is the question

with the regular iambic rhythm disrupted half-way through the line. Think of the verse-form as a basic, underlying pulse in the verse rather than a straightjacket which constricts freedom of expression. At times of high tension, and for deliberate dramatic effect, Shakespeare sometimes allows the verse-form to break down altogether. For example in Hamlet's soliloquy after he has met the ghost, he exclaims 'O most pernicious woman!' (Act 1, scene 5, line 111) in the middle of a speech which is otherwise in pentameters.

Now let us look at how the meaning is built up over several lines. This is part of a speech of Hamlet's, early in the play, taken from a soliloquy in which he is decrying his widowed mother's over-hasty re-marriage:

> Must I remember? Why, she would hang on him
> As if increase of appetite had grown
> By what it fed on; and yet, within a month –
> Let me not think on't. Frailty, thy name is woman!

> (Act 1, scene 2, lines 145–8)

How many of these lines, incidentally, conform exactly to the pattern of the iambic pentameter? Notice also that although the extract consists of three sentences, only one of them ends at the end of a line. There is no punctuation between 'Why, she' and 'fed on', indicating that you should read on rapidly with a barely discernible pause at the line-ends. A line clearly does not necessarily make sense by itself. One of the best ways to read Shakespeare *badly* is to read each line separately, ignoring the punctuation or lack of it. Far better is to read to the punctuation, while keeping the pulse of the verse in the back of your mind.

Although most of the verse in the play is unrhymed, Shakespeare often uses a pair of rhyming lines to signal the end of a scene. The play within the play, 'The Murder of Gonzago', is written in rhymed iambic pentameters.

There are also many passages in the play in prose. Hamlet often speaks prose in scenes where he is pretending to be mad, as does Ophelia when she is genuinely mad. Hamlet also uses prose when addressing characters who are not of noble birth like the gravedigger and the players, or to people for whom he feels contempt, like Rosencrantz, Guildenstern and Osric.

Images

In all Shakespeare's plays there is constant use of *imagery* or *figurative* language such as *similes, metaphors* and *personification*. The difference between figurative and non-figurative language is illustrated economically in the single line of Hamlet's which opens Act 1, scene 4: 'The air bites shrewdly; it is very cold.' First, Hamlet personifies the air as a beast with sharp teeth, and then he says what he means in plain language.

Simile, where one thing is described as being *like* another, is frequently used. For example, Gertrude at one point describes Hamlet as:

> Mad as the sea and wind, when both contend
> Which is the mightier.

(Act 4, scene 1, lines 7–8)

In Act 1, scene 5, lines 21–4, the Ghost tells Hamlet that he is about to tell him a tale which will 'Make thy two eyes, like stars, start from their spheres,' and later, make his hair stand on end 'Like quills upon the fretful porpentine'.

Shakespeare also uses metaphor, where one thing is described as *being* another, as in Hamlet's remark: 'Denmark's a prison' or when he addresses the subterranean voice of the ghost as 'old mole'.

The playwright's use of metaphor can make the text resonate with meaning. After the exit of the tiresome, pedantic, self-important Osric in Act 5, scene 2, Horatio remarks: 'This lapwing runs away with the shell on his head' (line 188). In comparing Osric to a lapwing chick, Horatio implies:

- Osric's immaturity, because he is a chick rather than an adult bird;
- Osric's precociousness, because lapwing chicks can walk very soon after hatching;
- Osric's stupidity, because although he can walk, he can't see where he is going because of the shell on his head.

The fact that I have used forty-four words to explain Shakespeare's ten demonstrates how skilfully compressed the meaning is!

Critics have discovered threads of connected and inter-related imagery running through the play. The most obvious are the constant references to disease, corruption and the overthrow of the laws of nature. Early in the play, Marcellus gives his opinion that: 'Something is rotten in the state of Denmark' (Act 1, scene 4, line 99) and many other examples can be found. Claudius, for example, is referred to as 'garbage' by the

Ghost, and as a 'mildew'd ear' and a 'canker' by Hamlet. Possibly the most revolting example is when Ophelia is referred to in terms of 'breeding maggots in a dead dog' by Hamlet.

Understanding the play

Speaking words correctly and looking out for figurative language will help you to understand what the language means. Here are some more ways to work out the meanings of words and phrases:

- **The words themselves**   Are they similar to modern words? Can you guess their meaning from this? Check the glossary for words that are new to you.
- **The context of the immediate lines**   Is there a general theme in the conversation or speech that might give you some clues?
- **The context of the scene**   Where and when is this scene taking place? What is the main action? Can you picture the scene and pick up clues from the setting?
- **The characters as you understand them**   When you saw this character before, was he or she funny, depressed, scared, serious? Can you guess at the sort of things this person might say and the sort of tone he or she is likely to adopt?

Don't worry if you don't understand every word. On your first reading, or hearing, what is important is getting the gist of what is being said. Shakespeare's language is very rich in its ideas and images. You do not have to understand it all at once: you can enjoy finding out more each time you revisit it.

The Tragedy of Hamlet, Prince of Denmark

Note to readers

The text itself is based, with some emendations, on that prepared by Professor Peter Alexander and adopted by the BBC for their production of *Hamlet*. We have, however, justified the openings of all speeches to the left. This procedure facilitates ease of reading (although we recognize that it tends to obscure the metrical regularity of some passages of dialogue) and is in any case the format in which the earliest editions of Shakespeare's works appeared.

CHARACTERS
in the play

CLAUDIUS, *King of Denmark*
HAMLET, *son to the former and nephew to the present King*
POLONIUS, *Lord Chamberlain*
HORATIO, *friend to Hamlet*
LAERTES, *son to Polonius*

VOLTEMAND	
CORNELIUS	
ROSENCRANTZ	
GUILDENSTERN	*Courtiers*
OSRIC	
A Gentleman	
A Priest	

MARCELLUS	*Officers*
BERNARDO	

FRANCISCO, *a soldier*
REYNALDO, *servant to Polonius*
Players
Two Clowns, *grave-diggers*
FORTINBRAS, *Prince of Norway*
A Norwegian Captain
English Ambassadors

GERTRUDE, *Queen of Denmark, and mother of Hamlet*
OPHELIA, *daughter to Polonius*

Ghost of Hamlet's Father

Lords, Ladies, Officers, Soldiers, Sailors, Messengers, *and* Attendants

---

The scene: *Denmark*

3

Hamlet (Edward Fox): Young Vic production, 1982.

Two soldiers are on guard at Elsinore Castle. Horatio arrives, asking them about a ghost they have seen. The ghost enters, a silent, warlike figure in the shape of old Hamlet, the recently-dead King of Denmark. Horatio decides to tell his friend Prince Hamlet, old Hamlet's son.

Claudius, brother of old Hamlet and now King of Denmark, is addressing his court. He is celebrating his marriage to his brother's widow, Gertrude. He sends ambassadors to the King of Norway to complain about Fortinbras's plans for war against Denmark.

Laertes, son of Claudius' chief minister, Polonius, seeks leave to return to Paris, which is granted. Claudius questions Hamlet about his gloomy appearance and behaviour. Hamlet says he is sincerely mourning his father's death. Left alone, he speaks of his despair and disgust at his mother's hasty marriage, less than two months after old Hamlet's death. Horatio arrives and tells Hamlet about the ghost. Hamlet decides to watch for the ghost himself that night.

Laertes says goodbye to his sister, Ophelia, warning her of getting too involved with Hamlet, who, as a prince, is unlikely to marry a commoner. Polonius arrives, and instructs his son about his behaviour in France. Laertes leaves, and Polonius tells Ophelia to spend less time with Hamlet. She says she will obey.

On the battlements, Hamlet waits for the ghost with Horatio and Marcellus. When Hamlet speaks to it, it beckons him, and Hamlet follows. The ghost reveals that he was murdered by Claudius, and demands to be revenged. He says that the official story – that he was bitten by a snake while sleeping in his orchard – is a lie. He was really killed by Claudius pouring poison into his ear.

Left alone, Hamlet vows to carry out the ghost's demand. Rejoined by Horatio and Marcellus, Hamlet swears them both to silence about what they have seen. He warns them that he might behave strangely in the future, but they are not even to hint that they know the cause.

s.d. **Elsinore**   a large castle on the east coast of Zealand, an island forming part of Denmark.

guard-platform   level space inside the castle used for mounting guns.

2 **Stand and unfold yourself**   stop and identify yourself.

6 **most carefully upon your hour**   punctually to change the guard.

Act One

Scene one

Elsinore. The guard-platform of the Castle.

FRANCISCO *at his post. Enter to him* BERNARDO.

BERNARDO
  Who's there?

FRANCISCO
  Nay, answer me. Stand and unfold yourself.

BERNARDO
  Long live the King!

FRANCISCO
  Bernardo?

BERNARDO
  He.   5

FRANCISCO
  You come most carefully upon your hour.

BERNARDO
  'Tis now struck twelve; get thee to bed, Francisco.

FRANCISCO
  For this relief much thanks. 'Tis bitter cold,
  And I am sick at heart.

BERNARDO
  Have you had quiet guard?   10

FRANCISCO
  Not a mouse stirring.

14 *rivals*   partners.

16 **ground**   country (i.e. Denmark).

17 **liegemen to the Dane**   loyal subjects of the King of Denmark.

18 **Give you good night**   (may God) give you a good night.

26 **A piece of him**   Horatio is offering Bernardo his hand in the dark.

BERNARDO
Well, good night.
If you do meet Horatio and Marcellus,
The rivals of my watch, bid them make haste.

Enter HORATIO *and* MARCELLUS.

FRANCISCO
I think I hear them. Stand, ho! Who is there?   15

HORATIO
Friends to this ground.

MARCELLUS
And liegemen to the Dane.

FRANCISCO
Give you good night.

MARCELLUS
O, farewell, honest soldier!
Who hath reliev'd you?   20

FRANCISCO
Bernardo hath my place.
Give you good night.

Exit

MARCELLUS
Holla, Bernardo!

BERNARDO
Say –
What, is Horatio there?   25

HORATIO
A piece of him.

30 *fantasy*   imagination.

31 *will not . . . him*   will not allow himself to believe anything.

32 *Touching*   about.

   of us   by us.

33 *entreated*   invited.

36 *approve our eyes*   confirm what we have seen.

39 *assail your ears*   try hard to convince you.

41 *What*   concerning those things.

44 *Last night of all*   only last night.

45 *yond same star*   Bernardo is pointing to a star that is now in the same place in the sky as it was last night when the Ghost appeared – thus preparing us for its reappearance.

46 *illume*   light up.

BERNARDO

Welcome, Horatio; welcome, good Marcellus.

HORATIO

What, has this thing appear'd again to-night?

BERNARDO

I have seen nothing.

MARCELLUS

Horatio says 'tis but our fantasy,   30
And will not let belief take hold of him
Touching this dreaded sight, twice seen of us:
Therefore I have entreated him along
With us to watch the minutes of this night,
That, if again this apparition come,   35
He may approve our eyes and speak to it.

HORATIO

Tush, tush, 'twill not appear.

BERNARDO

Sit down awhile,
And let us once again assail your ears,
That are so fortified against our story,   40
What we have two nights seen.

HORATIO

Well, sit we down,
And let us hear Bernardo speak of this.

BERNARDO

Last night of all,
When yond same star that's westward from the pole 45
Had made his course t' illume that part of heaven
Where now it burns, Marcellus and myself,
The bell then beating one –

49 *Peace, break thee off*   hush, stop talking.

50 *In the same figure*   it has the same appearance as last night.

51 *Thou art a scholar*   Horatio, as a scholar, could speak Latin, the language used in the exorcism of ghosts.

52 *'a*   he.

53 *harrows*   tears into me (like the teeth of a harrow into the earth).

54 *It would be spoke to*   it wants to be spoken to.

56 *usurp'st*   intrudes on. The ghost has upset the peace of the night, and taken on the appearance of the dead king, who should be at rest.

58 *buried Denmark*   the dead King of Denmark.

59 *sometime*s   formerly.

  charge   command.

Enter Ghost.

MARCELLUS

Peace, break thee off; look where it comes again.

BERNARDO

In the same figure, like the King that's dead.   50

MARCELLUS

Thou art a scholar; speak to it, Horatio.

BERNARDO

Looks 'a not like the King? Mark it, Horatio.

HORATIO

Most like. It harrows me with fear and wonder.

BERNARDO

It would be spoke to.

MARCELLUS

Question it, Horatio.   55

HORATIO

What art thou that usurp'st this time of night
Together with that fair and warlike form
In which the majesty of buried Denmark
Did sometimes march? By heaven I charge thee,
    speak!

MARCELLUS

It is offended.   60

BERNARDO

See, it stalks away.

HORATIO

Stay! speak, speak! I charge thee, speak!

                                        Exit Ghost

13

65 **fantasy** imagination.

66 **on't** about it.

67–9 **I might not. . .own eyes** I would not believe this without the undeniable evidence ('true avouch') of my senses ('sensible'), my own eyes.

73 **Norway** king of Norway, the elder Fortinbras.

74 **parle** conference, which led to fighting.

75 **sledded Polacks** Polish army, equipped with sledges.

77 **jump** precisely.

78 **martial stalk** military stride.

79 **In what. . .know not** I do not know exactly what one should do about this.

80 **in the gross. . .opinion** my view in general terms is.

81 **bodes** foretells.

   eruption upheaval.

82 **Good now** well now (starting a new phase of the conversation, maybe after a pregnant pause).

84 **nightly. . .the land** every night puts the people of Denmark to work.

MARCELLUS

'Tis gone, and will not answer.

BERNARDO

How now, Horatio! You tremble and look pale.
Is not this something more than fantasy?   65
What think you on't?

HORATIO

Before my God, I might not this believe
Without the sensible and true avouch
Of mine own eyes.

MARCELLUS

Is it not like the King?   70

HORATIO

As thou art to thyself:
Such was the very armour he had on
When he the ambitious Norway combated;
So frown'd he once when, in an angry parle,
He smote the sledded Polacks on the ice.   75
'Tis strange.

MARCELLUS

Thus twice before, and jump at this dead hour,
With martial stalk hath he gone by our watch.

HORATIO

In what particular thought to work I know not;
But, in the gross and scope of mine opinion,   80
This bodes some strange eruption to our state.

MARCELLUS

Good now, sit down, and tell me, he that knows,
Why this same strict and most observant watch
So nightly toils the subject of the land;

15

85 **why**   why there is.

   daily cast of brazen cannon   daily manufacture of brass cannons.

86 **mart**   trade.

87 **impress**   forcible recruitment.

   sore task   hard labour.

88 **Does not...week**   the ship builders work a seven-day week, with no time off on Sunday.

89 **toward**   about to happen.

90 **joint-labourer**   fellow worker.

93 **whisper goes so**   rumour has it.

94 **even but now**   just now.

96 **prick'd on...pride**   goaded on by ambition to be thought as worthy.

97 **Dar'd to the combat**   challenged to single combat.

   Hamlet   the dead king, whose ghost has just appeared.

98 **so**   i.e. valiant.

   this side...world   everyone in this part of the world.

99 **compact**   treaty.

100 **heraldry**   the recognised codes of chivalry.

102 **he stood seiz'd of**   which belonged to him personally.

103 **Against....moiety competent**   matching this, an equal area of land.

104 **gaged**   wagered.

   which had return'd   which would have been transferred.

106 **cov'nant**   treaty (the one mentioned on line 99).

107 **carriage...design'd**   terms of the agreement.

108 **young Fortinbras**   the dead King of Norway's son.

109 **unimproved mettle**   unrestrained courage.

110 **skirts**   outlying parts.

111–2 **Shark'd...diet**   indiscriminately rounded up (as a 'shark' feeds on anything) a bunch ('list') of determined ruffians ('lawless resolutes') willing to do anything for regular meals ('food and diet').

113 **stomach**   danger.

114 **state**   rulers.

And why such daily cast of brazen cannon,   85
And foreign mart for implements of war;
Why such impress of shipwrights, whose sore task
Does not divide the Sunday from the week;
What might be toward, that this sweaty haste
Doth make the night joint-labourer with the day: 90
Who is't that can inform me?

HORATIO
That can I:
At least, the whisper goes so. Our last king,
Whose image even but now appear'd to us,
Was, as you know, by Fortinbras of Norway,   95
Thereto prick'd on by a most emulate pride,
Dar'd to the combat; in which our valiant Hamlet –
For so this side of our known world esteem'd him –
Did slay this Fortinbras; who, by a seal'd compact,
Well ratified by law and heraldry,   100
Did forfeit, with his life, all those his lands
Which he stood seiz'd of, to the conqueror;
Against the which a moiety competent
Was gaged by our king; which had return'd
To the inheritance of Fortinbras,   105
Had he been vanquisher; as, by the same
   cov'nant
And carriage of the article design'd,
His fell to Hamlet. Now, sir, young Fortinbras,
Of unimproved mettle hot and full,
Hath in the skirts of Norway, here and there, 110
Shark'd up a list of lawless resolutes,
For food and diet, to some enterprise
That hath a stomach in't; which is no other,
As it doth well appear unto our state,
But to recover of us, by strong hand   115

17

116 **terms compulsatory**   conditions that Denmark is forced to accept.

119 **source of**   reason for.

    head   fountain-head, from which a river flows. Metaphorically, the meaning is again the 'source'.

120 **post-haste**   urgent activity.

    romage   busy bustling about.

122 **Well may it sort**   this may well be the reason.

    portentous figure   ghost which is an omen.

124 **question**   cause.

125 **mote**   speck of dust.

126 **most high. . .Rome**   the time when Rome was at the peak of its power: 'palmy' because the palm was a symbol of victory.

    mightiest Julius   Julius Caesar (c.101–44 BC), the story of whose assassination is told in the play by Shakespeare which bears his name.

128 **tenantless**   unoccupied, without dead bodies.

    sheeted   shrouded.

130 **As**   as well as (although the text is difficult to make precise grammatical sense of here, and may be corrupt).

    stars with trains of fire   comets.

131 **Disasters**   this has a special significance in astrology, meaning an unlucky or unfavourable position in the sky or aspect of a star or planet.

    moist star   the moon.

132 **Neptune's empire**   the sea. Neptune was the Roman god of the sea.

133 **sick almost to doomsday**   almost as dark as it is prophesied that it will be when Christ comes again to judge the living and the dead.

134 **precurse**   forerunner.

135 **harbingers**   announcers of an arrival.

    still   always.

    fates   classical goddesses of destiny.

136 **omen coming on**   approaching prophetic sign (i.e. the ghost).

138 **climatures**   regions.

140 **I'll cross. . .blast me**   I will cross its path, even if it curses me. It was thought that by crossing the path of a ghost one risked being put in its power.

And terms compulsatory, those foresaid lands
So by his father lost; and this, I take it,
Is the main motive of our preparations,
The source of this our watch, and the chief head
Of this post-haste and romage in the land.   120

BERNARDO

I think it be no other but e'en so.
Well may it sort, that this portentous figure
Comes armed through our watch: so like the King
That was and is the question of these wars.

HORATIO

A mote it is to trouble the mind's eye.   125
In the most high and palmy state of Rome,
A little ere the mightiest Julius fell,
The graves stood tenantless, and the sheeted dead
Did squeak and gibber in the Roman streets;
As, stars with trains of fire, and dews of blood,   130
Disasters in the sun; and the moist star
Upon whose influence Neptune's empire stands
Was sick almost to doomsday with eclipse;
And even the like precurse of fear'd events,
As harbingers preceding still the fates   135
And prologue to the omen coming on,
Have heaven and earth together demonstrated
Unto our climatures and countrymen.

Re-enter Ghost.

But, soft, behold! Lo, where it comes again!
I'll cross it, though it blast me. Stay, illusion.   140

Ghost *spreads its arms.*

If thou hast any sound or use of voice,
Speak to me.

19

144 **grace to me**   bring me credit.

146 **art privy to**   have secret knowledge of.

147 **happily**   by chance.

149 **uphoarded**   hoarded up.

150 **Extorted treasure. . .earth**   treasure taken by force and buried.

s.d. **The cock crows**   a sign that dawn is breaking. Ghosts were believed to
return to purgatory at dawn.

153 **partisan**   spear with an axe-like head.

154 **stand**   remain.

158 **being so majestical**   because it (the ghost) looks so majestic.

159 **the show of**   a display of.

161 **malicious mockery**   wicked and useless.

If there be any good thing to be done,
That may to thee do ease and grace to me.
Speak to me.   145
If thou art privy to thy country's fate,
Which happily foreknowing may avoid,
O, speak!
Or if thou hast uphoarded in thy life
Extorted treasure in the womb of earth,   150
For which, they say, you spirits oft walk in death,

The cock crows.

Speak of it. Stay, and speak. Stop it, Marcellus.

MARCELLUS
Shall I strike at it with my partisan?

HORATIO
Do, if it will not stand.

BERNARDO
'Tis here!   155

HORATIO
'Tis here!

MARCELLUS
'Tis gone!

Exit Ghost

We do it wrong, being so majestical,
To offer it the show of violence;
For it is, as the air, invulnerable,   160
And our vain blows malicious mockery.

BERNARDO
It was about to speak, when the cock crew.

164 *fearful summons*   terrifying command.

165 *trumpet*   trumpeter.

169 *extravagant and erring*   wandering.

170 *confine*   place of confinement.

171 *This present object*   this sight we have just witnessed (i.e. the ghost's rapid departure).

probation   proof.

173–4 *ever 'gainst. . .celebrated*   always, in preparation for Christmas.

175 *bird of dawning*   cock.

176 *abroad*   away from its proper resting place.

177 *wholesome*   healthy.

strike   exert an evil influence.

178 *takes*   strikes down.

179 *gracious*   touched with divine grace.

181 *in russet mantle*   wearing a rust-coloured robe.

182 *yon*   yonder, over there.

183 *Break. . .up*   let's disperse our guard.

185 *young Hamlet*   to distinguish him from old Hamlet, whose ghost we have just seen.

188 *needful in our loves*   necessary because of the love we have for him.

190 *convenient*   conveniently.

HORATIO

And then it started like a guilty thing
Upon a fearful summons. I have heard
The cock, that is the trumpet to the morn,   165
Doth with his lofty and shrill-sounding throat
Awake the god of day; and at his warning,
Whether in sea or fire, in earth or air,
Th' extravagant and erring spirit hies
To his confine; and of the truth herein   170
This present object made probation.

MARCELLUS

It faded on the crowing of the cock.
Some say that ever 'gainst that season comes
Wherein our Saviour's birth is celebrated,
This bird of dawning singeth all night long;   175
And then, they say, no spirit dare stir abroad,
The nights are wholesome, then no planets strike,
No fairy takes, nor witch hath power to charm,
So hallowed and so gracious is that time.

HORATIO

So have I heard, and do in part believe it.   180
But look, the morn, in russet mantle clad,
Walks o'er the dew of yon high eastward hill.
Break we our watch up; and, by my advice,
Let us impart what we have seen to-night
Unto young Hamlet; for, upon my life,   185
This spirit, dumb to us, will speak to him.
Do you consent we shall acquaint him with it,
As needful in our loves, fitting our duty?

MARCELLUS

Let's do't, I pray; and I this morning know
Where we shall find him most convenient.   190

Exeunt

23

s.d. **Flourish**   sound of ceremonial trumpets, a fanfare.

1 **Hamlet**   i.e. old Hamlet.

   our   my (Claudius is using the 'royal plural').

2 **green**   fresh.

   us befitted   was fitting for us.

4 **contracted**   drawn together.

   one brow of woe   universal mourning.

5 **discretion**   reason.

   nature   natural feelings of grief.

8 **sometime**   former.

   sister   i.e. sister-in-law.

9 **jointress**   widow who holds her late husband's property for her lifetime.

10 **defeated joy**   first of a series of figures of speech in which Claudius
   describes his simultaneous mourning for his brother and wooing of
   Gertrude.

11 **auspicious**   happy.

   dropping   weeping.

12 **dirge**   a funeral song.

13 **dole**   sorrow.

14 **Taken to wife**   married.

   barr'd   rejected.

15 **better wisdoms**   superior judgements; Claudius is anxious not to be seen to
   be acting without his court's support.

15–16 **freely gone. . .affair along**   agreed willingly with this marriage.

17 **that you know**   what you should know already.

18 **weak supposal of our worth**   low estimation of our strength.

20 **disjoint and out of frame**   disorganised.

21 **Co-leagued**   linked.

   dream of his advantage   mistaken fancy that he is stronger.

23 **Importing**   concerning.

24 **with all bands of law**   all the binding formalities of law.

Scene two

Elsinore. The Castle.

Flourish. Enter CLAUDIUS KING OF DENMARK, GERTRUDE THE QUEEN, *and* Councillors, *including* POLONIUS, *his son* LAERTES, VOLTEMAND, CORNELIUS, *and* HAMLET.

KING

Though yet of Hamlet our dear brother's death
The memory be green; and that it us befitted
To bear our hearts in grief, and our whole kingdom
To be contracted in one brow of woe;
Yet so far hath discretion fought with nature   5
That we with wisest sorrow think on him,
Together with remembrance of ourselves.
Therefore our sometime sister, now our queen,
Th' imperial jointress to this warlike state,
Have we, as 'twere with a defeated joy,   10
With an auspicious and a dropping eye,
With mirth in funeral, and with dirge in marriage,
In equal scale weighing delight and dole,
Taken to wife; nor have we herein barr'd
Your better wisdoms, which have freely gone   15
With this affair along. For all, our thanks.
Now follows that you know; young Fortinbras,
Holding a weak supposal of our worth,
Or thinking by our late dear brother's death
Our state to be disjoint and out of frame,   20
Co-leagued with this dream of his advantage –
He hath not fail'd to pester us with message
Importing the surrender of those lands
Lost by his father, with all bands of law,
To our most valiant brother. So much for him.   25

25

26 *and for* and for the reason.

27 *writ* written.

28 *Norway* i.e to the King of Norway.

29 *impotent* powerless.

   bed-rid confined to his sick-bed.

30 *suppress* stop.

31 *gait* actions.

31–3 *in that the levies. . .subject* because all the troops mustered are subjects of the King of Norway, he can prevent their use by Fortinbras.

37 *business* do business, negotiate.

38 *delated articles* clearly-stated terms. Cornelius and Voltemand are to be messengers rather than ambassadors.

39 *let your haste commend your duty* let your speed demonstrate your loyalty.

41 *We doubt it nothing* we do not doubt it.

43 *suit* request, petition.

44 *speak of reason* make a reasonable request.

   the Dane the King of Denmark.

45 *lose your voice* waste your breath.

   thou less formal than 'you', corresponding to the French 'tu' or German 'du'.

46 *That shall. . .asking?* that I would not have given you freely even if you had not asked for it.

47 *native* closely related.

48 *instrumental* useful.

Now for ourself, and for this time of meeting,
Thus much the business is: we have here writ
To Norway, uncle of young Fortinbras –
Who, impotent and bed-rid, scarcely hears
Of this his nephew's purpose – to suppress   30
His further gait herein, in that the levies,
The lists, and full proportions, are all made
Out of his subject; and we here dispatch
You, good Cornelius, and you, Voltemand,
For bearers of this greeting to old Norway;   35
Giving to you no further personal power
To business with the King more than the scope
Of these delated articles allow.
Farewell; and let your haste commend your duty.

CORNELIUS ⎫
VOLTEMAND ⎭

In that and all things we will show our duty.   40

KING

We doubt it nothing, heartily farewell.

Exeunt VOLTEMAND *and* CORNELIUS

And now, Laertes, what's the news with you?
You told us of some suit; what is't, Laertes?
You cannot speak of reason to the Dane
And lose your voice. What wouldst thou beg,
   Laertes,   45
That shall not be my offer, not thy asking?
The head is not more native to the heart,
The hand more instrumental to the mouth,
Than is the throne of Denmark to thy father.
What wouldst thou have, Laertes?   50

27

51 *dread*   revered, held in awe.

54 *duty*   loyalty.

57 *bow them*   submit themselves.

59 *'A hath*   he has.

   slow   reluctant.

60 *laboursome petition*   laborious, persistent requests.

61 *will*   wishes.

   seal'd my hard consent   gave my hard-won permission.

63 *Take thy fair hour*   make the most of this good opportunity.

   time be thine   your time is your own.

64 *And thy. . .thy will*   spend your time as your conscience ('best graces') tells you to.

65 *cousin*   nephew. The word was formerly used for any close relative.

   son   stepson.

66 *A little more. . .than kind*   more than a distant relative and yet less than a close member of the family. (There is a pun on 'kind', which also means 'well disposed' or 'friendly'.)

67 *clouds*   i.e. clouds of grief or mourning.

68 *too much in the sun*   in the sunshine of the king's approval, with a pun on 'sun'/'son', as Claudius has called him his son (see note to line 65).

69 *nighted colour*   black clothes of mourning, and melancholy behaviour.

70 *Denmark*   the King of Denmark.

71–2 *Do not for ever. . .the dust*   Hamlet in his sorrow looks only at the ground.

71 *vailed lids*   downcast eyes.

LAERTES

My dread lord,
Your leave and favour to return to France;
From whence though willingly I came to Denmark
To show my duty in your coronation,
Yet now, I must confess, that duty done,   55
My thoughts and wishes bend again toward
   France,
And bow them to your gracious leave and pardon.

KING

Have you your father's leave? What says Polonius?

POLONIUS

'A hath, my lord, wrung from me my slow leave
By laboursome petition; and at last   60
Upon his will I seal'd my hard consent.
I do beseech you, give him leave to go.

KING

Take thy fair hour, Laertes; time be thine,
And thy best graces spend it at thy will!
But now, my cousin Hamlet, and my son –   65

HAMLET

(*Aside*) A little more than kin, and less than kind.

KING

How is it that the clouds still hang on you?

HAMLET

Not so, my lord; I am too much in the sun.

QUEEN

Good Hamlet, cast thy nighted colour off,
And let thine eye look like a friend on Denmark.   70
Do not for ever with thy vailed lids

29

73 **'tis common**   death is common to us all.

74 **nature**   life.

77 **particular**   special.

79 **alone**   only.

   inky   black.

80 **customary suits**   the clothes I usually wear now.

81 **windy suspiration. . .breath**   forced sighs.

82 **fruitful river in the eye**   abundant tears.

83 **haviour of the visage**   expression of the face.

84 **forms, moods, shapes**   outwardly visible signs.

85 **denote**   represent.

86 **play**   i.e. act, like an actor, without sincere feeling.

87 **passes show**   surpasses outward expression.

88 **These but. . .woe**   these, the mere clothing and behaviour associated with mourning.

92 **bound**   was bound.

93 **term**   suitable period of time.

94 **obsequious**   sorrow suitable for funeral rites or obsequies.

   persever   persist. The stress is on the second syllable.

95 **condolement**   sorrow.

96 **impious**   disrespectful.

97 **incorrect**   not corrected by submitting to the will of God.

Seek for thy noble father in the dust.
Thou know'st 'tis common – all that lives must die,
Passing through nature to eternity.

HAMLET

Ay, madam, it is common.   75

QUEEN

If it be,
Why seems it so particular with thee?

HAMLET

Seems, madam! Nay, it is; I know not seems.
'Tis not alone my inky cloak, good mother,
Nor customary suits of solemn black,   80
Nor windy suspiration of forc'd breath,
No, nor the fruitful river in the eye,
Nor the dejected haviour of the visage,
Together with all forms, moods, shapes of grief,
That can denote me truly. These, indeed, seem;   85
For they are actions that a man might play;
But I have that within which passes show –
These but the trappings and the suits of woe.

KING

'Tis sweet and commendable in your nature,
   Hamlet,
To give these mourning duties to your father;   90
But you must know your father lost a father;
That father lost lost his; and the survivor bound,
In filial obligation, for some term
To do obsequious sorrow. But to persever
In obstinate condolement is a course   95
Of impious stubbornness; 'tis unmanly grief;
It shows a will most incorrect to heaven,
A heart unfortified, a mind impatient,

98 *unfortified*   lacking courage in adversity.

99 *simple*   stupid.

unschool'd   undisciplined by knowledge of philosophy or theology.

100–1 *is as common. . .to sense*   i.e. death is as much a part of everyone's experience as any common thing.

103 *fault to heaven*   an offence against God.

106 *who*   i.e. reason.

still   always.

107 *corse*   dead body.

109 *unprevailing*   useless.

111 *most immediate to our throne*   next in line to the throne.

114 *impart toward*   bestow upon.

For   as for.

115 *school*   university.

Wittenberg   a university town in Germany.

116 *retrograde to our desire*   against my wishes.

117 *beseech you bend you*   beg you to make yourself willing.

118 *eye*   sight.

120 *lose her prayers*   beg in vain.

125 *accord*   agreement.

126 *in grace whereof*   in honour of which.

127–9 *No jocund health. . .bruit again*   no joyful toast ('jocund health') that the King of Denmark drinks today will pass without the great cannon being fired, so that the noise of the King's revelry ('rouse') will be echoed by the sky ('heaven shall bruit again').

An understanding simple and unschool'd;
For what we know must be, and is as common   100
As any the most vulgar thing to sense,
Why should we in our peevish opposition
Take it to heart? Fie! 'tis a fault to heaven,
A fault against the dead, a fault to nature,
To reason most absurd; whose common theme   105
Is death of fathers, and who still hath cried,
From the first corse till he that died to-day,
'This must be so'. We pray you throw to earth
This unprevailing woe, and think of us
As of a father; for let the world take note   110
You are the most immediate to our throne;
And with no less nobility of love
Than that which dearest father bears his son
Do I impart toward you. For your intent
In going back to school in Wittenberg,   115
It is most retrograde to our desire;
And we beseech you bend you to remain
Here, in the cheer and comfort of our eye,
Our chiefest courtier, cousin, and our son.

QUEEN

Let not thy mother lose her prayers, Hamlet: 120
I pray thee stay with us; go not to Wittenberg.

HAMLET

I shall in all my best obey you, madam.

KING

Why, 'tis a loving and a fair reply.
Be as ourself in Denmark. Madam, come;
This gentle and unforc'd accord of Hamlet   125
Sits smiling to my heart; in grace whereof,
No jocund health that Denmark drinks to-day

33

132 *resolve*   dissolve.

133 *the Everlasting*   God.

134 *canon*   divine law.

   self-slaughter   suicide. The Sixth Commandment, 'Thou shalt not kill', was thought to prohibit suicide as well as murder.

137 *Fie on't!*   shame on it!

138 *rank and gross*   foul and coarse.

139 *merely*   completely.

141 *this*   i.e. Claudius.

142 *Hyperion*   in early Greek mythology, the father of the sun.

   to   compared to.

   satyr   one of a race of half-man, half-goat creatures, much given to drunkenness and promiscuity, and so a fitting choice considering Hamlet's opinion of Claudius.

143 *between*   allow.

146–7 *As if increase. . .fed on*   as if her desire for him had increased the more she had of what should have satisfied it.

149 *ere*   before.

151 *Niobe*   in Greek mythology, a Queen of Thebes who wept so much at the death of her fourteen children that she was transformed into a rock, which continued to weep.

152 *wants discourse of reason*   lacks the capacity for rational thought.

155 *Hercules*   mythical Greek hero of enormous strength and courage.

But the great cannon to the clouds shall tell,
And the King's rouse the heaven shall bruit again,
Re-speaking earthly thunder. Come away.   130

Flourish. Exeunt all but HAMLET

HAMLET
O, that this too too solid flesh would melt,
Thaw, and resolve itself into a dew!
Or that the Everlasting had not fix'd
His canon 'gainst self-slaughter! O God! God!
How weary, stale, flat, and unprofitable,   135
Seem to me all the uses of this world!
Fie on't! Ah, fie! 'tis an unweeded garden,
That grows to seed; things rank and gross in
   nature
Possess it merely. That it should come to this!
But two months dead! Nay, not so much, not two. 140
So excellent a king that was to this
Hyperion to a satyr; so loving to my mother,
That he might not beteem the winds of heaven
Visit her face too roughly. Heaven and earth!
Must I remember? Why, she would hang on him 145
As if increase of appetite had grown
By what it fed on; and yet, within a month –
Let me not think on't. Frailty, thy name is woman! –
A little month, or ere those shoes were old
With which she followed my poor father's body,   150
Like Niobe, all tears – why she, even she –
O God! a beast that wants discourse of reason
Would have mourn'd longer – married with my
   uncle,
My father's brother; but no more like my father
Than I to Hercules. Within a month,   155

156 **unrighteous** insincere.

157 **left. . .eyes** left the redness ('flushing') of her sore ('galled') eyes.

158–9 **post With such dexterity** hasten with such eagerness.

159 **incestuous** marriage to a dead brother's widow was regarded as incest, and against religious law, even though the couple were unrelated by blood.

166 **I'll change that name with you** I will exchange the name of 'servant' for that of 'friend'.

167 **make you from** are you doing away from.

170 **even** evening.

172 **truant disposition** an inclination to play truant.

Ere yet the salt of most unrighteous tears
Had left the flushing in her galled eyes,
She married. O, most wicked speed, to post
With such dexterity to incestuous sheets!
It is not, nor it cannot come to good.   160
But break, my heart, for I must hold my tongue.

Enter HORATIO, MARCELLUS, *and* BERNARDO.

HORATIO
Hail to your lordship!

HAMLET
I am glad to see you well.
Horatio – or I do forget myself.

HORATIO
The same, my lord, and your poor servant ever.   165

HAMLET
Sir, my good friend. I'll change that name with
   you.
And what make you from Wittenberg, Horatio?
Marcellus?

MARCELLUS
My good lord!

HAMLET
I am very glad to see you. (*To* BERNARDO) Good
   even, sir. –   170
But what, in faith, make you from Wittenberg?

HORATIO
A truant disposition, good my lord.

HAMLET
I would not hear your enemy say so;

177 **affair**   business.

178 **teach you to drink deep**   a bitter reference to the King's frequent drunkenness.

182 **hard upon**   closely; shortly after.

183–4 **The funeral bak'd-meats. . .marriage tables**   the left-overs from the hot food served at the funeral were served cold at the wedding feast.

185 **dearest foe**   most deadly enemy.

186 **Or ever**   before.

190 **'a**   he.

191 **'A was a man. . .all**   all things considered, he had the essential qualities of a man.

Nor shall you do my ear that violence,
To make it truster of your own report   175
Against yourself. I know you are no truant.
But what is your affair in Elsinore?
We'll teach you to drink deep ere you depart.

HORATIO
My lord, I came to see your father's funeral.

HAMLET
I prithee do not mock me, fellow-student;   180
I think it was to see my mother's wedding.

HORATIO
Indeed, my lord, it followed hard upon.

HAMLET
Thrift, thrift, Horatio! The funeral bak'd-meats
Did coldly furnish forth the marriage tables.
Would I had met my dearest foe in heaven   185
Or ever I had seen that day, Horatio!
My father – methinks I see my father.

HORATIO
Where, my lord?

HAMLET
In my mind's eye, Horatio.

HORATIO
I saw him once; 'a was a goodly king.   190

HAMLET
'A was a man, take him for all in all,
I shall not look upon his like again.

HORATIO
My lord, I think I saw him yester-night.

197 **Season your admiration**   control your amazement.

198 **attent**   attentive.

206 **at point**   in readiness.

  cap-a-pe   from head to foot.

209 **oppress'd**   troubled.

210 **distill'd**   transformed.

211 **act**   effect.

213 **dreadful**   fearful.

215 **delivered**   told.

216 **Form**   and shape.

218 **like**   like one another (than the ghost was to Hamlet's father).

HAMLET

Saw who?

HORATIO

My lord, the King your father.   195

HAMLET

The King my father!

HORATIO

Season your admiration for a while
With an attent ear, till I may deliver,
Upon the witness of these gentlemen,
This marvel to you.   200

HAMLET

For God's love, let me hear.

HORATIO

Two nights together had these gentlemen,
Marcellus and Bernardo, on their watch,
In the dead waste and middle of the night,
Been thus encount'red. A figure like your father, 205
Armed at point exactly, cap-a-pe,
Appears before them, and with solemn march
Goes slow and stately by them; thrice he walk'd
By their oppress'd and fear-surprised eyes,
Within his truncheon's length; whilst they, distill'd 210
Almost to jelly with the act of fear,
Stand dumb and speak not to him. This to me
In dreadful secrecy impart they did;
And I with them the third night kept the watch;
Where, as they had delivered, both in time,   215
Form of the thing, each word made true and good,
The apparition comes. I knew your father;
These hands are not more like.

224 *it* its.

224–5 *did address. . .speak* start to move as if it wanted to speak.

231 *writ down in our duty* part of our duty to you.

HAMLET

But where was this?

MARCELLUS

My lord, upon the platform where we watch.   220

HAMLET

Did you not speak to it?

HORATIO

My lord, I did;
But answer made it none; yet once methought
It lifted up it head and did address
Itself to motion, like as it would speak;   225
But even then the morning cock crew loud,
And at the sound it shrunk in hast away
And vanish'd from our sight.

HAMLET

'Tis very strange.

HORATIO

As I do live, my honour'd lord, 'tis true;   230
And we did think it writ down in our duty
To let you know of it.

HAMLET

Indeed, indeed, sirs, but this troubles me.
Hold you the watch to-night?

ALL

We do, my lord.   235

HAMLET

Arm'd, say you?

ALL

Arm'd, my lord.

241 **beaver up**   visor raised.

249 **amaz'd**   stunned, bewildered. The word was stronger in Shakespeare's day.

HAMLET
From top to toe?

ALL
My lord, from head to foot.

HAMLET
Then saw you not his face?   240

HORATIO
O yes, my lord; he wore his beaver up.

HAMLET
What, look'd he frowningly?

HORATIO
A countenance more in sorrow than in anger.

HAMLET
Pale or red?

HORATIO
Nay, very pale.   245

HAMLET
And fix'd his eyes upon you?

HORATIO
Most constantly.

HAMLET
I would I had been there.

HORATIO
It would have much amaz'd you.

HAMLET
Very like, very like. Stay'd it long?   250

251 *tell*   count to.

254 *grizzl'd*   grey.

256 *A sable silver'd*   deep black with streaks of silver-grey.

258 *Perchance*   perhaps.

259 *warr'nt*   guarantee.

262 *hold my peace*   keep quiet.

263 *hitherto*   up until now.

   conceal'd   kept quiet about.

264 *Let it. . .still*   see that you carry on keeping it a secret.

265 *whatsomever*   whatever.

   hap   happen.

266 *Give it. . .no tongue*   think about it, but don't talk about it.

267 *requite your loves*   reward your loyalty.

HORATIO

While one with moderate haste might tell a
hundred.

BOTH

Longer, longer.

HORATIO

Not when I saw't.

HAMLET

His beard was grizzl'd – no?

HORATIO

It was, as I have seen it in his life,   255
A sable silver'd.

HAMLET

I will watch to-night;
Perchance 'twill walk again.

HORATIO

I warr'nt it will.

HAMLET

If it assume my noble father's person,   260
I'll speak to it, though hell itself should gape
And bid me hold my peace. I pray you all,
If you have hitherto conceal'd this sight,
Let it be tenable in your silence still;
And whatsomever else shall hap to-night,   265
Give it an understanding, but no tongue;
I will requite your loves. So, fare you well –
Upon the platform, 'twixt eleven and twelve,
I'll visit you.

ALL

Our duty to your honour.   270

273 **doubt**   suspect.

  I **necessaries**   luggage.

    embark'd   loaded onto a ship.

  2 **as the winds give benefit**   when the winds are favourable.

  3 **And convey is assistant**   and when a suitable ship is leaving.

  6 **For**   as for.

6–7 **trifling. . .blood**   Laertes is warning Ophelia to treat Hamlet's attentions
      ('favour') as not meant seriously ('trifling'), but just a passing fancy
      ('fashion') brought on by a sexual impulse ('toy in blood').

  8 **violet**   Laertes compares Hamlet's love to a violet, a pretty but short-lived
      flower of the spring.

    primy   in its prime, the springtime.

10 **suppliance of a minute**   pastime: that which supplies the desires of the
      moment.

HAMLET

Your loves, as mine to you; farewell.

Exeunt all but HAMLET

My father's spirit in arms! All is not well.
I doubt some foul play. Would the night were
    come!
Till then sit still, my soul. Foul deeds will rise,
Though all the earth o'erwhelm them, to men's
    eyes.   275

Exit

Scene three

Elsinore. The house of Polonius.

Enter LAERTES *and* OPHELIA *his sister.*

LAERTES

My necessaries are embark'd. Farewell.
And, sister, as the winds give benefit
And convoy is assistant, do not sleep,
But let me hear from you.

OPHELIA

Do you doubt that?   5

LAERTES

For Hamlet, and the trifling of his favour,
Hold it a fashion and a toy in blood,
A violet in the youth of primy nature,
Forward not permanent, sweet not lasting.
The perfume and suppliance of a minute;   10
No more.

14 *crescent* when it is growing.

15 *thews* sinews.

 temple waxes body (the soul's 'temple') grows.

16 *inward service* inner faculties.

17 **Grows wide withal** grow bigger as well: the mind and soul grow at the same rate as the body. It is unclear what Laertes means here, but perhaps he is hinting that as Hamlet matures he may change his mind about Ophelia.

18 *cautel* act of deceit.

19 *virtue of his will* sincerity of his desire.

 fear suspect.

20 **His greatness weigh'd** bearing in mind his high rank.

 his will. . .own he cannot follow his own desires.

21 *subject to* ruled by.

22 *unvalued person* unimportant people, commoners.

23 **Carve for himself** take what he wants.

 choice i.e. choice of a wife.

24 *sanity* soundness.

25 *circumscrib'd* restricted.

26 *voice and yielding* opinion and consent.

 that body i.e the state.

28 **It fits. . .believe it** it is proper for you to believe it only as far.

30 **May give his saying deed** may match his words with actions.

31 *main voice. . .withal* general public opinion goes along with.

33 *credent* gullible.

 list listen to.

34 *chaste treasure* virginity.

35 *unmast'red importunity* uncontrolled and persistent requests.

37 *keep you. . .affection* do not go as far as your natural feelings would want.

39 *chariest* most cautious.

 prodigal enough quite extravagant enough.

41 *Virtue. . .strokes* the personified figure of Virtue herself does not escape ('scapes not') malicious ('calumnious') slander.

OPHELIA
  No more but so?

LAERTES
  Think it no more;
  For nature crescent does not grow alone
  In thews and bulk, but as this temple waxes,   15
  The inward service of the mind and soul
  Grows wide withal. Perhaps he loves you now,
  And now no soil nor cautel doth besmirch
  The virtue of his will; but you must fear,
  His greatness weigh'd, his will is not his own;   20
  For he himself is subject to his birth:
  He may not, as unvalued persons do,
  Carve for himself; for on his choice depends
  The sanity and health of this whole state;
  And therefore must his choice be circumscrib'd   25
  Unto the voice and yielding of that body
  Whereof he is the head. Then if he says he loves
      you,
  It fits your wisdom so far to believe it
  As he in his particular act and place
  May give his saying deed; which is no further   30
  Than the main voice of Denmark goes withal.
  Then weigh what loss your honour may sustain,
  If with too credent ear you list his songs,
  Or lose your heart, or your chaste treasure open
  To his unmast'red importunity. *fock eachother*   35
  Fear it, Ophelia, fear it, my dear sister;
  And keep you in the rear of your affection,
  Out of the shot and danger of desire.
  The chariest maid is prodigal enough
  If she unmask her beauty to the moon.   40
  Virtue itself scapes not calumnious strokes;

42–3 **The canker. . .disclos'd**   the canker-worm damages ('galls') the tender young plants of spring too often before their buds ('buttons') are open ('disclos'd').

44–5 **And in. . .imminent**   and infectious diseases ('contagious blastments') are most likely to strike in childhood.

47 **to**   against.

50 **ungracious pastors**   ungodly priests.

52 **Whiles**   while.

   puff'd   swollen.

53 **dalliance**   careless pleasure.

54 **recks not his own rede**   does not follow his own advice.

55 **O, fear me not!**   don't worry about me.

58 **Occasion smiles upon a second leave**   opportunity has blessed me with a chance to say goodbye again.

60 **The wind sits. . .your sail**   the wind is blowing in the right direction for you to depart.

61 **stay'd for**   they are waiting for you.

62–3 **these few precepts. . .character**   make sure that you remember these few pieces of advice.

63 **Give thy thoughts no tongue**   don't tell people what you're thinking.

64 **Nor any unproportion'd thought his act**   and do not put any ill-considered ('unproportion'd') thought into action.

65 **familiar**   friendly.

   vulgar   available to everyone alike, regardless of status.

66 **and their adoption tried**   when their friendship has been tested.

67 **Grapple**   grasp.

The canker galls the infants of the spring
Too oft before their buttons be disclos'd;
And in the morn and liquid dew of youth
Contagious blastments are most imminent.   45
Be wary, then; best safety lies in fear;
Youth to itself rebels, though none else near.

OPHELIA

I shall the effect of this good lesson keep
As watchman to my heart. But, good my brother,
Do not, as some ungracious pastors do,   50
Show me the steep and thorny way to heaven,
Whiles, like a puff'd and reckless libertine,
Himself the primrose path of dalliance treads
And recks not his own rede.

LAERTES

O, fear me not!   55

Enter POLONIUS.

I stay too long. But here my father comes.
A double blessing is a double grace;
Occasion smiles upon a second leave.

POLONIUS

Yet here, Laertes! Aboard, aboard, for shame!
The wind sits in the shoulder of your sail,   60
And you are stay'd for. There – my blessing with
    thee!
And these few precepts in thy memory
Look thou character. Give thy thoughts no tongue,
Nor any unproportion'd thought his act.
Be thou familiar, but by no means vulgar.   65
Those friends thou hast, and their adoption tried,
Grapple them to thy soul with hoops of steel;

68–9 **But do not. . .courage**   do not wear out your capacity to make friends ('dull thy palm') by easily accepting every newly-arrived and untried ('new-hatch'd, unfledg'd') young gentleman ('courage').

70 **entrance to**   starting.

71 **Bear't**   conduct it.

opposed   your adversary.

72 **Give every man thy ear**   listen to everyone.

73 **censure**   opinion.

74 **habit**   clothes.

75 **not express'd in fancy**   not of an extravagant passing fashion.

77 **station**   position in society.

78 **Are of a most select. . .in that**   the sense of this line is obscure, and the text is probably corrupt. The meaning appears to be that the French nobility are careful about their clothes.

81 **dulls**   blunts.

my blessing season this in thee!   may my blessing bring the advice I have given to ripeness ('season') in you.

87 **tend**   wait.

But do not dull thy palm with entertainment
Of each new-hatch'd, unfledg'd courage. Beware
Of entrance to a quarrel; but, being in, 70
Bear't that th' opposed may beware of thee.
Give every man thy ear, but few thy voice;
Take each man's censure, but reserve thy judgment.
Costly thy habit as thy purse can buy,
But not express'd in fancy; rich, not gaudy; 75
For the apparel oft proclaims the man;
And they in France of the best rank and station
Are of a most select and generous choice in that.
Neither a borrower nor a lender be;
For loan oft loses both itself and friend, 80
And borrowing dulls the edge of husbandry.
This above all – to thine own self be true,
And it must follow, as the night the day,
Thou canst not then be false to any man.
Farewell; my blessing season this in thee! 85

LAERTES
Most humbly do I take my leave, my lord.

POLONIUS
The time invites you; go, your servants tend.

LAERTES
Farewell, Ophelia; and remember well
What I have said to you.

OPHELIA
'Tis in my memory lock'd, 90
And you yourself shall keep the key of it.

94 **touching** about.

95 **Marry** a mild oath, a shortened version of 'By the Virgin Mary'.

bethought remembered.

98 **audience** attention.

free generous.

99 **put on me** told to me.

102 **behoves** is suitable for. Polonius is telling Ophelia that she does not understand that because she is a commoner and not of royal blood, Hamlet cannot have serious or honourable intentions towards her.

103 **Give me up** tell me.

104–5 **tenders Of his affection** offers of love.

106 **green** immature.

107 **Unsifted** inexperienced.

LAERTES
Farewell.

Exit

POLONIUS
What is't, Ophelia, he hath said to you?

OPHELIA
So please you, something touching the Lord
Hamlet.

POLONIUS
Marry, well bethought!   95
'Tis told me he hath very oft of late
Given private time to you; and you yourself
Have of your audience been most free and
bounteous.
If it be so – as so 'tis put on me,
And that in way of caution – I must tell you   100
You do not understand yourself so clearly
As it behoves my daughter and your honour.
What is between you? Give me up the truth.

OPHELIA
He hath, my lord, of late made many tenders
Of his affection to me.   105

POLONIUS
Affection! Pooh! You speak like a green girl,
Unsifted in such perilous circumstance.
Do you believe his tenders, as you call them?

OPHELIA
I do not know, my lord, what I should think.

POLONIUS
Marry, I will teach you: think yourself a baby   110

111 **ta'en these tenders for true pay**   taken these offers of money for actual payment.

112 **sterling**   of true value.

Tender yourself   value yourself.

113–4 **not to crack. . .thus**   not to make the word out of breath by over-using it. The image is of an animal being made breathless in hunting ('running') it.

114 **tender me a fool**   make a fool of me (for being the father of a daughter who has been seduced).

116 **fashion**   manner.

117 **fashion**   Polonius picks up Ophelia's last word and uses it against her, giving it the sense of a passing fancy, as Laertes used it in line 7 of this scene.

118 **given countenance**   confirmed.

120 **springes to catch woodcocks**   snares to catch silly birds. This was a proverbial phrase, meaning traps to catch fools. Polonius thinks this is what Hamlet's vows are.

121 **the blood burns**   sexual passions are aroused.

prodigal   lavishly.

122–5 **These blazes. . .take for fire**   Polonius is warning Ophelia not to mistake the sudden flashes of Hamlet's sexual passion ('blazes') for the constant fire of true love.

126 **something scanter**   somewhat less generous.

127–8 **Set your entreatments. . .to parle**   do not talk to him whenever he demands to see you. The metaphor suggests that Ophelia is a town under siege, negotiating surrender ('entreatments') on the orders ('command to parle') of Hamlet, the besieger.

130 **larger tether**   longer rein. As a prince, and as a man, he has more freedom.

132 **brokers**   go-betweens in matters of love.

133 **Not of that dye which their investments show**   of deceptive appearance. The image is of priests whose essential character ('dye') is not that suggested by their clothing ('investments').

134 **implorators of unholy suits**   persuaders to wicked deeds.

135 **Breathing**   whispering.

pious bonds   marriage contracts.

136 **This is for all**   once and for all.

That you have ta'en these tenders for true pay
Which are not sterling. Tender yourself more
    dearly;
Or – not to crack the wind of the poor phrase,
Running it thus – you'll tender me a fool.

OPHELIA

My lord, he hath importun'd me with love   115
In honourable fashion.

POLONIUS

Ay, fashion you may call it; go to, go to.

OPHELIA

And hath given countenance to his speech, my
    lord,
With almost all the holy vows of heaven.

POLONIUS

Ay, springes to catch woodcocks! I do know,   120
When the blood burns, how prodigal the soul
Lends the tongue vows. These blazes, daughter,
Giving more light than heat – extinct in both,
Even in their promise, as it is a-making –
You must not take for fire. From this time   125
Be something scanter of your maiden presence;
Set your entreatments at a higher rate
Than a command to parle. For Lord Hamlet,
Believe so much in him, that he is young,
And with a larger tether may he walk   130
Than may be given you. In few, Ophelia,
Do not believe his vows; for they are brokers,
Not of that dye which their investments show,
But mere implorators of unholy suits,
Breathing like sanctified and pious bonds,   135
The better to beguile. This is for all –

138 *slander*   misuse.

140 **Look to't**   see that you obey.

  I charge you   I command you.

  Come your ways   come with me.

1 *shrewdly*   sharply.

2 *eager*   keen, sharp.

4 *it lacks of twelve*   it is just before midnight.

5 *it is struck*   i.e. the clock has struck midnight.

6 *season*   time.

7 *held his wont to walk*   usually walked.

s.d. *pieces*   cannon.

I would not, in plain terms, from this time forth
Have you so slander any moment leisure
As to give words or talk with the Lord Hamlet.
Look to't, I charge you. Come your ways.   140

OPHELIA
I shall obey, my lord.

Exeunt

Scene four

Elsinore. The guard-platform of the Castle.

Enter HAMLET, HORATIO, *and* MARCELLUS.

HAMLET
The air bites shrewdly; it is very cold.

HORATIO
It is a nipping and an eager air.

HAMLET
What hour now?

HORATIO
I think it lacks of twelve.

MARCELLUS
No, it is struck.   5

HORATIO
Indeed? I heard it not. It then draws near the season
Wherein the spirit held his wont to walk.

A flourish of trumpets, and two pieces go off.

What does this mean, my lord?

9 **doth wake** is staying up late.

 takes his rouse is carousing.

10 **Keeps wassail** is drinking toasts and feasting.

 swagg'ring up-spring reels riotous drunken dancing.

11 **Rhenish** German wine from the Rhineland.

13 **triumph of his pledge** celebration of his toast.

17 **to the manner born** used to customs like these from my birth.

18 **More honour'd in the breach than the observance** it would more honourable
   to break it ('breach') than to observe it.

19–20 **This heavy-headed. . .nations** this drunken reveling which leaves us with
   hangovers ('heavy-headed') gives us a bad reputation ('traduc'd and
   tax'd') among people from other countries.

21 **clepe** call.

 swinish phrase words implying we behave like pigs.

22 **Soil our addition** stain our reputation.

 takes removes.

23 **perform'd at height** carried out perfectly.

24 **pith and marrow** the essence.

 attribute reputation.

26 **for. . .nature** because of an inherited characteristic inclining them to vice.

27 **As** for instance.

 wherein for which.

28 **his** its.

29 **o'ergrowth** over-development.

 complexion characteristic.

30 **pales and forts** barricades and defences.

31 **o'er-leavens** puts out of balance.

32 **form of plausive manners** pattern of socially acceptable behaviour.

34 **fortune's star** the destiny luck has given them.

35 **His** i.e. their (still referring to the 'particular men' in line 25).
 virtues else other virtues.

36 **undergo** experience.

37 **general censure** popular opinion.

62

HAMLET

The King doth wake to-night and takes his rouse,
Keeps wassail, and the swagg'ring up-spring reels,　10
And, as he drains his draughts of Rhenish down,
The kettle-drum and trumpet thus bray out
The triumph of his pledge.

HORATIO

Is it a custom?

HAMLET

Ay, marry is't;　15
But to my mind, though I am native here
And to the manner born, it is a custom
More honour'd in the breach than the observance.
This heavy-headed revel east and west
Makes us traduc'd and tax'd of other nations;　20
They clepe us drunkards, and with swinish phrase
Soil our addition; and, indeed, it takes
From our achievements, though perform'd at
　height,
The pith and marrow of our attribute.
So, oft it chances in particular men　25
That, for some vicious mole of nature in them,
As in their birth, wherein they are not guilty,
Since nature cannot choose his origin;
By the o'ergrowth of some complexion,
Oft breaking down the pales and forts of reason;　30
Or by some habit that too much o'er-leavens
The form of plausive manners – that these men,
Carrying, I say, the stamp of one defect,
Being nature's livery or fortune's star,
His virtues else, be they as pure as grace,　35
As infinite as man may undergo,
Shall in the general censure take corruption

38–40 **The dram. . .his own scandal**   this passage does not make perfect sense in any of the early editions of the play, and must be corrupt. The general sense is something like 'the tiny piece of evil ('dram of eale') often spoils the whole person and his reputation'.

42 **ministers of grace**   messengers of God's grace.

43 **spirit of health**   good spirit.

   goblin damn'd   spirit condemned to hell.

46 **questionable shape**   form inviting questions (i.e. that of his father).

50 **canoniz'd**   buried according to the laws of the church.

   hearsed in death   placed in a coffin when you died.

51 **cerements**   grave clothes or shrouds.

52 **enurn'd**   entombed.

53 **op'd**   opened.

55 **corse**   corpse.

   complete steel   a full set of armour.

56 **glimpses of the moon**   moonlight.

57 **fools of nature**   people made fools of because their understanding is limited by the fact that they are still natural or living, unlike the ghost.

58 **horridly**   dreadfully.

   disposition   feelings.

62 **impartment**   communication.

64

From that particular fault. The dram of eale
Doth all the noble substance of a doubt
To his own scandal.   40

Enter Ghost.

HORATIO

Look, my lord, it comes.

HAMLET

Angels and ministers of grace defend us!
Be thou a spirit of health or goblin damn'd,
Bring with thee airs from heaven or blasts from hell,
Be thy intents wicked or charitable,   45
Thou com'st in such a questionable shape
That I will speak to thee. I'll call thee Hamlet,
King, father, royal Dane. O answer me!
Let me not burst in ignorance, but tell
Why thy canoniz'd bones, hearsed in death,   50
Have burst their cerements; why the sepulchre
Wherein we saw thee quietly enurn'd
Hath op'd his ponderous and marble jaws
To cast thee up again. What may this mean
That thou, dead corse, again in complete steel   55
Revisits thus the glimpses of the moon,
Making night hideous, and we fools of nature
So horridly to shake our disposition
With thoughts beyond the reaches of our souls?
Say, why is this? wherefore? What should we do? 60

Ghost *beckons* HAMLET.

HORATIO

It beckons you to go away with it,
As if it some impartment did desire
To you alone.

65 **removed ground**   remote, secluded place.

71 **I do not set my life at a pin's fee**   I do not value my life more than the cost
    of a pin.

72 **And for**   and as for.

75 **flood**   sea.

77 **beetles**   overhangs.

79 **deprive your sovereignty of reason**   take away reason from its control over
    your actions.

81 **toys of desperation**   fanciful notions of despair leading to suicide.

MARCELLUS

Look with what courteous action
It waves you to a more removed ground.   65
But do not go with it.

HORATIO

No, by no means.

HAMLET

It will not speak; then I will follow it.

HORATIO

Do not, my lord.

HAMLET

Why, what should be the fear?   70
I do not set my life at a pin's fee;
And for my soul, what can it do to that,
Being a thing immortal as itself?
It waves me forth again; I'll follow it.

HORATIO

What if it tempt you toward the flood, my lord,   75
Or to the dreadful summit of the cliff
That beetles o'er his base into the sea,
And there assume some other horrible form,
Which might deprive your sovereignty of reason
And draw you into madness? Think of it: 80
The very place puts toys of desperation,
Without more motive, into every brain
That looks so many fathoms to the sea
And hears it roar beneath.

HAMLET

It waves me still.   85
Go on; I'll follow thee.

67

91 **arture**   artery.

92 **hardy**   strong.

  Nemean lion   in Greek mythology, one of the twelve labours of Hercules was to kill a huge, ferocious lion that was terrorising the valley of Nemea.

  nerve   sinews.

93 **Unhand**   let me go. Marcellus and Horatio are holding Hamlet back.

94 **lets**   hinders.

96 **waxes**   grows.

97 **fit**   fitting.

98 **Have after**   follow him.

MARCELLUS

You shall not go, my lord.

HAMLET

Hold off your hands.

HORATIO

Be rul'd; you shall not go.

HAMLET

My fate cries out, 90
And makes each petty arture in this body
As hardy as the Nemean lion's nerve.

Ghost *beckons*.

Still am I call'd. Unhand me, gentlemen.
By heaven, I'll make a ghost of him that lets me.
I say, away! Go on; I'll follow thee. 95

Exeunt Ghost *and* HAMLET

HORATIO

He waxes desperate with imagination.

MARCELLUS

Let's follow; 'tis not fit thus to obey him.

HORATIO

Have after. To what issue will this come?

MARCELLUS

Something is rotten in the state of Denmark.

HORATIO

Heaven will direct it. 100

MARCELLUS

Nay, let's follow him.

Exeunt

2 **Mark me** listen carefully.

4 **my hour** i.e. dawn, when he must return to purgatory.

10 **bound** ready: but the ghost takes him to mean obliged when it replies 'So art thou to revenge'.

Scene five

Elsinore. The battlements of the Castle.

Enter Ghost *and* HAMLET

HAMLET
Whither wilt thou lead me? Speak, I'll go no
further.

GHOST
Mark me.

HAMLET
I will.

GHOST
My hour is almost come,
When I to sulph'rous and tormenting flames   5
Must render up myself.

HAMLET
Alas, poor ghost!

GHOST
Pity me not, but lend thy serious hearing
To what I shall unfold.

HAMLET
Speak; I am bound to hear.   10

GHOST
So art thou to revenge, when thou shalt hear.

HAMLET
What?

GHOST
I am thy father's spirit,

14 **Doom'd**   sentenced.

15 **fast**   be imprisoned.

16 **days of nature**   lifetime.

17 **But that**   if it were not for the fact that.

20 **harrow up**   cut to pieces with a harrow, a heavy farming tool used for breaking up the soil after ploughing.

21 **start from their spheres**   jump out of their sockets.

22 **locks**   i.e. locks of hair.

23 **particular**   individual.

24 **fretful porpentine**   angry porcupine.

25 **eternal blazon**   picture of the secrets of eternity.

  be   i.e. be made known.

26 **List**   listen.

29 **unnatural**   a word with much stronger connotations to Shakespeare's audience. The murder of a brother was an especially vicious crime, going against 'nature'.

31 **in the best**   at best. Even the least reprehensible murder is foul.

33 **Haste me to know't**   let me know about it at once.

34 **meditation**   thought.

36 **I find thee apt**   I approve of your attitude.

37–8 **And duller. . .Lethe wharf**   and you would be more sluggish ('duller') than the fleshy plant ('fat weed') that grows on the banks ('wharf') of the river Lethe. In Greek mythology, the Lethe was a river in the underworld. Dead souls drank of its waters, and this caused them to forget their past existence.

Doom'd for a certain term to walk the night,
And for the day confin'd to fast in fires,   15
Till the foul crimes done in my days of nature
Are burnt and purg'd away. But that I am forbid
To tell the secrets of my prison-house,
I could a tale unfold whose lightest word
Would harrow up thy soul, freeze thy young blood,   20
Make thy two eyes, like stars, start from their
    spheres,
Thy knotted and combined locks to part,
And each particular hair to stand an end,
Like quills upon the fretful porpentine,
But this eternal blazon must not be   25
To ears of flesh and blood. List, list, O, list!
If thou didst ever thy dear father love –

HAMLET

O God!

GHOST

Revenge his foul and most unnatural murder.

HAMLET

Murder!   30

GHOST

Murder most foul, as in the best it is:
But this most foul, strange, and unnatural.

HAMLET

Haste me to know't, that I, with wings as swift
As meditation or the thoughts of love,
May sweep to my revenge.   35

GHOST

I find thee apt;
And duller shouldst thou be than the fat weed

40 *'Tis given out*   the story has been put about.

41 *whole ear of Denmark*   all the people of Denmark.

42 *forged process*   false account.

43 *Rankly abus'd*   grossly deceived.

46 *prophetic*   Hamlet has evidently already guessed that foul play was involved in his father's death.

56–7 *decline Upon*   descend to.

60 *shape of heaven*   disguised as an angel.

61 *to a radiant angel link'd*   married to an angel.

62 *sate itself in a celestial bed*   satisfy itself sexually with a heavenly partner.

63 *prey on garbage*   feed on filth. In this extended metaphor, the ghost compares itself to the 'radiant angel', Gertrude to 'lust' and Claudius to 'garbage'.

67 *secure hour*   at the time that I felt safest.

68 *hebona*   a poison.

    vial   small glass vessel.

That roots itself in ease on Lethe wharf,
Wouldst thou not stir in this. Now, Hamlet, hear:
'Tis given out that, sleeping in my orchard,   40
A serpent stung me; so the whole ear of Denmark
Is by a forged process of my death
Rankly abus'd; but know, thou noble youth,
The serpent that did sting thy father's life
Now wears his crown.   45

HAMLET
O my prophetic soul!
My uncle!

GHOST
Ay, that incestuous, that adulterate beast,
With witchcraft of his wits, with traitorous gifts –
O wicked wit and gifts that have the power   50
So to seduce! – won to his shameful lust
The will of my most seeming virtuous queen.
O Hamlet, what a falling off was there,
From me, whose love was of that dignity
That it went hand in hand even with the vow   55
I made to her in marriage; and to decline
Upon a wretch whose natural gifts were poor
To those of mine!
But virtue, as it never will be moved,
Though lewdness court it in a shape of heaven,   60
So lust, though to a radiant angel link'd,
Will sate itself in a celestial bed
And prey on garbage.
But soft! methinks I scent the morning air.
Brief let me be. Sleeping within my orchard,   65
My custom always of the afternoon,
Upon my secure hour thy uncle stole,
With juice of cursed hebona in a vial,

70 **leprous distilment** distilled liquid causing effects like those of leprosy.

72 **quicksilver** mercury.

73 **gates and alleys** veins and arteries. The body is being compared to a city.

74 **posset** clot.

75 **eager** sharp or sour additions which would make the milk curdle.

77 **tetter bark'd about** eruptions and boils broke out on his skin, like bark on a tree.

78 **lazar-like** like someone suffering from leprosy.

81 **dispatch'd** deprived.

82 **Cut off** killed.

   blossoms of my sin while my sins were still in full bloom. Old Hamlet was killed so quickly that he was unable to repent his sins before death, making the time he has to spend in purgatory longer.

83 **Unhous'led** without having received the sacrament.

   disappointed unprepared.

   unanel'd unannointed.

85 **imperfections on my head** sins unpardoned.

87 **nature** natural feelings as a son.

89 **luxury** lechery.

90 **act** i.e. of revenge.

92 **aught** anything (the object of 'contrive').

   heaven i.e. God's judgement.

93 **thorns that in her bosom lodge** i.e. her own guilty conscience.

95 **matin** morning.

96 **gins** begins.

   his i.e. the glowworm's.

   uneffectual weak.

98 **host of heaven** army of angels.

And in the porches of my ears did pour
The leperous distilment; whose effect   70
Holds such an enmity with blood of man
That swift as quicksilver it courses through
The natural gates and alleys of the body;
And with a sudden vigour it doth posset
And curd, like eager droppings into milk,   75
The thin and wholesome blood. So did it mine;
And a most instant tetter bark'd about,
Most lazar-like, with vile and loathsome crust,
All my smooth body.
Thus was I, sleeping, by a brother's hand   80
Of life, of crown, of queen, at once dispatch'd;
Cut off even in the blossoms of my sin,
Unhous'led, disappointed, unanel'd;
No reck'ning made, but sent to my account
With all my imperfections on my head.   85
O, horrible! O, horrible! most horrible!
If thou hast nature in thee, bear it not;
Let not the royal bed of Denmark be
A couch for luxury and damned incest.
But, howsomever thou pursuest this act,   90
Taint not thy mind, nor let thy soul contrive
Against thy mother aught; leave her to heaven,
And to those thorns that in her bosom lodge
To prick and sting her. Fare thee well at once.
The glowworm shows the matin to be near,   95
And gins to pale his uneffectual fire.
Adieu, adieu, adieu! Remember me.

Exit

HAMLET
O all you host of heaven! O earth! What else?

77

99 *couple*   include.

100 *instant*   instantly.

103 *distracted globe*   confused head.

105 *trivial fond*   insignificant and foolish.

106 *saws*   wise proverbs.

all forms, all pressures past   images and impressions of the past.

113 *meet it is*   it is appropriate.

121 *secure him*   keep him safe.

And shall I couple hell? O, fie! Hold, hold, my
   heart;
And you, my sinews, grow not instant old,   100
But bear me stiffly up. Remember thee!
Ay, thou poor ghost, whiles memory holds a seat
In this distracted globe. Remember thee!
Yea, from the table of my memory
I'll wipe away all trivial fond records,   105
All saws of books, all forms, all pressures past,
That youth and observation copied there,
And thy commandment all alone shall live
Within the book and volume of my brain,
Unmix'd with baser matter. Yes, by heaven!   110
O most pernicious woman!
O villain, villain, smiling, damned villain!
My tables – meet it is I set it down
That one may smile, and smile, and be a villain;
At least I am sure it may be so in Denmark.   115

Writing

So, uncle, there you are. Now to my word:
It is 'Adieu, adieu! Remember me'.
I have sworn't.

HORATIO
   (*Within*) My lord, my lord!

Enter HORATIO *and* MARCELLUS.

MARCELLUS
   Lord Hamlet!   120

HORATIO
   Heavens secure him!

HAMLET
   So be it!

124 **Come, bird, come**   Hamlet makes a joke of Marcellus's cry, answering as if
       he is a falconer calling his hawk.

132 **once**   ever.

136 **But he's an arrant knave**   that is not a complete scoundrel. Hamlet is
       uncertain whether to reveal the ghost's secret, and is playing for time.

MARCELLUS
Illo, ho, ho, my lord!

HAMLET
Hillo, ho, ho, boy! Come, bird, come.

MARCELLUS
How is't, my noble lord?   125

HORATIO
What news, my lord?

HAMLET
O, wonderful!

HORATIO
Good my lord, tell it.

HAMLET
No; you will reveal it.

HORATIO
Not I, my lord, by heaven!   130

MARCELLUS
Nor I, my lord.

HAMLET
How say you, then; would heart of man once think
    it?
But you'll be secret?

BOTH
Ay, by heaven, my lord!

HAMLET
There's never a villain dwelling in all Denmark   135
But he's an arrant knave.

140 *circumstance*   formality.

142 *point*   direct.

150 *Saint Patrick*   an appropriate saint to swear by because he is the patron
saint of error and confusion as well as the gatekeeper of purgatory, to
which the ghost is returning.

152 *honest ghost*   i.e. not an evil spirit.

154 *O'ermaster't*   overcome it.

156 *Give*   grant.

HORATIO

There needs no ghost, my lord, come from the
    grave
To tell us this.

HAMLET

Why, right; you are in the right;
And so, without more circumstance at all,   140
I hold it fit that we shake hands and part;
You, as your business and desire shall point
    you –
For every man hath business and desire,
Such as it is; and for my own poor part,
Look you, I will go pray.   145

HORATIO

These are but wild and whirling words, my lord.

HAMLET

I am sorry they offend you, heartily;
Yes, faith, heartily.

HORATIO

There's no offence, my lord.

HAMLET

Yes, by Saint Patrick, but there is, Horatio,   150
And much offence too. Touching this vision
    here –
It is an honest ghost, that let me tell you.
For your desire to know what is between us,
O'ermaster't as you may. And now, good friends,
As you are friends, scholars, and soldiers,   155
Give me one poor request.

HORATIO

What is't, my lord? We will.

163 **Upon my sword**   because the hilt of a sword forms a cross.

167 **truepenny**   honest fellow.

168 **cellarage**   space under the stage.

HAMLET

Never make known what you have seen to-night.

BOTH

My lord, we will not.

HAMLET

Nay, but swear't.   160

HORATIO

In faith, My lord, not I.

MARCELLUS

Nor I, my lord, in faith.

HAMLET

Upon my sword.

MARCELLUS

We have sworn, my lord, already.

HAMLET

Indeed, upon my sword, indeed.   165

GHOST

(*Cries under the stage*) Swear.

HAMLET

Ha, ha, boy! say'st thou so? Art thou there,
  truepenny?
Come on. You hear this fellow in the cellarage;
Consent to swear.

HORATIO

Propose the oath, my lord.   170

HAMLET

Never to speak of this that you have seen,
Swear by my sword.

174 *Hic et ubique?*   (Latin) here and everywhere?

181 *pioneer*   military tunneller, who undermines enemy positions.

183 *as a stranger give it welcome*   accept it without asking too many questions.

187 *so help you mercy*   as you hope to receive God's mercy.

188 *How*   however.

   some'er   sometimes.

190 *put an antic disposition on*   behave in an eccentric manner.

192 *encumb'red*   folded.

193 *doubtful phrase*   ambiguous or mysterious remark.

194 *an if*   if.

GHOST

(*Beneath*) Swear.

HAMLET

Hic et ubique? Then we'll shift our ground.
Come hither, gentlemen,   175
And lay your hands again upon my sword.
Swear by my sword
Never to speak of this that you have heard.

GHOST

(*Beneath*) Swear, by his sword.

HAMLET

Well said, old mole! Canst work i' th' earth so fast? 180
A worthy pioneer! Once more remove, good
    friends.

HORATIO

O day and night, but this is wondrous strange!

HAMLET

And therefore as a stranger give it welcome.
There are more things in heaven and earth,
    Horatio,
Than are dreamt of in your philosophy.   185
But come.
Here, as before, never, so help you mercy,
How strange or odd some'er I bear myself –
As I perchance hereafter shall think meet
To put an antic disposition on –   190
That you, at such times, seeing me, never shall,
With arms encumb'red thus, or this head-shake,
Or by pronouncing of some doubtful phrase,
As 'Well, well, we know' or 'We could, an if we
    would'

195 **list** wished.

There be. . .might there are people, who if they chose to. . .

196 **note** indicate.

203 **friending** friendship.

206 **The time is out of joint** the present time is unsettled and disordered.

Or 'If we list to speak' or 'There be, an if they
    might'   195
Or such ambiguous giving out, to note
That you know aught of me – this do swear,
So grace and mercy at your most need help you.

GHOST

(*Beneath*) Swear.

HAMLET

Rest, rest, perturbed spirit! So, gentlemen,   200
With all my love I do commend me to you;
And what so poor a man as Hamlet is
May do t'express his love and friending to you,
God willing, shall not lack. Let us go in together;
And still your fingers on your lips, I pray.   205
The time is out of joint. O cursed spite,
That ever I was born to set it right!
Nay, come, let's go together.

                                           Exeunt

Claudius, Polonius and Gertrude: Young Vic, 1982.

Act 2: summary

[handwritten annotation in margin: He doesn't trust his son, or he could also be ? concerned of him]

Two months have passed. Polonius tells a servant to go to Paris to spy on Laertes. Ophelia tells her father that when she last met Hamlet, he appeared to be mad. Polonius interprets this as the symptoms of frustrated love, and decides to tell Claudius.

Claudius and Gertrude have sent for Rosencrantz and Guildenstern, who are old friends of Hamlet's, to find out the reason for his strange behaviour.

The ambassador Claudius sent to Norway reports that Fortinbras's preparations for war against Denmark have been stopped by the king. Instead, Fortinbras plans to wage war against Poland.

Polonius reads out to Gertrude and Claudius a love letter from Hamlet. Ophelia has given it to her father and he proposes that they spy on the couple together. Polonius speaks to Hamlet, who appears mad, but as Polonius remarks, 'there is method in't' (scene 2, line 220–1). Rosencrantz and Guildenstern enter and, when questioned, admit to Hamlet that they have been sent by Claudius and Gertrude. Hamlet tells them of his sour and depressed state of mind.

A company of actors arrives at the castle, and Hamlet greets them warmly. He asks for a demonstration of their skill, and the First Player recites some lines about the death of Priam in the Trojan War. Hamlet asks that they perform 'The Murder of Gonzago' the next night, and include in it an extra speech which Hamlet himself will write.

Alone, Hamlet condemns himself for his failure so far to have obeyed the ghost's demands for revenge, accusing himself of cowardice. His plan now is to have the actors perform a story similar to the murder of his father. He will observe the king's behaviour during the play, and if he looks guilty, this will confirm the ghost's story.

3 **marvellous** very.

8 **Enquire me** i.e. for me.

Danskers Danes.

9 **keep** live.

11 **encompassment and drift of question** roundabout method of enquiry.

12–13 **come you. . .touch it** you will learn more (of Laertes) than specific questions ('particular demands') would tell you.

14 **Take you** pretend to have.

Act Two

Scene one

Elsinore. The house of Polonius.

Enter POLONIUS *and* REYNALDO.

POLONIUS
  Give him this money and these notes, Reynaldo.

REYNALDO
  I will, my lord.

POLONIUS
  You shall do marvellous wisely, good Reynaldo,
  Before you visit him, to make inquire
  Of his behaviour.   5

REYNALDO
  My lord, I did intend it.

POLONIUS
  Marry, well said; very well said. Look you, sir,
  Enquire me first what Danskers are in Paris;
  And how, and who, what means, and where they
     keep,
  What company, at what expense; and finding   10
  By this encompassment and drift of question
  That they do know my son, come you more nearer
  Than your particular demands will touch it.
  Take you, as 'twere, some distant knowledge of
     him;
  As thus: 'I know his father and his friends,   15
  And in part him'. Do you mark this, Reynaldo?

20 **put on him** attribute to him.

21 **forgeries** slanders.

rank foul.

23 **usual slips** commonplace minor vices.

24 **noted** recognised.

26 **gaming** gambling.

28 **Drabbing** associating with prostitutes.

30 **season it in the charge** tone down the severity of the accusation.

32 **incontinency** complete promiscuity.

33 **quaintly** subtly.

34 **taints of liberty** faults natural to freedom.

36 **savageness in unreclaimed blood** wildness of untamed passion.

37 **Of general assault** which affects all young people.

REYNALDO
  Ay, very well, my lord.

POLONIUS
  'And in part him – but' you may say 'not well;
  But if 't be he I mean, he's very wild;
  Addicted so and so'; and there put on him   20
  What forgeries you please; marry, none so rank
  As may dishonour him; take heed of that;
  But, sir, such wanton, wild, and usual slips
  As are companions noted and most known
  To youth and liberty.   25

REYNALDO
  As gaming, my lord.

POLONIUS
  Ay, or drinking, fencing, swearing, quarrelling,
  Drabbing – you may go so far.

REYNALDO
  My lord, that would dishonour him.

POLONIUS
  Faith, no; as you may season it in the charge.   30
  You must not put another scandal on him,
  That he is open to incontinency;
  That's not my meaning. But breathe his faults so
    quaintly
  That they may seem the taints of liberty;
  The flash and outbreak of a fiery mind,   35
  A savageness in unreclaimed blood,
  Of general assault.

REYNALDO
  But, my good lord –

42 **fetch of warrant**   justified trick.

43 **slight sullies**   mild faults.

44 **soil'd wi' th' working**   blemished in the course of its natural use.

46 **party in converse**   the person you are talking to.

   sound   i.e. sound out.

47 **Having ever**   if he has ever.

   prenominate crimes   minor faults we have just been talking about.

48 **the youth you breathe of**   i.e. Laertes.

49 **closes with you in this consequence**   confides in you in the following way.

51 **addition**   title.

54 **'a**   he.

POLONIUS

Wherefore should you do this?

REYNALDO

Ay, my lord, I would know that.   40

POLONIUS

Marry, sir, here's my drift,
And I believe it is a fetch of warrant;
You laying these slight sullies on my son,
As 'twere a thing a little soil'd wi' th' working,
Mark you,   45
Your party in converse, him you would sound,
Having ever seen in the prenominate crimes
The youth you breathe of guilty, be assur'd
He closes with you in this consequence –
'Good sir' or so, or 'friend' or 'gentleman'   50
According to the phrase or the addition
Of man and country.

REYNALDO

Very good, my lord.

POLONIUS

And then, sir, does 'a this – 'a does –
What was I about to say? By the mass,   55
I was about to say something; where did I leave?

REYNALDO

At 'closes in the consequence', at 'friend or so' and
  'gentleman'

POLONIUS

At 'closes in the consequence' – ay, marry,
He closes thus: 'I know the gentleman;
I saw him yesterday, or t'other day,   60

97

62 *o'ertook in's rouse*   overcome with drunkenness.

65 *Videlicet*   that is to say.

67 *of*   by.

   reach   insight.

68 *windlasses*   roundabout ways (a hunting term).

   assays of bias   indirect attempts.

69 *indirections*   indirect methods.

   directions   people's intentions.

71 *have me*   understand me.

73 *God buy ye*   God redeem your soul (goodbye).

75 *Observe his inclination in yourself*   make direct observation of his behaviour.

77 *ply his music*   have liberty to do as he wishes.

Or then, or then; with such, or such; and, as you
   say,
There was 'a gaming; there o'ertook in's rouse;
There falling out at tennis'; or perchance
'I saw him enter such a house of sale'
Videlicet, a brothel, or so forth. See you now   65
Your bait of falsehood take this carp of truth;
And thus do we of wisdom and of reach,
With windlasses and with assays of bias,
By indirections find directions out;
So, by my former lecture and advice,   70
Shall you my son. You have me, have you not?

REYNALDO
My lord, I have.

POLONIUS
God buy ye; fare ye well.

REYNALDO
Good my lord!

POLONIUS
Observe his inclination in yourself.   75

REYNALDO
I shall, my lord.

POLONIUS
And let him ply his music.

REYNALDO
Well, my lord.

POLONIUS
Farewell!

Exit REYNALDO

99

83 **closet**   private sitting room.

84 **doublet all ubrac'd**   shirt all unfastened.

85 **fouled**   dirty.

86 **down-gyved**   hanging down round his ankles like fetters.

88 **purport**   meaning.

99 **As 'a**   as if he.

101 **waving**   moving.

Enter OPHELIA.

How now, Ophelia! What's the matter?   80

OPHELIA

O my lord, my lord, I have been so affrighted!

POLONIUS

With what, i' th' name of God?

OPHELIA

My lord, as I was sewing in my closet,
Lord Hamlet, with his doublet all unbrac'd,
No hat upon his head, his stockings fouled,   85
Ungart'red and down-gyved to his ankle;
Pale as his shirt, his knees knocking each other,
And with a look so piteous in purport
As if he had been loosed out of hell
To speak of horrors – he comes before me.   90

POLONIUS

Mad for thy love?

OPHELIA

My lord, I do not know,
But truly I do fear it.

POLONIUS

What said he?

OPHELIA

He took me by the wrist, and held me hard;   95
Then goes he to the length of all his arm,
And, with his other hand thus o'er his brow,
He falls to such perusal of my face
As 'a would draw it. Long stay'd he so.
At last, a little shaking of mine arm,   100
And thrice his head thus waving up and down,

101

103 **bulk** body.

108 **bended** directed.

110 **ecstasy** madness.

111 **property** quality.

fordoes destroys.

121 **quoted** observed.

122 **wreck** seduce.

beshrew my jealousy! a curse on my suspicion.

123–4 **it is as proper. . .opinions** it is as characteristic ('proper') of our old age to go too far in our scheming.

127–8 **This must be known. . .utter love** this must be made known to the king, because if it were kept secret ('kept close') it might cause us more grief than would the hate it will provoke when we reveal it.

He rais'd a sigh so piteous and profound
As it did seem to shatter all his bulk
And end his being. That done, he lets me go,
And, with his head over his shoulder turn'd,   105
He seem'd to find his way without his eyes:
For out adoors he went without their helps
And to the last bended their light on me.

POLONIUS

Come, go with me, I will go seek the King.
This is the very ecstasy of love,   110
Whose violent property fordoes itself,
And leads the will to desperate undertakings
As oft as any passion under heaven
That does afflict our natures. I am sorry –
What, have you given him any hard words of
    late?   115

OPHELIA

No, my good lord; but, as you did command,
I did repel his letters, and denied
His access to me.

POLONIUS

That hath made him mad.
I am sorry that with better heed and judgment   120
I had not quoted him. I fear'd he did but trifle,
And meant to wreck thee; but beshrew my
    jealousy!
By heaven, it is as proper to our age
To cast beyond ourselves in our opinions
As it is common for the younger sort   125
To lack discretion. Come, go we to the King.
This must be known; which, being kept close,
    might move

2 **Moreover that**   besides the fact that.

6 **Sith nor**   since neither.

10 **deem of**   judge.

12 **sith**   afterwards.

    haviour   behaviour.

13 **vouchsafe your rest**   agree to remain.

16 **occasion**   chance.

18 **open'd**   made known.

More grief to hide than hate to utter love.
Come.

Exeunt

Scene two

Elsinore. The Castle.

Flourish. Enter KING, QUEEN, ROSENCRANTZ,
GUILDENSTERN, *and* Attendants.

KING
Welcome, dear Rosencrantz and Guildenstern!
Moreover that we much did long to see you,
The need we have to use you did provoke
Our hasty sending. Something have you heard
Of Hamlet's transformation; so I call it,   5
Sith nor th' exterior nor the inward man
Resembles that it was. What it should be,
More than his father's death, that thus hath put
    him
So much from th' understanding of himself,
I cannot deem of. I entreat you both   10
That, being of so young days brought up with him,
And sith so neighboured to his youth and haviour,
That you vouchsafe your rest here in our court
Some little time; so by your companies
To draw him on to pleasures, and to gather,   15
So much as from occasion you may glean,
Whether aught to us unknown afflicts him thus
That, open'd, lies within our remedy.

QUEEN
Good gentlemen, he hath much talk'd of you;

21 **adheres**   is close to.

22 **gentry**   courtesy.

24 **supply**   assistance.

profit   benefit.

our hope   i.e. our hope to find out what is troubling Hamlet.

26 **fits**   is suitable for.

28 **of**   over.

29–30 **Put your dread. . .entreaty**   express your wishes, which we are bound to respect, more as a command than as a request.

32 **in the full bent**   completely.

40 **practices**   what we do.

And sure I am two men there is not living   20
To whom he more adheres. If it will please you
To show us so much gentry and good will
As to expend your time with us awhile
For the supply and profit of our hope,
Your visitation shall receive such thanks   25
As fits a king's remembrance.

ROSENCRANTZ
　　Both your Majesties
Might, by the sovereign power you have of us,
Put your dread pleasures more into command
Than to entreaty.   30

GUILDENSTERN
　　But we both obey,
And here give up ourselves, in the full bent,
To lay our service freely at your feet,
To be commanded.

KING
Thanks, Rosencrantz and gentle Guildenstern.   35

QUEEN
Thanks, Guildenstern and gentle Rosencrantz.
And I beseech you instantly to visit
My too much changed son. Go, some of you,
And bring these gentlemen where Hamlet is.

GUILDENSTERN
Heavens make our presence and our practices   40
Pleasant and helpful to him!

QUEEN
　　Aye amen!

Exeunt ROSENCRANTZ, GUILDENSTERN, *and some* Attendants

45 *still* always.

47 *hold* value.

50 *policy* the business of politics.

55 *fruit* i.e. the final course.

56 *grace* honour.

58 *head* origin.

distemper mental disorder.

59 *doubt* suspect.

the main i.e. the main one.

61 *sift him* examine him (Polonius) closely.

Enter POLONIUS.

POLONIUS

Th' ambassadors from Norway, my good lord,
Are joyfully return'd.

KING

Thou still hast been the father of good news.   45

POLONIUS

Have I, my lord? I assure you, my good liege,
I hold my duty, as I hold my soul,
Both to my God and to my gracious King;
And I do think – or else this brain of mine
Hunts not the trail of policy so sure   50
As it hath us'd to do – that I have found
The very cause of Hamlet's lunacy.

KING

O, speak of that; that do I long to hear.

POLONIUS

Give first admittance to th' ambassadors;
My news shall be the fruit to that great feast.   55

KING

Thyself do grace to them, and bring them in.

Exit POLONIUS

He tells me, my dear Gertrude, he hath found
The head and source of all your son's distemper.

QUEEN

I doubt it is no other but the main,
His father's death and our o'erhasty marriage.   60

KING

Well, we shall sift him.

63 **brother**   i.e. fellow king.

64 **desires**   good wishes.

65 **Upon our first**   as soon as he had heard what we said.

66 **to him appear'd**   he was under the impression.

67 **preparation 'gainst the Polack**   expedition prepared to fight the Poles.

70 **impotence**   weakness.

71 **falsely borne in hand**   deceitfully taken advantage of.

   arrests   orders to stop warlike preparations.

73 **in fine**   in conclusion.

75 **give th'assay of arms**   make a military attack.

77 **fee**   allowance, salary.

78 **commission**   permission and order.

80 **entreaty**   request.

81 **quiet pass**   permission to pass peacefully.

83 **regards**   conditions.

85 **likes us**   pleases me.

86 **more considered time**   when we have more time to consider it.

Re-enter POLONIUS, *with* VOLTEMAND *and* CORNELIUS.

Welcome, my good friends!
Say, Voltemand, what from our brother Norway?

VOLTEMAND
Most fair return of greetings and desires.
Upon our first, he sent out to suppress   65
His nephew's levies; which to him appear'd
To be a preparation 'gainst the Polack;
But, better look'd into, he truly found
It was against your Highness. Whereat griev'd,
That so his sickness, age, and impotence,   70
Was falsely borne in hand, sends out arrests
On Fortinbras; which he, in brief, obeys;
Receives rebuke from Norway; and, in fine,
Makes vow before his uncle never more
To give th' assay of arms against your Majesty.   75
Whereon old Norway, overcome with joy,
Gives him threescore thousand crowns in annual
   fee,
And his commission to employ those soldiers,
So levied as before, against the Polack;
With an entreaty, herein further shown.   80

Gives a paper.

That it might please you to give quiet pass
Through your dominions for this enterprise,
On such regards of safety and allowance
As therein are set down.

KING
It likes us well;   85
And at our more considered time we'll read,
Answer, and think upon this business.

111

92 **expostulate**   discuss, debate.

96 **soul of wit**   essence of intelligence.

97 **limbs and outward flourishes**   less essential outward parts.

102 **More matter with less art**   more substance with less rhetoric, or get to the point!

105 **figure**   figure of speech.

109 **defect**   mental disorder, fault.

111 **Thus it remains, and the remainder thus**   this is the situation as it is, and now follows the remainder of my analysis of it.

112 **Perpend**   consider.

113 **while she is mine**   until she is married.

115 **gather, and surmise**   put this together with what I have told you and draw your conclusions.

Meantime we thank you for your well-took labour.
Go to your rest; at night we'll feast together.
Most welcome home!   90

    Exeunt Ambassadors *and* Attendants

POLONIUS
This business is well ended.
My liege, and madam, to expostulate
What majesty should be, what duty is,
Why day is day, night night, and time is time,
Were nothing, but to waste night, day, and time.   95
Therefore, since brevity is the soul of wit,
And tediousness the limbs and outward flourishes,
I will be brief. Your noble son is mad.
Mad call I it; for, to define true madness,
What is't but to be nothing else but mad?   100
But let that go.

QUEEN
More matter with less art.

POLONIUS
Madam, I swear I use no art at all.
That he's mad, 'tis true: 'tis true 'tis pity;
And pity 'tis 'tis true. A foolish figure!   105
But farewell it, for I will use no art,
Mad let us grant him, then; and now remains
That we find out the cause of this effect;
Or rather say the cause of this defect,
For this effect defective comes by cause.   110
Thus it remains, and the remainder thus.
Perpend.
I have a daughter – have while she is mine –
Who in her duty and obedience, mark,
Hath given me this. Now gather, and surmise.   115

117 **beautified**   made beautiful, which, in proximity to 'celestial' and 'my soul's idol' is probably a pun on beatified, meaning made blessed.

122 **stay awhile**   bear with me.

   be faithful   read the letter accurately.

123 **Doubt**   suspect.

127 **ill at these numbers**   no good at writing verse.

128 **reckon**   count.

130–1 **whilst this machine is to him**   for as long as his body is his own.

133 **more above**   in addition.

134 **As they fell out**   as they took place.

Reads.

'To the celestial, and my soul's idol, the most
beautified Ophelia.' That's an ill phrase, a vile
phrase; 'beautified' is a vile phrase. But you shall
hear. Thus:

Reads.

'In her excellent white bosom, these, &c.'   120

QUEEN

Came this from Hamlet to her?

POLONIUS

Good madam, stay awhile; I will be faithful.

Reads.

'Doubt thou the stars are fire;
   Doubt that the sun doth move;
Doubt truth to be a liar;   125
   But never doubt I love.
O dear Ophelia, I am ill at these numbers.
I have not art to reckon my groans; but that I love
thee best, O most best, believe it. Adieu.
   Thine evermore, most dear lady, whilst   130
this machine is to him, HAMLET.'
This, in obedience, hath my daughter shown me;
And more above, hath his solicitings,
As they fell out by time, by means, and place,
All given to mine ear.   135

KING

But how hath she
Receiv'd his love?

140 **fain**   willingly.

141 **When**   if when.

145 **play'd the desk or table-book**   merely recorded what I knew rather than reported it.

146 **given my heart a winking**   chose to ignore.

147 **idle**   careless.

148 **round**   directly.

149 **bespeak**   speak to.

150 **out of thy star**   above your sphere, i.e. social status.

151 **prescripts**   commands.

152 **resort**   attempts to visit her.

157 **watch**   sleeplessness.

158 **lightness**   light-headedness.

   declension   decline.

162 **like**   likely.

POLONIUS

What do you think of me?

KING

As of a man faithful and honourable.

POLONIUS

I would fain prove so. But what might you think, 140
When I had seen this hot love on the wing,
As I perceiv'd it, I must tell you that,
Before my daughter told me – what might you,
Or my dear Majesty your queen here, think,
If I had play'd the desk or table-book;   145
Or given my heart a winking, mute and dumb;
Or look'd upon this love with idle sight –
What might you think? No, I went round to work,
And my young mistress thus I did bespeak:
'Lord Hamlet is a prince out of thy star;   150
This must not be'. And then I prescripts gave her,
That she should lock herself from his resort,
Admit no messengers, receive no tokens.
Which done, she took the fruits of my advice;
And he repelled, a short tale to make,   155
Fell into a sadness, then into a fast,
Thence to a watch, thence into a weakness,
Thence to a lightness, and, by this declension,
Into the madness wherein now he raves
And all we mourn for.   160

KING

Do you think 'tis this?

QUEEN

It may be, very like.

167 *Take this from this*   Polonius points to his head and his shoulders.

170 *centre*   centre of the world.

171 *try*   judge, examine the case.

173 *lobby*   ante-room or corridor outside the throne-room.

175 *loose*   release.

176 *Be you and I*   let us be.

  arras   tapestry used as a wall-hanging.

178 *thereon*   for this reason.

179 *assistant for a state*   advisor or minister of the king.

POLONIUS

Hath there been such a time – I would fain know
    that –
That I have positively said ''Tis so',
When it prov'd otherwise?   165

KING

Not that I know.

POLONIUS

Take this from this, if this be otherwise.
If circumstances lead me, I will find
Where truth is hid, though it were hid indeed
Within the centre.   170

KING

How may we try it further?

POLONIUS

You know sometimes he walks four hours together,
Here in the lobby.

QUEEN

So he does, indeed.

POLONIUS

At such a time I'll loose my daughter to him.   175
Be you and I behind an arras then;
Mark the encounter: if he love her not,
And be not from his reason fall'n thereon,
Let me be no assistant for a state,
But keep a farm and carters.   180

KING

We will try it.

Enter HAMLET, *reading on a book*.

119

182 **poor wretch**   poor fellow (a term of affection).

184 **board him presently**   address him immediately.

186 **God-a-mercy**   thank you.

188 **fish-monger**   Hamlet may mean a pimp or seller of women, or he may be accusing Polonius of trying to 'fish out' his secrets, or he may be using the first word that enters his head in an attempt to seem mad.

196 **a good kissing carrion**   flesh good for kissing. The sun's kisses were thought to cause the dead dog to become pregnant with maggots. To add to this verbal mixture of references to sex and death, 'carrion' is also slang for a prostitute.

QUEEN
But look where sadly the poor wretch comes reading.

POLONIUS
Away, I do beseech you, both away:
I'll board him presently. O, give me leave.

Exeunt KING *and* QUEEN

How does my good Lord Hamlet?   185

HAMLET
Well, God-a-mercy.

POLONIUS
Do you know me, my lord?

HAMLET
Excellent well; you are a fish-monger.

POLONIUS
Not I, my lord.

HAMLET
Then I would you were so honest a man.   190

POLONIUS
Honest, my lord!

HAMLET
Ay, sir; to be honest, as this world goes, is to be
one man pick'd out of ten thousand.

POLONIUS
That's very true, my lord.

HAMLET
For if the sun breed maggots in a dead dog, being 195
a good kissing carrion – Have you a daughter?

199–200 **But as your daughter may conceive**   Hamlet continues with mad logic: if the sun can cause a dead dog to bear maggots, can it not make a girl pregnant?

200 **look to't**   take care.

201 **How say you by that?**   what do you mean by that?

204 **extremity**   distress.

208 **matter**   subject.

209 **Between who?**   Hamlet takes 'matter' to mean quarrel or trouble.

213 **purging thick amber**   discharging yellowish pus.

214 **plumtree gum**   the sap which oozes from plum trees.

215 **hams**   thighs.

217 **hold it not honesty**   do not consider it proper.

POLONIUS

    I have, my lord.

HAMLET

    Let her not walk i' th' sun.
    Conception is a blessing. But as your daughter
    may conceive – friend, look to't.   200

POLONIUS

    How say you by that? (*Aside*) Still harping on my
    daughter. Yet he knew me not at first; 'a said I was
    a fish-monger. 'A is far gone, far gone. And truly
    in my youth I suff'red much extremity for love.
    Very near this. I'll speak to him again. – What do 205
    you read, my lord?

HAMLET

    Words, words, words.

POLONIUS

    What is the matter, my lord?

HAMLET

    Between who?

POLONIUS

    I mean, the matter that you read, my lord.   210

HAMLET

    Slanders, sir; for the satirical rogue says here that
    old men have grey beards; that their faces are
    wrinkled; their eyes purging thick amber and
    plumtree gum; and that they have a plentiful lack
    of wit, together with most weak hams – all which, 215
    sir, though I most powerfully and potently believe,
    yet I hold it not honesty to have it thus set down;

221 **out of the air**   indoors. One cure for madness was thought to be to confine the patient to a small, dark room.

223 **pregnant**   full of meaning.

224 **happiness**   aptness.

226 **prosperously be delivered of**   express with such clarity.

231 **withal**   with.

for you yourself, sir, shall grow old as I am, if, like
a crab, you could go backward.

POLONIUS

(*Aside*) Though this be madness, ~~yet there is method~~ 220
~~in't.~~ – Will you walk out of the air, my lord?

HAMLET

Into my grave?

POLONIUS

Indeed, that's out of the air. (*Aside*) How pregnant
sometimes his replies are! a happiness that often
madness hits on, which reason and sanity could 225
not so prosperously be delivered of. I will leave
him, and suddenly contrive the means of meeting
between him and my daughter. – My lord, I will
take my leave of you.

HAMLET

You cannot, sir, take from me anything that I will 230
more willingly part withal – except my life, except
my life, except my life.

Enter ROSENCRANTZ *and* GUILDENSTERN.

POLONIUS

Fare you well, my lord.

HAMLET

These tedious old fools!

POLONIUS

You go to seek the Lord Hamlet; there he is.   235

ROSENCRANTZ

(*To* POLONIUS) God save you, sir!

Exit POLONIUS

125

242 **indifferent**   ordinary.

244 **On fortune's cap we are not the very button**   we are not the most fortunate men in the world.

248 **her favours**   because they are neither at the summit ('cap') of fortune nor at her feet, they are around her middle (genitals).

249 **privates**   i.e. private parts.

251 **strumpet**   prostitute. Fortune gives favours to all, but is faithful to no one.

GUILDENSTERN

My honour'd lord!

ROSENCRANTZ

My most dear lord!

HAMLET

My excellent good friends! How dost thou, Guildenstern? Ah, Rosencrantz! Good lads, how do you 240
both?

ROSENCRANTZ

As the indifferent children of the earth.

GUILDENSTERN

Happy in that we are not over-happy;
On fortune's cap we are not the very button.

HAMLET

Nor the soles of her shoe?   245

ROSENCRANTZ

Neither, my lord.

HAMLET

Then you live about her waist, or in the middle of
her favours?

GUILDENSTERN

Faith, her privates we.

HAMLET

In the secret parts of Fortune? O, most true; she 250
is a strumpet. What news?

ROSENCRANTZ

None, my lord, but that the world's grown
honest.

127

254 **doomsday near**   the Day of Judgement must be near, because only that would cause the world to 'grow honest'.

261 **confines**   places of confinement.

262 **wards**   areas.

HAMLET

Then is doomsday near. But your news is not true.
Let me question more in particular. What have 255
you, my good friends, deserved at the hands of
Fortune, that she sends you to prison hither?

GUILDENSTERN

Prison, my lord!

HAMLET

Denmark's a prison.

ROSENCRANTZ

Then is the world one.   260

HAMLET

A goodly one; in which there are many confines,
wards, and dungeons, Denmark being one o' th'
worst.

ROSENCRANTZ

We think not so, my lord.

HAMLET

Why, then, 'tis none to you; for there is nothing 265
either good or bad, but thinking makes it so. To
me it is a prison.

ROSENCRANTZ

Why, then your ambition makes it one; 'tis too
narrow for your mind.

HAMLET

O God, I could be bounded in a nutshell and 270
count myself a king of infinite space, were it not
that I have bad dreams.

279–80 **beggars bodies. . .beggars' shadows**   if Rosencrantz is correct in saying that ambition is the shadow of a shadow, then beggars, because they have no ambition, have real bodies, while kings and heroes, who are ambitiously straining to reach beyond human limitations ('outstretch'd') are beggars' shadows. This exchange, from line 273 onwards, is an example of a sort of witty playing with ideas fashionable among educated people in Shakespeare's day. It takes the appearance of a logical argument without asking to be taken literally.

281 **fay**   faith.

reason   debate, carry on with this argument.

282 **wait upon you**   accompany you.

283 **sort**   classify, categorise.

285 **most dreadfully attended**   very badly served by my servants.

286 **beaten way**   well-worn path.

what make you   what are you doing.

291 **too dear a half-penny**   too expensive at a half-penny (i.e. worth very little).

→ The dreams aren't important.

GUILDENSTERN

Which dreams indeed are ambition; for the very
substance of the ambitious is merely the shadow
of a dream.   275

HAMLET

A dream itself is but a shadow.

ROSENCRANTZ

Truly, and I hold ambition of so airy and light a
quality that it is but a shadow's shadow.

HAMLET

Then are our beggars bodies, and our monarchs
and outstretch'd heroes the beggars' shadows. Shall 280
we to th' court? for, by my fay, I cannot reason.

BOTH

We'll wait upon you.

HAMLET

No such matter. I will not sort you with the rest
of my servants; for, to speak to you like an honest
man, I am most dreadfully attended. But, in the 285
beaten way of friendship, what make you at
Elsinore?

ROSENCRANTZ

To visit you, my lord; no other occasion.

HAMLET

Beggar that I am, I am even poor in thanks; but
I thank you; and sure, dear friends, my thanks are 290
too dear a half-penny. Were you not sent for? Is
it your own inclining? Is it a free visitation? Come,
come, deal justly with me. Come, come; nay,
speak.

131

296 **but to th' purpose**   but let's get to the point.

299 **colour**   disguise.

302 **conjure**   ask you very seriously.

303 **consonancy**   similar upbringing.

305–6 **by what more. . .you withal**   by whatever feeling there is between us that could make you want to answer, more than a skilled cross-examiner ('proposer') could.

306 **even**   straightforward.

309 **I have an eye of you**   I must keep an eye on you.

310 **hold not off**   do not remain silent.

314 **moult no feather**   remain intact.

316 **foregone all custom of exercises**   given up my usual sports and pastimes.

GUILDENSTERN

What should we say, my lord?   295

HAMLET

Why any thing, but to th' purpose: you were sent
for; and there is a kind of confession in your looks,
which your modesties have not craft enough to
colour; I know the good King and Queen have sent
for you.   300

ROSENCRANTZ

To what end, my lord?

HAMLET

That you must teach me. But let me conjure you
by the rights of our fellowship, by the consonancy
of our youth, by the obligation of our ever-
preserved love, and by what more dear a better 305
proposer can charge you withal, be even and direct
with me, whether you were sent for or no?

ROSENCRANTZ

(*Aside to* GUILDENSTERN) What say you?

HAMLET

(*Aside*) Nay, then, I have an eye of you. – If you
love me, hold not off.   310

GUILDENSTERN

My lord, we were sent for.

HAMLET

I will tell you why; so shall my anticipation
prevent your discovery, and your secrecy to the
King and Queen moult no feather. I have of late
– but wherefore I know not – lost all my mirth, 315
forgone all custom of exercises; and indeed it goes

133

317–8 **goodly frame**   fine structure.

318 **sterile promontory**   barren piece of land sticking out into the sea.

320 **brave**   splendid.

321 **fretted with golden fire**   decorated with the light of the sun and stars.

325 **form and moving**   shape and movement.

express   well-made.

326 **apprehension**   perception and understanding.

327 **paragon**   supreme example.

328–9 **quintessence of dust**   highest and most perfect embodiment of physical matter.

336 **lenten entertainment**   meagre hospitality, as would be given during the fasting time of Lent.

337 **coted**   overtook.

340 **tribute on me**   money from me.

341 **foil and target**   sword and shield.

342 **gratis**   without payment.

342 **humorous man**   actor playing the parts of eccentrics.

344 **tickle a' th' sere**   easily moved to laughter.

so heavily with my disposition that this goodly
frame, the earth, seems to me a sterile promontory;
this most excellent canopy the air, look you, this
brave o'er-hanging firmament, this majestical roof 320
fretted with golden fire – why, it appeareth no
other thing to me than a foul and pestilent congre-
gation of vapours. What a piece of work is a man!
How noble in reason! how infinite in faculties! in
form and moving, how express and admirable! in 325
action, how like an angel! in apprehension, how
like a god! the beauty of the world! the paragon
of animals! And yet, to me, what is this quintessence of dust? Man delights not me – no, nor
woman neither, though by your smiling you seem 330
to say so.

ROSENCRANTZ

My lord, there was no such stuff in my thoughts.

HAMLET

Why did ye laugh, then, when I said 'Man delights
not me'?

ROSENCRANTZ

To think, my lord, if you delight not in man, what 335
lenten entertainment the players shall receive from
you. We coted them on the way; and hither are
they coming to offer you service.

HAMLET

He that plays the king shall be welcome – his
Majesty shall have tribute on me; the adventurous 340
knight shall use his foil and target; the lover shall
not sigh gratis; the humorous man shall end his
part in peace; the clown shall make those laugh
whose lungs are tickle a' th' sere; and the lady

345 *freely*   openly.

349 *residence*   staying in their own town.

351 *inhibition*   being banned from their own theatre.

352 *late innovation*   recent conspiracy.

353 *estimation*   reputation.

354 **Are they so followed?**   are they still attracting the same audiences?

356 *rusty*   out of practice.

357 **their endeavour keeps in the wonted place**   their efforts are as successful as ever.

358 *eyrie*   nest of a bird of prey.

   children   a reference to a company of boy actors who were popular in Shakespeare's day, and which often presented satirical, politically controversial plays. The following discussion of them, down to line 380, is a sort of in-joke about the rivalry between Shakespeare's company and the boys. It has no particular relevance to the plot of **Hamlet**.

   eyases   young hawks.

359 **cry out on the top of the question**   can be heard above all other voices in debate.

360 *tyrannically*   excessively, as an actor playing a tyrant would be.

361 **berattle the common stages**   noisily assail the public playhouses.

363 **many wearing rapiers**   many fashionable young men.

363 **afraid of goose quills**   are afraid of what the satirical playwrights who work for the boys' company might have written about them (with their 'goose quills').

365 *escoted*   paid.

   quality   profession of actors.

366 **no longer than they can sing?**   only until their voices break?

shall say her mind freely, or the blank verse shall 345
halt for't. What players are they?

ROSENCRANTZ

Even those you were wont to take such delight in
– the tragedians of the city.

HAMLET

How chances it they travel? Their residence, both
in reputation and profit, was better both ways.   350

ROSENCRANTZ

I think their inhibition comes by the means of the
late innovation.

HAMLET

Do they hold the same estimation they did when
I was in the city? Are they so followed?

ROSENCRANTZ

No, indeed, are they not.   355

HAMLET

How comes it? Do they grow rusty?

ROSENCRANTZ

Nay, their endeavour keeps in the wonted pace;
but there is, sir, an eyrie of children, little eyases,
that cry out on the top of question, and are most
tyrannically clapp'd for't. These are now the 360
fashion, and so berattle the common stages – so
they call them – that many wearing rapiers are
afraid of goose quills and dare scarce come thither.

HAMLET

What, are they children? Who maintains 'em?
How are they escoted? Will they pursue the quality 365
no longer than they can sing? Will they not say

137

368 *common players*   i.e. adult actors.

368–9 *if their means are no better*   if they can't find any more profitable employment.

370 *succession*   future profession.

373 *tarre them*   urge them on.

373–4 *no money bid for argument*   no money put up for new plays.

374–5 *went to cuffs*   came to blows.

378 *carry it away*   gain the victory.

379 *Hercules and his load*   the sign outside Shakespeare's Globe Theatre showed Hercules with a globe on his shoulders: hence, this means that Shakespeare is comically admitting that the boys' company is winning their battle for audiences against their rivals at The Globe.

382 *mows*   grimaces, rude faces.

384 *picture in little*   miniature portrait (i.e. on coins of these values).

385 *'Sblood*   (mild oath) literally, by God's blood.

385–6 *more than natural*   beyond the usual.

afterwards, if they should grow themselves to
common players — as it is most like, if their means
are no better — their writers do them wrong to
make them exclaim against their own succession? 370

ROSENCRANTZ

Faith, there has been much to-do on both sides;
and the nation holds it no sin to tarre them to
controversy. There was for a while no money bid
for argument, unless the poet and the player went
to cuffs in the question. 375

HAMLET

Is't possible?

GUILDENSTERN

O, there has been much throwing about of brains.

HAMLET

Do the boys carry it away?

ROSENCRANTZ

Ay, that they do, my lord — Hercules and his load
too. 380

HAMLET

It is not very strange; for my uncle is King of
Denmark, and those that would make mows at him
while my father lived give twenty, forty, fifty, a
hundred ducats apiece for his picture in little.
'Sblood, there is something in this more than 385
natural, if philosophy could find it out.

A flourish.

GUILDENSTERN

There are the players.

389 *appurtenance*   proper accompaniment.

390 *fashion*   customary outward show.

390–1 *comply with you in this garb*   observe the expected formalities to you in this manner ('garb').

391 *my extent*   i.e. the extent of my welcome.

393 *entertainment*   friendly reception.

397 *north-north-west*   when the wind is blowing from this direction.

398 *I know a hawk from a handsaw*   Hamlet means that most of the time his judgement is as good as anyone's. There is much speculation among editors about what the 'hawk' and the 'handsaw' actually are: the 'handsaw', for example, may be a misprint for hernshaw, an alternative name for a heron.

399 *Well be with you*   i.e. good day.

401 *great baby*   i.e. Polonius.

402 *swaddling clouts*   bandages wrapped around newborn babies.

403 *Happily*   perhaps.

406 *You say right. . .*   Hamlet says this loudly so that Polonius will not suspect that he was the subject of Hamlet's conversation with Rosencrantz and Guildenstern.

HAMLET

Gentlemen, you are welcome to Elsinore. Your
hands, come then; th' appurtenance of welcome is
fashion and ceremony. Let me comply with you in 390
this garb; lest my extent to the players, which, I
tell you, must show fairly outwards, should more
appear like entertainment than yours. You are
welcome. But my uncle-father and aunt-mother are
deceived. 395

GUILDENSTERN

In what, my dear lord?

HAMLET

I am but mad north-north-west; when the wind is
southerly I know a hawk from a handsaw.

Re-enter POLONIUS.

POLONIUS

Well be with you, gentlemen!

HAMLET

Hark you, Guildenstern, and you too – at each ear 400
a hearer: that great baby you see there is not yet
out of his swaddling clouts.

ROSENCRANTZ

Happily he is the second time come to them; for
they say an old man is twice a child.

HAMLET

I will prophesy he comes to tell me of the players; 405
mark it. You say right, sir: a Monday morning;
'twas then indeed.

POLONIUS

My lord, I have news to tell you.

409 **Roscius**   a famous Roman actor.

412 **Buzz, buzz!**   impolite exclamation meaning something like 'Tell us something we don't know already!'

414 **on his ass**   punning on arse, and mocking Polonius's 'Upon my honour'.

418–9 **scene individable or poem unlimited**   these refer to the conventions of ancient Greek playwrights, described by the philosopher Aristotle, to confine the action of a play to one place and to a single day, and covering a single story. A play which does this is said to preserve the unities. A 'scene individable' preserves the unities, while a 'poem unlimited' does not.

419 **Seneca**   Roman writer of tragedies.

    Plautus   Roman writer of comedies.

420 **the law of writ**   plays preserving the unities.

    the liberty   plays not preserving the unities.

422 **Jephthah**   an Old Testament leader of Israel, who sacrificed his daughter.

427 **passing**   extremely.

HAMLET

My lord, I have news to tell you. When Roscius
was an actor in Rome –   410

POLONIUS

The actors are come hither, my lord.

HAMLET

Buzz, buzz!

POLONIUS

Upon my honour –

HAMLET

Then came each actor on his ass –

POLONIUS

The best actors in the world, either for tragedy, 415
comedy, history, pastoral, pastoral-comical, historical-pastoral, tragical-historical, tragical-comical-
historical-pastoral, scene individable, or poem
unlimited. Seneca cannot be too heavy nor Plautus
too light. For the law of writ and the liberty, these 420
are the only men.

HAMLET

O Jephthah, judge of Israel, what a treasure hadst
thou!

POLONIUS

What a treasure had he, my lord?

HAMLET

Why –   425
'One fair daughter, and no more,
The which he loved passing well'.

432 **follows not**   does not follow logically, but also is not the next line of the
ballad about Jephthah Hamlet began in lines 426–7.

435 **lot**   chance.

wot   knows.

438 **row**   stanza.

pious chanson   religious (because it is a story from the Bible) ballad.

439 **abridgement**   what will cut me short, but an 'abridgement' is also an
entertainment.

442 **valanc'd**   fringed i.e. with a beard.

443 **beard**   confront.

444 **young lady**   a boy actor.

445 **nearer to heaven**   i.e. taller.

446 **altitude of a chopine**   the height of a pair of high-heeled shoes.

447–8 **uncurrent gold**   piece of gold that is no longer legal tender because it has a
crack in it reaching within the circle surrounding the sovereign's head.

448 **crack'd within the ring**   broken. Boys could no longer play women's parts
once their voices had broken.

449 **We'll e'en to't**   we'll get straight down to it.

449–50 **like French falconers**   the English thought French falconers were over-
anxious to launch their falcons at the first thing that came along, rather
than wait for suitable prey.

POLONIUS

(*Aside*) Still on my daughter.

HAMLET

Am I not i' th' right, old Jephthah?

POLONIUS

If you call me Jephthah, my lord, I have a 430
daughter that I love passing well.

HAMLET

Nay, that follows not.

POLONIUS

What follows then, my lord?

HAMLET

Why –
    'As by lot, God wot'   435
and then, you know,
    'It came to pass, as most like it was'.
The first row of the pious chanson will show you
more; for look where my abridgement comes.

Enter the Players.

You are welcome, masters; welcome, all. – I am 440
glad to see thee well. – Welcome, good friends. –
O, my old friend! Why thy face is valanc'd since
I saw thee last; com'st thou to beard me in
Denmark? – What, my young lady and mistress!
By'r lady, your ladyship is nearer to heaven than 445
when I saw you last by the altitude of a chopine.
Pray God, your voice, like a piece of uncurrent
gold, be not crack'd within the ring. – Masters,
you are all welcome. We'll e'en to't like French
falconers, fly at anything we see. We'll have a 450

145

451 **straight**   straight away.

452 **quality**   skills as an actor.

457 **caviary to the general**   wasted on the common people, as caviare ('caviary') would be.

459 **cried in the top of**   were superior to.

460 **digested**   composed.

461 **modesty**   restraint.

    cunning   skill.

462 **sallets**   tasty morsels; spicey or bawdy passages.

465 **honest method**   straightforward presentation of the story.

466 **more handsome than fine**   more fittingly and satisfyingly attractive than showy or flashy.

467 **chiefly**   particularly.

    Æneas' tale   the story told by Aeneas, one of King Priam's sons, to Dido, Queen of Carthage, about the death of his father during the fall of the city of Troy. The source is in Book II of Virgil's Aeneid.

471 **rugged**   long-haired, ferocious-looking.

    Pyrrhus   the Greek soldier who killed Priam.

    Hyrcanian beast   tiger. Hyrcania is in modern Iran, and was thought in ancient times to be the home of many wild and dangerous beasts.

473 **sable**   black (because covered in hair).

475 **ominous horse**   the wooden horse in which the Greeks entered Troy.

478 **total gules**   completely red.

    trick'd   covered.

Is he checking or is he a coward?

speech straight. Come, give us a taste of your quality; come, a passionate speech.

1 PLAYER
What speech, my good lord?

HAMLET
I heard thee speak me a speech once, but it was never acted; or, if it was, not above once; for the 455 play, I remember, pleas'd not the million; 'twas caviary to the general. But it was – as I received it, and others whose judgments in such matters cried in the top of mine – an excellent play, well digested in the scenes, set down with as much 460 modesty as cunning. I remember one said there were no sallets in the lines to make the matter savoury, nor no matter in the phrase that might indict the author of affectation; but call'd it an honest method, as wholesome as sweet, and by 465 very much more handsome than fine. One speech in it I chiefly lov'd: 'twas Æneas' tale to Dido; and thereabout of it especially where he speaks of Priam's slaughter. If it live in your memory, begin at this line – let me see, let me see: 470

'The rugged Pyrrhus, like th' Hyrcanian beast,'
'Tis not so; it begins with Pyrrhus.

'The rugged Pyrrhus, he whose sable arms,
Black as his purpose, did the night resemble
When he lay couched in the ominous horse, 475
Hath now this dread and black complexion smear'd
With heraldry more dismal; head to foot
Now is he total gules, horridly trick'd
With blood of fathers, mothers, daughters, sons,

147

480 **Bak'd and impasted. . .streets**   turned into a thick paste by the heat of the dry streets.

482 **their lord's**   i.e. Priam, who as king was lord of the streets of Troy.

483 **o'er-sized with coagulate gore**   covered with congealing blood.

484 **carbuncles**   red jewel stones, which were supposed to glow in the dark.

489 **Anon**   soon.

him   i.e. Priam.

490 **Striking too short at Greeks**   old Priam is too weak to wound his Greek enemies.

492 **Repugnant to command**   disobeying orders.

495 **senseless Ilium**   Ilium was the royal palace within Troy; 'senseless' means without senses rather than stupid.

498 **Takes prisoner Pyrrhus' ear**   i.e. the noise of the palace collapsing catches Pyrrhus' attention.

499 **declining**   descending.

milky   white-haired.

501 **as a painted tyrant**   not moving, like a painting of a tyrant.

502 **like a neutral to his will and matter**   like one indifferent ('neutral') to his own desires ('will') and business ('matter').

504 **against**   before.

505 **rack**   clouds.

508 **region**   heavens.

Bak'd and impasted with the parching streets,   480
That lend a tyrannous and damned light
To their lord's murder. Roasted in wrath and fire,
And thus o'er-sized with coagulate gore,
With eyes like carbuncles, the hellish Pyrrhus
Old grandsire Priam seeks.'   485

So proceed you.

POLONIUS
Fore God, my lord, well spoken, with good accent
and good discretion.

1 PLAYER
'Anon he finds him
Striking too short at Greeks; his antique sword,   490
Rebellious to his arm, lies where it falls,
Repugnant to command. Unequal match'd,
Pyrrhus at Priam drives, in rage strikes wide;
But with the whiff and wind of his fell sword
Th' unnerved father falls. Then senseless Ilium,   495
Seeming to feel this blow, with flaming top
Stoops to his base, and with a hideous crash
Takes prisoner Pyrrhus' ear. For, lo! his sword,
Which was declining on the milky head
Of reverend Priam, seem'd i' th' air to stick.   500
So, as a painted tyrant, Pyrrhus stood
And, like a neutral to his will and matter,
Did nothing.
But as we often see, against some storm,
A silence in the heavens, the rack stand still,   505
The bold winds speechless, and the orb below
As hush as death, anon the dreadful thunder
Doth rend the region; so, after Pyrrhus' pause,
A roused vengeance sets him new a-work;

149

510 **Cyclops'** in classical mythology, the Cyclops were a race of one-eyed giants who assisted Vulcan in making armour for the gods.

511 **Mars** the Roman god of war.

proof eterne everlasting strength.

514 **strumpet** prostitute.

515 **synod** council.

516 **fellies** parts of the rim.

517 **nave** hub.

520 **It shall to the barber's** i.e. we'll cut it.

521 **He's** i.e. Polonius. Hamlet is now talking to the player.

jig a short comical performance.

tale of bawdry smutty story.

522 **Hecuba** Priam's wife, Queen of Troy.

523 **mobled** veiled.

527 **bisson rheum** blinding tears.

clout piece of cloth.

528 **late** recently.

529 **o'er-teemed** worn out with child-bearing.

531 **Who** whoever.

with tongue in venom steep'd with bitter speech, as if their tongue had been soaked ('steep'd') in poison ('venom').

532 **state** power, rule.

And never did the Cyclops' hammers fall   510
On Mars's armour, forg'd for proof eterne,
With less remorse than Pyrrhus' bleeding sword
Now falls on Priam.
Out, out, thou strumpet, Fortune! All you gods,
In general synod, take away her power;   515
Break all the spokes and fellies from her wheel,
And bowl the round nave down the hill of heaven,
As low as to the fiends.'

POLONIUS

This is too long.

HAMLET

It shall to the barber's, with your beard. Prithee 520
say on. He's for a jig, or a tale of bawdry, or he
sleeps. Say on; come to Hecuba.

1 PLAYER

'But who, ah, who had seen the mobled queen – '

HAMLET

'The mobled queen'?

POLONIUS

That's good; 'mobled queen' is good.   525

1 PLAYER

'Run barefoot up and down, threat'ning the flames
With bisson rheum; a clout upon that head
Where late the diadem stood, and for a robe,
About her lank and all o'er-teemed loins,
A blanket, in the alarm of fear caught up –   530
Who this had seen, with tongue in venom steep'd,
'Gainst Fortune's state would treason have
    pronounc'd.
But if the gods themselves did see her then,

151

538 *milch*   produce milk (i.e. tears).

   burning eyes of heaven   the sun, moon and stars.

539 *passion*   pity.

540 *whe'er*   whether.

   he   referring to Hamlet, who has been visibly moved by the player's speech.

   turn'd   changed.

544 *bestowed*   accommodated.

545 *abstract*   summary.

546 *you were better*   it would be better for you.

548 *their desert*   what they deserve.

549 *God's bodykins*   (mild oath) by God's body.

550 *after*   according to

552 *bounty*   generosity.

When she saw Pyrrhus make malicious sport
In mincing with his sword her husband's limbs,   535
The instant burst of clamour that she made –
Unless things mortal move them not at all –
Would   have   made   milch   the   burning   eyes   of
    heaven,
And passion in the gods.'

POLONIUS

Look whe'er he has not turn'd his colour, and has 540
tears in 's eyes. Prithee no more.

HAMLET

'Tis well; I'll have thee speak out the rest of this
soon. – Good my lord, will you see the players well
bestowed? Do you hear: let them be well used; for
they are the abstract and brief chronicles of the 545
time; after your death you were better have a bad
epitaph than their ill report while you live.

POLONIUS

My lord, I will use them according to their desert.

HAMLET

God's bodykins, man, much better. Use every man
after his desert, and who shall scape whipping? 550
Use them after your own honour and dignity: the
less they deserve, the more merit is in your bounty.
Take them in.

POLONIUS

Come, sirs.

HAMLET

Follow him, friends. We'll hear a play to-morrow. 555
Dost thou hear me, old friend; can you play 'The
Murder of Gonzago'?

153

559 *ha't*   have it, see it performed.

   for a need   if necessary.

569 **Good buy**   goodbye.

570 **peasant**   low, unworthy man. Frequently a term of abuse.

573 **Could force his soul. . .conceit**   could make his innermost feelings correspond
     so closely to what he was imagining. . .

574 *her*   i.e. his soul's.

   visage wann'd   face grew pale.

575 **in's aspect**   in his expression.

576 **function**   action of his body.

577 **forms to his conceit**   gestures suitable to his imaginative performance.

1 PLAYER

Ay, my lord.

HAMLET

We'll ha't to-morrow night. You could, for a need,
study a speech of some dozen or sixteen lines 560
which I would set down and insert in't, could you
not?

1 PLAYER

Ay, my lord.

HAMLET

Very well. Follow that lord; and look you mock him
not.   565

Exeunt POLONIUS *and* Players

My good friends, I'll leave you till night. You are
welcome to Elsinore.

ROSENCRANTZ

Good my lord!

Exeunt ROSENCRANTZ *and* GUILDENSTERN

HAMLET

Ay, so God buy to you! Now I am alone.
O, what a rogue and peasant slave am I!   570
Is it not monstrous that this player here,
But in a fiction, in a dream of passion,
Could force his soul so to his own conceit
That from her working all his visage wann'd;
Tears in his eyes, distraction in's aspect.   575
A broken voice, and his whole function suiting
With forms to his conceit? And all for nothing!
For Hecuba!
What's Hecuba to him or he to Hecuba,

155

583 **cleave the general ear with horrid speech**   split the audience's ears with terrifying words.

584 **free**   innocent (i.e. those free from guilt).

585 **Confound**   confuse.

588 **muddy-mettl'd**   dull spirited.

   peak   mope about.

589 **unpregnant of my cause**   unprepared to pursue my mission.

592 **defeat**   act of destruction.

593 **pate**   head.

595–6 **gives me the lie. . .the lungs**   accuses me of an out-and-out falsehood.

598 **'Swounds**   (oath) by God's wounds.

599 **pigeon-liver'd**   a coward. Pigeons or doves were thought to be gentle birds because their livers do not secrete gall, which was considered to be the bodily fluid which produced courage.

600 **To make oppression bitter**   to make the oppression of others bitter to myself.

601 **'a**   have.

   region kites   scavenging birds of the air.

603 **kindless**   unnatural.

605 **brave**   noble. Hamlet is ironically condemning himself for the empty ranting he has just been indulging in.

609 **drab**   prostitute.

610 **scullion**   lowly kitchen maid.

611 **About**   get to work.

That he should weep for her? What would he do, 580
Had he the motive and the cue for passion
That I have? He would drown the stage with tears.
And cleave the general ear with horrid speech;
Make mad the guilty, and appal the free,
Confound the ignorant, and amaze indeed 585
The very faculties of eyes and ears.
Yet I,
A dull and muddy-mettl'd rascal, peak,
Like John-a-dreams, unpregnant of my cause,
And can say nothing; no, not for a king 590
Upon whose property and most dear life
A damn'd defeat was made. Am I a coward?
Who calls me villain, breaks my pate across,
Plucks off my beard and blows it in my face,
Tweaks me by the nose, gives me the lie i' th'
    throat 595
As deep as to the lungs? Who does me this?
Ha!
'Swounds, I should take it; for it cannot be
But I am pigeon-liver'd and lack gall
To make oppression bitter, or ere this 600
I should 'a fatted all the region kites
With this slave's offal. Bloody, bawdy villain!
Remorseless, treacherous, lecherous, kindless
    villain!
O, vengeance!
Why, what an ass am I! This is most brave, 605
That I, the son of a dear father murder'd,
Prompted to my revenge by heaven and hell,
Must, like a whore, unpack my heart with words,
And fall a-cursing like a very drab,
A scullion! Fie upon't! foh! 610
About, my brains. Hum – I have heard

157

613 **cunning** skilful presentation.

614 **presently** immediately.

615 **proclaim'd** owned up to.

620 **tent him to the quick** probe him to the tenderest part of his wound.
blench turn pale.

626 **Abuses** deceives.

627 **relative** conclusive.

the idea!

That guilty creatures, sitting at a play,
Have by the very cunning of the scene
Been struck so to the soul that presently
They have proclaim'd their malefactions;   615
For murder, though it have no tongue, will speak
With most miraculous organ. I'll have these
    players   *It makes them confess.*
Play something like the murder of my father
Before mine uncle. I'll observe his looks;
I'll tent him to the quick. If 'a do blench,   620
I know my course. The spirit that I have seen
May be a devil; and the devil hath power
T' assume a pleasing shape; yea, and perhaps
Out of my weakness and my melancholy,
As he is very potent with such spirits,   625
Abuses me to damn me. I'll have grounds
More relative than this. The play's the thing
Wherein I'll catch the conscience of the King.

Exit

*Al is de waarheid nog zogo, dan
komt hy wel*

*Als hy een spice vertelt dan weet ik
wel wat ik moet doen.*

De geest kan wel 'n duivel zyn...

I have to be careful → DOUBT

*He's both a ⎯ soldier
                    to be
  ° I want∂sure   thinker °
that I have the right
information, because otherwise I
go the hell!*   159
    ↳ be damned.

Gertrude (Virginia McKenna) and Hamlet (Roger Rees): Royal Shakespeare Company production, 1985–85.

Rosencrantz and Guildenstern have been unable to discover the reason for Hamlet's madness. Polonius tells Ophelia to meet Hamlet while he and Claudius spy on them. Hamlet enters, deep in thought; seeing Ophelia, he roughly tells her to enter a nunnery. Claudius's observation of the scene convinces him that love is not the cause of Hamlet's eccentric behaviour, and fears that he may be in danger. He decides to send Hamlet away to England.

The king, queen and courtiers arrive to watch the play. At the point where the murderer pours poison into his victim's ear, Claudius starts up guiltily and leaves.

Rosencrantz and Guildenstern bring Hamlet a request from Gertrude for a private conversation. Alone, Hamlet reveals that his desire for revenge is re-sharpened, but that he will not physically harm his mother.

Claudius tells Rosencrantz and Guildenstern that they must accompany Hamlet to England. Polonius tells Claudius of Hamlet's planned meeting with Gertrude, and that he will eavesdrop on them. Left alone, Claudius reveals his guilty conscience and tries to pray. Hamlet enters, and seeing Claudius undefended, considers killing him. He decides not to: if Claudius were to die in prayer, his soul might not go to hell.

Polonius tells Gertrude of his plan to spy on Hamlet, and hides. Hamlet enters, and when he speaks violently to her, Gertrude calls for help. Polonius calls out too, and Hamlet, taking him for the king, kills him. Hamlet rages at his mother for her over-hasty marriage, and she begins to acknowledge her faults. The ghost appears to Hamlet and reminds him of his neglected task of vengeance — Gertrude can neither see nor hear it. Hamlet tells his mother to stop sleeping with Claudius, and not to reveal that he is only feigning madness. Gertrude agrees to the second demand. Hamlet leaves, dragging the body of Polonius behind him.

1 **drift of conference**   manipulation of the conversation.

2 **puts on this confusion**   assumes this madness.

7 **forward to be sounded**   willing to be questioned.

8 **crafty madness**   contrived appearance of madness.

13 **forcing of his disposition**   i.e. he forced himself to be polite to them.

14 **Niggard of question**   reluctant to start a conversation.

Guildernsteen and Rosencrantz seem to be a bit more clever than Hamlet thought.

Ze weten dat hij de madness speelt.

Act Three

Elsinore. The Castle.

Enter KING, QUEEN, POLONIUS, OPHELIA, ROSENCRANTZ, *and* GUILDENSTERN.

KING
And can you by no drift of conference
Get from him why he puts on this confusion,
Grating so harshly all his days of quiet
With turbulent and dangerous lunacy?

ROSENCRANTZ
He does confess he feels himself distracted,   5
But from what cause 'a will by no means speak.

GUILDENSTERN
Nor do we find him forward to be sounded;
But, with a crafty madness, keeps aloof
When we would bring him on to some confession
Of his true state.   10

QUEEN
Did he receive you well?

ROSENCRANTZ
Most like a gentleman.

GUILDENSTERN
But with much forcing of his disposition.

ROSENCRANTZ
Niggard of question; but of our demands
Most free in his reply.   15

16–17 **assay him To any pastime**   attempt to get him to take part in some sport or amusement.

19 **o'er-raught**   overtook.

26 **matter**   play.

29 **give him a further edge**   make him even keener on this.

33 **closely**   secretly.

35 **Affront**   meet face to face with.

36 **espials**   spies.

37 **bestow**   place.

39 **gather by him, as he is behav'd**   gather from the way he behaves.

QUEEN

Did you assay him
To any pastime?

ROSENCRANTZ

Madam, it so fell out that certain players
We o'er-raught on the way. Of these we told him;
And there did seem in him a kind of joy   20
To hear of it. They are here about the court,
And, as I think, they have already order
This night to play before him.

POLONIUS

'Tis most true;
And he beseech'd me to entreat your Majesties   25
To hear and see the matter.

KING

With all my heart; and it doth much content me
To hear him so inclin'd.
Good gentlemen, give him a further edge,
And drive his purpose into these delights.   30

ROSENCRANTZ

We shall, my lord.

Exeunt ROSENCRANTZ *and* GUILDENSTERN

KING

Sweet Gertrude, leave us too;
For we have closely sent for Hamlet hither,
That he, as 'twere by accident, may here
Affront Ophelia.   35
Her father and myself – lawful espials –
Will so bestow ourselves that, seeing unseen,
We may of their encounter frankly judge,
And gather by him, as he is behav'd,

46 *wonted way*   usual behaviour.

47 *To both your honours*   to the credit of you both.

49 *Gracious*   my gracious lord.

50 *book*   evidently a prayer book, from what follows.

51 *show of such an exercise*   the pretence of being at prayers.

51–2 *may colour Your loneliness*   may explain why you are alone.

53 *too much proved*   too often found.

58 *plast'ring art*   skilful make-up.

59 *thing that helps it*   i.e. the plaster that covers it up.

60 *painted*   feigned, hypocritical.

If't be th' affliction of his love or no   40
That thus he suffers for.

QUEEN

I shall obey you;
And for your part, Ophelia, I do wish
That your good beauties be the happy cause
Of Hamlet's wildness; so shall I hope your virtues   45
Will bring him to his wonted way again,
To both your honours.

OPHELIA

Madam, I wish it may.

Exit QUEEN

POLONIUS

Ophelia, walk you here. – Gracious, so please you,
We will bestow ourselves. – Read on this book;   50
That show of such an exercise may colour
Your loneliness. – We are oft to blame in this:
'Tis too much prov'd, that with devotion's visage
And pious action we do sugar o'er
The devil himself.   55

KING

(*Aside*) O, 'tis too true!
How smart a lash that speech doth give my
    conscience!
The harlot's cheek, beautied with plast'ring art,
Is not more ugly to the thing that helps it
Than is my deed to my most painted word.   60
O heavy burden!

POLONIUS

I hear him coming; let's withdraw, my lord.

Exeunt KING *and* POLONIUS

63 **To be, or not to be** Hamlet is debating, perhaps, whether to take action to revenge his father's death, which would in all probability result in him losing his own life, or to leave things as they are. This leads him to question whether life is worth living at all.

68 **No more** i.e. death is no more than sleep.

to say let us suppose.

70 **That flesh is heir to** that are natural parts of our lives.

consummation ending.

72 **rub** snag.

74 **shuffled off this mortal coil** discarded the turmoil ('coil') of this present life ('mortal coil').

75 **give us pause** make us pause for thought.

respect consideration.

76 **makes calamity of so long life** makes calamities last so long (because we are reluctant to end them by committing suicide).

77 **scorns of time** insults of life.

78 **contumely** insolence.

80 **office** people in official positions.

81 **of** from.

82 **quietus** release (from life, i.e. by suicide).

83 **bare bodkin** unsheathed dagger.

fardels burdens.

86 **bourn** boundaries.

90 **conscience** conscious thought, reflection.

91 **native hue** natural colour.

92 **sicklied o'er** turned a sickly colour.

pale cast pale tinge.

168

Enter HAMLET.

[Handwritten: Do I want to be on earth any longer, to live or not.]

HAMLET

[Handwritten: Speaking exam]

To be, or not to be – that is the question;
Whether 'tis nobler in the mind to suffer
The slings and arrows of outrageous fortune,   65
Or to take arms against a sea of troubles,
And by opposing end them? To die, to sleep –
No more; and by a sleep to say we end
The heart-ache and the thousand natural shocks
That flesh is heir to. 'Tis a consummation   70
Devoutly to be wish'd. To die, to sleep;
To sleep, perchance to dream. Ay, there's the rub;
For in that sleep of death what dreams may come,
When we have shuffled off this mortal coil,
Must give us pause. There's the respect   75
That makes calamity of so long life;
For who would bear the whips and scorns of time,
Th' oppressor's wrong, the proud man's contumely,
The pangs of despis'd love, the law's delay,
The insolence of office, and the spurns   80
That patient merit of th' unworthy takes,
When he himself might his quietus make
With a bare bodkin? Who would these fardels
    bear,
To grunt and sweat under a weary life,
But that the dread of something after death –   85
The undiscover'd country, from whose bourn
No traveller returns – puzzles the will,
And makes us rather bear those ills we have
Than fly to others that we know not of?
Thus conscience does make cowards of us all;   90
And thus the native hue of resolution
Is sicklied o'er with the pale cast of thought,

[Handwritten right margin: a whole list of horrible things that can happen to a man]

[Handwritten right margin: Why? We don't know what will happen at the other end?]

[Handwritten bottom: Should I want to go on with this suffering life or should I kill myself to resolve all the problems.]

93 **pitch**   height.

    moment   momentousness.

94 **With this regard**   when thought about in this way.

95 **Soft you now!**   softly!

96 **orisons**   prayers.

101 **remembrances**   love tokens.

107–8 **words of so sweet. . .more rich**   words so sweetly arranged that they made the love tokens more precious.

108 **their perfume lost**   now that they are no longer perfumed by your 'sweet breath'.

110 **wax**   become.

112 **honest**   a virgin.

114 **fair**   beautiful.

And enterprises of great pitch and moment,
With this regard, their currents turn awry *~aret*
And lose the name of action. – Soft you now!   95
The fair Ophelia. – Nymph, in thy orisons
Be all my sins rememb'red.   *↳ prayers*

OPHELIA

Good my lord,
How does your honour for this many a day?

HAMLET

I humbly thank you; well, well, well.   100

OPHELIA

My lord, I have remembrances of yours
That I have longed long to re-deliver.
I pray you now receive them.

HAMLET

No, not I;
I never gave you aught.   105

OPHELIA

My honour'd lord, you know right well you did,
And with them words of so sweet breath compos'd
As made the things more rich; their perfume lost,
Take these again; for to the noble mind
Rich gifts wax poor when givers prove unkind.   110
There, my lord.

HAMLET

Ha, ha! Are you honest?

OPHELIA

My lord?

HAMLET

Are you fair?

117 **admit no discourse to**   allow no conversation with.

118 **commerce**   friendly communication.

121 **bawd**   prostitute.

122 **translate**   transform.

   his   its.

123 **sometime**   once.

124 **the time gives it proof**   recent events have proved it to be true. Hamlet is thinking of his mother's behaviour.

127 **inoculate our old stock. . .of it**   be grafted onto our corrupt nature so that we can no longer taste ('relish') it.

131 **indifferent honest**   reasonably virtuous.

135 **beck**   command.

OPHELIA

What means your lordship?   115

HAMLET

That if you be honest and fair, your honesty should
admit no discourse to your beauty.

OPHELIA

Could beauty, my lord, have better commerce than
with honesty?

HAMLET

Ay, truly; for the power of beauty will sooner 120
transform honesty from what it is to a bawd than
the force of honesty can translate beauty into his
likeness. This was sometime a paradox, but now
the time gives it proof. I did love you once.

OPHELIA

Indeed, my lord, you made me believe so.   125

HAMLET

You should not have believ'd me; for virtue cannot
so inoculate our old stock but we shall relish of it.
I loved you not.

OPHELIA

I was the more deceived.

HAMLET

Get thee to a nunnery. Why wouldst thou be a 130
breeder of sinners? I am myself indifferent honest,
but yet I could accuse me of such things that it
were better my mother had not borne me: I am
very proud, revengeful, ambitious; with more
offences at my beck than I have thoughts to put 135
them in, imagination to give them shape, or time

138–9 **_arrant knaves_** complete rogues.

147 **_calumny_** false accusation.

150 **_monsters_** cuckolds.

153 **_paintings_** cosmetics.

155 **_jig and amble_** prance about and mince seductively.

lisp speak in an affected way.

156 **_nickname_** give affected pet names to.

156–7 **_make your wantonness your ignorance_** make your flirtatious affectation the excuse for your stupid behaviour.

to act them in. What should such fellows as I do
crawling between earth and heaven? We are arrant
knaves, all; believe none of us. Go thy ways to a
nunnery. Where's your father? 140

OPHELIA

At home, my lord.

HAMLET

Let the doors be shut upon him, that he may play
the fool nowhere but in's own house. Farewell.

OPHELIA

O, help him, you sweet heavens!

HAMLET

If thou dost marry, I'll give thee this plague for thy 145
dowry· be thou as chaste as ice, as pure as snow,
thou shalt not escape calumny. Get thee to a
nunnery, go, farewell. Or, if thou wilt needs marry,
marry a fool; for wise men know well enough what
monsters you make of them. To a nunnery, go; and 150
quickly too. Farewell.

OPHELIA

O heavenly powers, restore him!

→ He knows he's been watched.

HAMLET

I have heard of your paintings too, well enough;
God hath given you one face, and you make your-)→ *make up*
selves another. You jig and amble, and you lisp, 155
and nickname God's creatures, and make your
wantonness your ignorance. Go to, I'll no more
on't; it hath made me mad. I say we will have no
more marriages: those that are married already, all

You may not have children

175

160 **but one**   i.e except Claudius.

164 **expectancy**   hope.

   rose   i.e. flower.

165 **glass of fashion and the mould of form**   the mirror of fashion and the model of good behaviour.

168 **music vows**   sweet-sounding promises.

170 **jangled**   i.e. rung discordantly and at random.

171 **blown**   full-flowering.

172 **Blasted with ecstasy**   blighted with madness.

174 **affections**   feelings.

176–7 **There's something. . .on brood**   his sadness is caused by him brooding about something.

178 **doubt**   fear.

   disclose   disclosure.

180 **quick determination**   a rapid decision.

182 **neglected tribute**   overdue taxes. This refers to the Danegeld, a tribute paid to Denmark by England from 991 A.D. onwards. In return for the payment, the Danes agreed not to invade England.

183 **Haply**   perhaps.

184 **variable objects**   a change of scene.

185 **something-settled**   somewhat settled.

but one, shall live; the rest shall keep as they are. 160
To a nunnery, go.

Exit.

OPHELIA
O, what a noble mind is here o'er thrown!
The courtier's, soldier's, scholar's, eye, tongue,
      sword;
Th' expectancy and rose of the fair state,
The glass of fashion and the mould of form,   165
Th' observ'd of all observers – quite, quite down!
And I, of ladies most deject and wretched,
That suck'd the honey of his music vows,
Now see that noble and most sovereign reason,
Like sweet bells jangled, out of time and harsh;   170
That unmatch'd form and feature of blown youth
Blasted with ecstasy. O, woe is me
T' have seen what I have seen, see what I see!

Re-enter KING *and* POLONIUS.

KING
Love! His affections do not that way tend;
Nor what he spake, though it lack'd form a little, 175
Was not like madness. There's something in his
      soul
O'er which his melancholy sits on brood;
And I do doubt the hatch and the disclose
Will be some danger; which to prevent
I have in quick determination   180
Thus set it down: he shall with speed to England
For the demand of our neglected tribute.
Haply the seas and countries different,
With variable objects, shall expel
This something-settled matter in his heart   185

186–7 **Wheron his brains. . .of himself** which he can't get out of his mind ('his
brains still beating') makes him behave in a way uncharacteristic of himself.

189 **grief** grievance.

195 **show his grief** disclose his grievance.

round blunt.

196 **in the ear** within earshot.

197 **find him not** fails to discover what is the matter with him.

1 **speech** i.e. the extra speech Hamlet has written for the play, first
mentioned in Act 2, scene 2, lines 559–62.

2 **trippingly** lightly.

mouth over-emphasise the words or ham it up.

3 **had as lief** would like it just as much if.

5 **use all** do everything.

Whereon his brains still beating puts him thus
From fashion of himself. What think you on't?

POLONIUS

It shall do well. But yet do I believe
The origin and commencement of his grief
Sprung from neglected love. How now, Ophelia!   190
You need not tell us what Lord Hamlet said;
We heard it all. My lord, do as you please;
But if you hold it fit, after the play
Let his queen mother all alone entreat him
To show his grief. Let her be round with him;   195
And I'll be plac'd, so please you, in the ear
Of all their conference. If she find him not,
To England send him; or confine him where
Your wisdom best shall think.

KING

It shall be so: 200
Madness in great ones must not unwatch'd go.

↳ We should let him killed
in England.

Exeunt

Scene two

Elsinore. The Castle.

Enter HAMLET *and three of the* Players.

↳ ok zou net zo lief
hebben dat iemand
anders mijn regels
spreekt

HAMLET

Speak the speech, I pray you, as I pronounc'd it
to you, trippingly on the tongue; but if you mouth
it, as many of our players do, I had as lief the
town-crier spoke my lines. Nor do not saw the air
too much with your hand, thus, but use all gently;   5

↳ the actor uses Hamlet's voice.

179

8 **beget** achieve.

9 **robustious** loud-mouthed.

10 **periwig-pated fellow** man wearing a wig, by implication an actor, because wigs were not commonly worn by men in Shakespeare's day.

11 **groundlings** audience standing in front of the stage, the cheapest part of the playhouse.

12 **capable of** able to understand and appreciate.

13 **inexplicable dumb-shows** mimes without any discernible point or reason.

14–15 **Termagant...Herod** villains from medieval morality or mystery plays, whose parts invited noisy and over-emphatic acting. Termagant was supposed to be a god of the Saracens, and Herod was the villainous, tyrannical king of Israel at the time of Christ's birth.

20 **modesty** balance, moderation.

21 **from** against.

23 **mirror up to nature** reveal the truth about the world.

26 **form and pressure** shape and impression.

this if this.

26–7 **come tardy off** badly executed.

27 **unskilful** those lacking judgement and education.

28–9 **the censure of the which one** the judgement of one of which.

36 **journeymen** day-labourers rather than skilled craftsmen. Hamlet is saying that these actors (the 'players' of line 31) performed so outrageously that he doubted they were human at all.

for in the very torrent, tempest, and, as I may say,
whirlwind of your passion, you must acquire and
beget a temperance that may give it smoothness.
O, it offends me to the soul to hear a robustious
periwig-pated fellow tear a passion to tatters, to   10
very rags, to split the ears of the groundlings, who,
for the most part, are capable of nothing but
inexplicable dumb shows and noise. I would have
such a fellow whipp'd for o'erdoing Termagant; it
out-herods Herod. Pray you avoid it.   15

1 PLAYER
  I warrant your honour.

HAMLET
  Be not too tame neither, but let your own discretion be your tutor. Suit the action to the word, the
  word to the action; with this special observance,
  that you o'erstep not the modesty of nature; for   20
  anything so o'erdone is from the purpose of
  playing, whose end, both at the first and now, was
  and is to hold, as 'twere, the mirror up to nature;
  to show virtue her own feature, scorn her own
  image, and the very age and body of the time his   25
  form and pressure. Now, this overdone or come
  tardy off, though it makes the unskilful laugh,
  cannot but make the judicious grieve; the censure
  of the which one must, in your allowance,
  o'erweigh a whole theatre of others. O, there be   30
  players that I have seen play – and heard others
  praise, and that highly – not to speak it profanely,
  that, neither having th' accent of Christians, nor
  the gait of Christian, pagan, nor man, have so
  strutted and bellowed that I have thought some of   35
  Nature's journeymen had made men, and not

181

39 *indifferently*   to some extent.

42 *clowns*   comic roles.

44 *quantity of barren spectators*   some stupid members of the audience.

46 *necessary question*   important part of the plot.

52 *presently*   at once.

made them well, they imitated humanity so
abominably.

1 PLAYER
I hope we have reform'd that indifferently with us,
sir. *onvruchtbare toeschouwers*   40
who are not so clever.

HAMLET
O, reform it altogether. And let those that play
your clowns speak no more than is set down for
them; for there be of them that will themselves
laugh, to set on some quantity of barren spectators
to laugh too, though in the meantime some   45
necessary question of the play be then to be
considered. That's villainous, and shows a most
pitiful ambition in the fool that uses it. Go, make
you ready.

Exeunt Players

Enter POLONIUS, ROSENCRANTZ, *and* GUILDENSTERN.

How now, my lord! Will the King hear this piece   50
of work?

POLONIUS
And the Queen too, and that presently.

HAMLET
Bid the players make haste.

Exit POLONIUS

Will you two help to hasten them?

ROSENCRANTZ
Ay, my lord.   55

Exeunt they two

183

58-9 **thou art e'en. . .cop'd withal**   you are as honest ('just') a man as I have ever met with ('cop'd withal') in my dealings with people ('conversation').

62 **advancement**   advantage to myself.

65 **candied**   sweetened (i.e. with flattery).

66 **crook**   bend.

pregnant   willing.

67 **thrift**   material advantage.

68 **mistress of her choice**   able to make up its own mind.

69 **distinguish her election**   discriminate between.

70 **seal'd thee**   marked you out.

71 **in suff'ring all, that suffers nothing**   undergoes every kind of hardship without revealing distress.

74 **blood**   emotions.

judgment   reason.

comeddled   blended.

75 **pipe**   musical instrument.

76 **stop**   hole, as in a flute or recorder, and hence musical note.

77 **passion's slave**   unable to control his emotions.

79 **Something too much**   enough.

HAMLET

What, ho, Horatio!

Enter HORATIO.

HORATIO

Here, sweet lord, at your service.

HAMLET

Horatio, thou art e'en as just a man
As e'er my conversation cop'd withal.

HORATIO

O my dear lord!   60

HAMLET

Nay, do not think I flatter;
For what advancement may I hope from thee,
That no revenue hast but thy good spirits
To feed and clothe thee? Why should the poor be
   flatter'd?
No, let the candied tongue lick absurd pomp,   65
And crook the pregnant hinges of the knee
Where thrift may follow fawning. Dost thou hear?
Since my dear soul was mistress of her choice
And could of men distinguish her election,
Sh'hath seal'd thee for herself; for thou hast been   70
As one, in suff'ring all, that suffers nothing;
A man that Fortune's buffets and rewards
Hast ta'en with equal thanks; and blest are those
Whose blood and judgment are so well comeddled
That they are not a pipe for Fortune's finger   75
To sound what stop she please. Give me that man
That is not passion's slave, and I will wear him
In my heart's core, ay, in my heart of heart,
As I do thee. Something too much of this.

84 **comment of thy soul**   your closest powers of observation.

85 **occulted**   hidden.

86 **unkennel**   reveal itself.

89 **stithy**   forge. Vulcan, the blacksmith of the classical gods, worked underground, and this, together with the smoke and flames of his fire, made him associated with hell, and thus 'foul' (line 88).

   heedful note   careful attention.

92 **censure of his seeming**   judgement of his appearance.

94 **steal aught**   gets away with anything.

95 **scape detecting**   escape detection.

   pay the theft   take the blame for it.

96 **be idle**   start feigning madness.

98 **How fares**   how are you? but Hamlet interprets it as meaning 'What food (fare) have you been eating?'

99 **chameleon**   it was believed that these lizards survived on air alone.

100 **promise-cramm'd**   the king has promised that Hamlet will inherit the crown, while Hamlet himself has promised to avenge his father's death.

   capons   castrated cockerels.

There is a play to-night before the King;   80
One scene of it comes near the circumstance
Which I have told thee of my father's
    death.
I prithee, when thou seest that act afoot,
Even with the very comment of thy soul
Observe my uncle. If his occulted guilt   85
Do not itself unkennel in one speech,
It is a damned ghost that we have seen,
And my imaginations are as foul
As Vulcan's stithy. Give him heedful note;
For I mine eyes will rivet to his face;   90
And, after, we will both our judgments join
In censure of his seeming.

HORATIO
Well, my lord.
If 'a steal aught the whilst this play is playing,
And scape detecting, I will pay the theft.   95

Enter trumpets and kettledrums. Danish march. Sound a flourish.
Enter KING, QUEEN, POLONIUS, OPHELIA, ROSENCRANTZ, GUIL-
DENSTERN, *and other* Lords *attendant, with the* Guard *carrying*
torches.

HAMLET
They are coming to the play; I must be idle.
Get you a place.

KING
How fares our cousin Hamlet?

HAMLET
Excellent, i' faith; of the chameleon's dish. I eat
the air, promise-cramm'd; you cannot feed capons 100
so.

102 **I have nothing with this answer**   I can make nothing of this answer.

102–3 **these words are not mine**   these words have nothing to do with my question.

111 **brute part**   brutal action.

capital a calf   fine a fool.

113 **stay upon your patience**   wait for your order to start.

115 **metal more attractive**   referring to Ophelia, who, he implies, draws him like a magnet.

117 **lie in your lap**   put my head on your lap or have sex with you. Hamlet's remark is provocatively ambiguous.

KING

I have nothing with this answer, Hamlet; these
words are not mine.

HAMLET

No, nor mine now. (*To* POLONIUS) My lord, you
play'd once i' th' university, you say?   105

POLONIUS

That did I, my lord, and was accounted a good
actor.

HAMLET

What did you enact?

POLONIUS

I did enact Julius Caesar; I was kill'd i' th' Capitol;
Brutus kill'd me.   110

HAMLET

It was a brute part of him to kill so capital a calf
there. Be the players ready?

ROSENCRANTZ

Ay, my lord; they stay upon your patience.

QUEEN

Come hither, my dear Hamlet, sit by me.

HAMLET

No, good mother; here's metal more attractive.   115

POLONIUS

(*To the* KING) O, ho! do you mark that?

HAMLET

Lady, shall I lie in your lap?

(*Lying down at* OPHELIA'*s feet*.)

121 **country matters**   (slang) sexual intercourse.

123 **fair thought**   good idea, or the thought of a beautiful woman ('fair').

125 **Nothing**   a pun on no thing, or penis, or alternatively, a woman's sexual organs were also known as a nothing from the shape of the number 0.

126 **merry**   indecent.

129 **your only jig-maker**   I am the only person who can amuse you.

131 **within's**   within this.

OPHELIA
  No, my lord.

HAMLET
  I mean, my head upon your lap?

OPHELIA
  Ay, my lord.   120

HAMLET
  Do you think I meant country matters?

OPHELIA
  I think nothing, my lord.

HAMLET
  That's a fair thought to lie between maids'
    legs.

OPHELIA
  What is, my lord?

HAMLET
  Nothing.   125

OPHELIA
  You are merry, my lord.

HAMLET
  Who, I?

OPHELIA
  Ay, my lord.

HAMLET
  O God, your only jig-maker! What should a man
  do but be merry? For look you how cheerfully my 130
  mother looks, and my father died within's two
  hours.

135 **suit of sables** clothes trimmed with costly black furs, rather than clothes for mourning.

138 **build churches** i.e. pay for the construction of churches where prayers would be said in his memory.

140 **hobby-horse** figure of a horse worn round the waist of a morris dancer.

140–1 **'For O, for O. . .forgot'** presumably a quotation from a ballad which has been lost.

s.d. **Hautboys** oboes.

Dumb Show mime.

s.d. **show of protestation** gesture indicating her love.

takes her up helps her to her feet.

declines leans.

makes passionate action makes gestures indicating grief.

143 **miching mallecho** an obscure phrase, but fortunately Hamlet himself tells us it means mischief. There is probably a connection with the Spanish word *malhecho*, meaning wickedness.

144 **Belike this show. . .the play** perhaps ('belike') this dumb show indicates ('imports') the plot ('argument') of the play.

OPHELIA

Nay, 'tis twice two months, my lord.

HAMLET

So long? Nay then, let the devil wear black, for I'll
have a suit of sables. O heavens! die two months 135
ago, and not forgotten yet? Then there's hope a
great man's memory may outlive his life half a
year; but, by'r lady, 'a must build churches, then;
or else shall 'a suffer not thinking on, with the
hobby-horse, whose epitaph is 'For O, for O, the 140
hobby-horse is forgot'!

The trumpet sounds. Hautboys play. The Dumb Show enters.

Enter a King *and a* Queen, *very lovingly; the* Queen *embracing
him and he her. She kneels, and makes show of protestation unto
him. He takes her up, and declines his head upon her neck. He
lies him down upon a bank of flowers; she, seeing him asleep,
leaves him. Anon comes in a* Fellow, *takes off his crown, kisses
it, pours poison in the sleeper's ears, and leaves him. The* Queen
returns; finds the King *dead, and makes passionate action. The*
Poisoner, *with some two or three* Mutes, *comes in again,
seeming to condole with her. The dead body is carried away. The*
Poisoner *woos the* Queen *with gifts: she seems harsh awhile, but
in the end accepts his love.*

Exeunt

OPHELIA

What means this, my lord?

HAMLET

Marry, this is miching mallecho; it means mischief.

OPHELIA

Belike this show imports the argument of the play.

s.d. **Prologue**   the actor who speaks the prologue to the play.

146 **keep counsel**   keep a secret.

148–9 **Be not you**   if you are not.

149 **show**   presumably Hamlet means, or at least Ophelia takes him to mean, take off your clothes.

151 **naught**   obscene, wicked.

156 **posy of a ring**   inscription on the inside of a ring.

159 **Phoebus' cart**   the sun.

160 **Neptune's salt wash**   the sea.

   Tellus' orbed ground   the earth.

Enter Prologue

HAMLET

We shall know by this fellow: the players cannot 145
keep counsel; they'll tell all.

OPHELIA

Will 'a tell us what this show meant?

HAMLET

Ay, or any show that you will show him. Be not
you asham'd to show, he'll not shame to tell you
what it means. 150

OPHELIA

You are naught, you are naught. I'll mark the
play.

PROLOGUE

For us, and for our tragedy,
Here stooping to your clemency,
We beg your hearing patiently. 155

Exit

HAMLET

Is this a prologue, or the posy of a ring?

OPHELIA

'Tis brief, my lord.

HAMLET

As woman's love.

Enter the Player King *and* Queen.

PLAYER KING

Full thirty times hath Phœbus' cart gone round
Neptune's salt wash and Tellus' orbed ground, 160

161 **borrowed sheen**   reflected light.

163 **Hymen**   the classical god of marriage.

164 **commutual**   together.

169 **distrust**   am worried (about you).

172–3 **hold quantity. . .extremity**   remain the same size in relation to one another, either being nothing ('aught') or excessive ('extremity').

174 **proof**   experience.

175 **And as my love is siz'd, my fear is so**   my love is great, so my fear is great also.

179 **My operant powers. . .to do**   the powers that work to keep me alive ('operant powers') are ceasing to do their job ('functions').

181 **haply**   perhaps.

183 **confound the rest**   may God curse what you were about to say.

187 **wormwood**   a bitter-tasting herb.

And thirty dozen moons with borrowed sheen
About the world have times twelve thirties been,
Since love our hearts and Hymen did our hands
Unite commutual in most sacred bands.

PLAYER QUEEN

So many journeys may the sun and moon   165
Make us again count o'er ere love be done!
But, woe is me, you are so sick of late,
So far from cheer and from your former state,
That I distrust you. Yet, though I distrust,
Discomfort you, my lord, it nothing must;   170
For women fear too much even as they love,
And women's fear and love hold quantity,
In neither aught, or in extremity.
Now, what my love is, proof hath made you know;
And as my love is siz'd, my fear is so.   175
Where love is great, the littlest doubts are fear;
Where little fears grow great, great love grows there.

PLAYER KING

Faith, I must leave thee, love and shortly too:
My operant powers their functions leave to do;
And thou shalt live in this fair world behind,   180
Honour'd, belov'd; and haply one as kind
For husband shalt thou –

PLAYER QUEEN

O, confound the rest!
Such love must needs be treason in my breast.
In second husband let me be accurst!   185
None wed the second but who kill'd the first.

HAMLET

That's wormwood, wormwood.

188 **instances**   motives.

  move   bring about.

189 **base respects of thrift**   the low promptings of greed.

192 **think**   believe.

194 **Purpose is but the slave to memory**   a firm decision ('purpose') is only carried out as long as it is remembered.

195 **Of violent birth, but poor validity**   they are born in a moment of extreme emotion, but have not the power to survive long.

196 **Which**   i.e. purpose.

  sticks on the tree   does not fall from the tree.

197 **mellow**   ripe.

198 **necessary**   inevitable.

199 **To pay ourselves. . .is debt**   to honour the promises that we have made to ourselves.

203 **enactures**   acts of putting into practice, i.e. the violent strength of these emotions causes acts which destroy the emotions themselves.

205 **slender accident**   insubstantial chance.

206 **This world is not for aye**   this life will not last for ever.

208 **to prove**   to be decided.

211 **The poor advanc'd**   the poor man who is promoted.

212 **hitherto**   to this extent.

214 **who not needs**   he who does not need.

  hollow   shallow, insincere.

  try   test.

215 **seasons**   turns him into.

218 **devices**   plans.

PLAYER QUEEN

> *The instances that second marriage move*
> *Are base respects of thrift, but none of love.*
> *A second time I kill my husband dead,*   190
> *When second husband kisses me in bed.*

PLAYER KING

> *I do believe you think what now you speak;*
> *But what we do determine oft we break.*
> *Purpose is but the slave to memory,*
> *Of violent birth, but poor validity;*   195
> *Which now, the fruit unripe, sticks on the tree;*
> *But fall unshaken when they mellow be.*
> *Most necessary 'tis that we forget*
> *To pay ourselves what to ourselves is debt.*
> *What to ourselves in passion we propose,*   200
> *The passion ending, doth the purpose lose.*
> *The violence of either grief or joy*
> *Their own enactures with themselves destroy.*
> *Where joy most revels grief doth most lament;*
> *Grief joys, joy grieves, on slender accident.*   205
> *This world is not for aye; nor 'tis not strange*
> *That even our loves should with our fortunes change;*
> *For 'tis a question left us yet to prove,*
> *Whether love lead fortune or else fortune love.*
> *The great man down, you mark his favourite flies;*   210
> *The poor advanc'd makes friends of enemies.*
> *And hitherto doth love on fortune tend;*
> *For who not needs shall never lack a friend,*
> *And who in want a hollow friend doth try,*
> *Directly seasons him his enemy.*   215
> *But, orderly to end where I begun,*
> *Our wills and fates do so contrary run*
> *That our devices still are overthrown;*

219 **ends** consequences.

220 **So think** i.e. so you may think now that.

221 **die thy thoughts** you will change your mind.

223 **Sport** amusement.

225 **anchor's cheer** meagre food of an anchorite or hermit.

230 **break it** i.e. the vow she has just made.

232 **beguile** charm away.

237 **protest too much** publicly promise.

Our thoughts are ours, their ends none of our own.
So think thou wilt no second husband wed;   220
But die thy thoughts when thy first lord is dead.

PLAYER QUEEN

Nor earth to me give food, nor heaven light,
Sport and repose lock from me day and night,
To desperation turn my trust and hope,
An anchor's cheer in prison be my scope,   225
Each opposite that blanks the face of joy
Meet what I would have well, and it destroy,
Both here and hence pursue me lasting strife,
If, once a widow, ever I be wife!

HAMLET

If she should break it now!   230

PLAYER KING

'Tis deeply sworn. Sweet, leave me here awhile;
My spirits grow dull, and fain I would beguile
The tedious day with sleep.

Sleeps.

PLAYER QUEEN

Sleep rock thy brain,
And never come mischance between us twain!   235

Exit

HAMLET

Madam, how like you this play?

QUEEN

The lady doth protest too much, methinks.

HAMLET

O, but she'll keep her word.

201

239 **no offence**   nothing offensive.

241 **offence**   Hamlet is punning on another meaning of offence, a crime.

244 **'The Mouse-trap'**   Hamlet knows that the real name of the play is 'The Murder of Gonzago' (Act 2, scene 2, line 556), but calls it 'The Mouse-trap' because he is using it to try to catch Claudius.

   Tropically   i.e. the title is derived from a trope, or figure of speech.

245 **image**   representation.

249 **free**   innocent.

   galled jade   broken down horse made sore from saddle or harness – although a 'jade' can also be a prostitute.

250 **withers**   shoulders of a horse.

   unwrung   not sore with rubbing.

253 **interpret**   provide a commentary: an interpreter spoke the lines of puppets in puppet shows.

254 **dallying**   exchanging endearments.

255 **keen**   witty, bitter.

256 **groaning**   groans of pain of a woman losing her virginity.

   take off mine edge   reduce my sexual appetite.

257 **Still better, and worse**   better because even more witty, worse because even more obscene.

KING

Have you heard the argument? Is there no offence
in't?   240

HAMLET

No, no; they do but jest, poison in jest; no offence
i' th' world.

KING

What do you call the play?

HAMLET

'The Mouse-trap'. Marry, how? Tropically. This
play is the image of a murder done in Vienna: 245
Gonzago is the duke's name; his wife, Baptista.
You shall see anon. 'Tis a knavish piece of work;
but what of that? Your Majesty, and we that have
free souls, it touches us not. Let the galled jade
wince, our withers are unwrung.   250

Enter LUCIANUS.

This is one Lucianus, nephew to the King.

OPHELIA

You are as good as a chorus, my lord.

HAMLET

I could interpret between you and your love, if I
could see the puppets dallying.

OPHELIA

You are keen, my lord, you are keen.   255

HAMLET

It would cost you a groaning to take off mine edge.

OPHELIA

Still better, and worse.

258 **mis-take your husbands**   deceitfully take your marriage vows (referring back to Ophelia's last comment, with its echo of for better or worse).

259 **pox**   a curse, short for a pox on you.

260 **the croaking raven**   a loose quotation from the anonymous old play, *The True Tragedy of Richard III*.

263 **Confederate season**   perfect opportunity.

   else no creature seeing   with no other creature to see except me.

265 **Hecat's ban**   the curse of Hecate, queen of witches.

267 **usurps**   overthrows.

269 **extant**   in existence.

273 **false fire**   blank ammunition.

275 **Give o'er**   stop.

HAMLET

So you mis-take your husbands. – Begin,
murderer; pox, leave thy damnable faces and
begin. Come; the croaking raven doth bellow for 260
revenge.

LUCIANUS

Thoughts black, hands apt, drugs fit and time
agreeing;
Confederate season, else no creature seeing;
Thou mixture rank, of midnight weeds collected,
With Hecat's ban thrice blasted, thrice infected, 265
Thy natural magic and dire property
On wholesome life usurps immediately.

(*Pours the poison in his ears.*)

HAMLET

'A poisons him i' th' garden for his estate. His
name's Gonzago. The story is extant, and written
in very choice Italian. You shall see anon how the 270
murderer gets the love of Gonzago's wife.

OPHELIA

The King rises.

HAMLET

What, frighted with false fire!

QUEEN

How fares my lord?

POLONIUS

Give o'er the play. 275

KING

Give me some light. Away!

278 **strucken**   wounded.

279 **hart ungalled**   unwounded deer.

280 **watch**   stay awake.

282 **this**   i.e. the play.

   forest of feathers   actors wore feathers, so this probably means a company of actors.

283 **turn Turk**   abandon.

284 **Provincial roses**   large rosettes.

   raz'd   slashed, with an open-work pattern.

285 **fellowship in a cry of players**   partnership in a company of actors.

288 **O Damon dear**   my dear friend.

289 **This realm dismantled was**   this country was deprived of.

290 **Jove himself**   i.e. old Hamlet.

291 **paiock**   the sense is not clear: maybe a form of peacock, a bird which was thought to be proud and lecherous, or a patchcock (a contemptible fellow). In either case, Hamlet is making an unflattering comparison between his father and Claudius.

292 **rhym'd**   i.e. found a rhyme-word for 'was'.

POLONIUS

Lights, lights, lights!

Exeunt all but HAMLET *and* HORATIO

HAMLET

Why, let the strucken deer go weep,
   The hart ungalled play;
For some must watch, while some must sleep; 280
   Thus runs the world away.
Would not this, sir, and a forest of feathers – if the
rest of my fortunes turn Turk with me – with two
Provincial roses on my raz'd shoes, get me a
fellowship in a cry of players, sir?   285

HORATIO

Half a share.

HAMLET

A whole one, I.
   For thou dost know, O Damon dear,
   This realm dismantled was
Of Jove himself; and now reigns here   290
   A very, very – paiock.

HORATIO

You might have rhym'd.

HAMLET

O good Horatio, I'll take the ghost's word for a
thousand pound. Didst perceive?

HORATIO

Very well, my lord.   295

HAMLET

Upon the talk of the poisoning.

300 **belike** perhaps.

perdy (oath) by God.

302 **vouchsafe** permit.

306 **retirement** he has retired to his private rooms.

distemp'red upset and angry.

307 **With drink, sir?** 'distemp'red' can also mean drunk.

308 **choler** anger.

311 **purgation** bleeding for medical reasons as a cure for 'choler'.

HORATIO

I did very well note him.

HAMLET

Ah, ha! Come, some music. Come, the
   recorders.
For if the King like not the comedy,
Why, then, belike he likes it not, perdy.   300
Come, some music.

Re-enter ROSENCRANTZ *and* GUILDENSTERN.

GUILDENSTERN

Good my lord, vouchsafe me a word with you.

HAMLET

Sir, a whole history.

GUILDENSTERN

The King, sir –

HAMLET

Ay, sir, what of him?   305

GUILDENSTERN

Is, in his retirement, marvellous distemp'red.

HAMLET

With drink, sir?

GUILDENSTERN

No, my lord, rather with choler.

HAMLET

Your wisdom should show itself more richer to
signify this to his doctor; for for me to put him to 310
his purgation would perhaps plunge him into far
more choler.

313 **frame**   order.

314 **start**   shy like a frightened horse.

320 **breed**   kind.

332 **admiration**   wonder.

GUILDENSTERN

Good my lord, put your discourse into some frame,
and start not so wildly from my affair.

HAMLET

I am tame sir. Pronounce. 315

GUILDENSTERN

The Queen, your mother, in most great affliction
of spirit, hath sent me to you.

HAMLET

You are welcome.

GUILDENSTERN

Nay, good my lord, this courtesy is not of the right
breed. If it shall please you to make me a whole- 320
some answer, I will do your mother's commandment; if not, your pardon and my return shall be
the end of my business.

HAMLET

Sir, I cannot.

ROSENCRANTZ

What, my lord? 325

HAMLET

Make you a wholesome answer; my wit's diseas'd.
But, sir, such answer as I can make, you shall
command; or rather as you say, my mother. Therefore no more, but to the matter: my mother, you
say – 330

ROSENCRANTZ

Then thus she says: your behaviour hath struck
her into amazement and admiration.

336 **closet** private room.

341 **pickers and stealers** hands.

342 **distemper** mental disorder.

343 **liberty** i.e. recovery.

345 **advancement** promotion.

347 **'While the grass grows'** the full proverb is 'While the grass grows, the horse starves'.

349 **musty** stale, overused.

350 **withdraw** to speak in private.

351–2 **recover the wind of me** get downwind of me (as a hunter does when stalking prey).

HAMLET

O wonderful son, that can so stonish a mother! But
is there no sequel at the heels of this mother's
admiration? Impart.   335

ROSENCRANTZ

She desires to speak with you in her closet ere you
go to bed.

HAMLET

We shall obey, were she ten times our mother.
Have you any further trade with us?

ROSENCRANTZ

My lord, you once did love me.   340

HAMLET

And do still, by these pickers and stealers.

ROSENCRANTZ

Good my lord, what is your cause of distemper?
You do surely bar the door upon your own liberty,
if you deny your griefs to your friend.

HAMLET

Sir, I lack advancement.   345

ROSENCRANTZ

How can that be, when you have the voice of the
King himself for your succession in Denmark?

HAMLET

Ay, sir, but 'While the grass grows' – the proverb
is something musty.

Re-enter the Players, *with recorders.*

O, the recorders! Let me see one. To withdraw 350
with you – why do you go about to recover the

353 **toil**   net.

354–5 **if my duty. . .unmannerly**   an obscure remark, which even Hamlet does not understand. Guildenstern possibly means something like: 'If I am too disrespectfully persistent in my attempts to serve you, it is because my love for you urges me not to stand on ceremony'.

357 **pipe**   recorder.

362 **I know no touch of it**   I don't know how to play it.

363 **ventages**   finger holes.

369 **unworthy a thing**   Hamlet is saying that Guildenstern insults him by assuming that he can 'play upon' him (i.e. manipulate him into disclosing the reason for his madness) when he cannot play upon so simple a thing as a recorder.

wind of me, as if you would drive me into a
toil?

GUILDENSTERN

O my lord, if my duty be too bold, my love is too
unmannerly.   355

HAMLET

I do not well understand that. Will you play upon
this pipe?

GUILDENSTERN

My lord, I cannot.

HAMLET

I pray you.

GUILDENSTERN

Believe me, I cannot.   360

HAMLET

I do beseech you.

GUILDENSTERN

I know no touch of it, my lord:

HAMLET

It is as easy as lying: govern these ventages with
your fingers and thumb, give it breath with your
mouth, and it will discourse most eloquent music. 365
Look you, these are the stops.

GUILDENSTERN

But these cannot I command to any utterance of
harmony; I have not the skill.

HAMLET

Why, look you now, how unworthy a thing you
make of me! You would play upon me; you would 370

373 **top of my compass**   highest note.

374 **little organ**   i.e. the recorder.

375 **'Sblood**   (oath) by God's blood.

377 **fret**   irritate, and also put fingers on the fretboard of a lute or guitar to produce a note.

386 **it is back'd**   has a back.

389 **Then I will come to my mother**   i.e. since you seem to be agreeing with everything I say, I will do as you ask.

seem to know my stops; you would pluck out the
heart of my mystery; you would sound me from my
lowest note to the top of my compass; and there
is much music, excellent voice, in this little organ,
yet cannot you make it speak. 'Sblood, do you 375
think I am easier to be play'd on than a pipe? Call
me what instrument you will, though you can fret
me, yet you cannot play upon me.

Re-enter POLONIUS.

God bless you, sir!

POLONIUS
My lord, the Queen would speak with you, and 380
presently.

HAMLET
Do you see yonder cloud that's almost in shape of
a camel?

POLONIUS
By th' mass, and 'tis like a camel indeed.

HAMLET
Methinks it is like a weasel.   385

POLONIUS
It is back'd like a weasel.

HAMLET
Or like a whale?

POLONIUS
Very like a whale.

HAMLET
Then I will come to my mother by and by.

390 *They fool me to the top of my bent*   they deceive me to the limit of my patience.

394 *witching time*   time when witches are about.

395 *churchyards yawn*   i.e. graves open.

399 *nature*   natural kind feelings of son to mother.

400 *Nero*   Roman emperor who arranged for his mother to be murdered.

403 *hypocrites*   Hamlet will utter savage threats to his mother with his 'tongue', while all the time his 'soul' will know that he would never actually carry them out.

404 *shent*   shamed.

405 *give them seals*   i.e. fit actions to the words.

| *I like him not*   I do not like his behaviour.

nor stands it safe with us   neither is it safe for us.

(*Aside*) They fool me to the top of my bent. – I will   390
come by and by.

POLONIUS
I will say so.

Exit POLONIUS

HAMLET
'By and by' is easily said. Leave me, friends.

Exeunt all but HAMLET

'Tis now the very witching time of night,
When churchyards yawn, and hell itself breathes
    out   395
Contagion to this world. Now could I drink hot
    blood,
And do such bitter business as the day
Would quake to look on. Soft! now to my mother.
O heart, lose not thy nature; let not ever
The soul of Nero enter this firm bosom.   400
Let me be cruel, not unnatural:
I will speak daggers to her, but use none.
My tongue and soul in this be hypocrites –
How in my words somever she be shent,
To give them seals never, my soul, consent!   405

Exit

Scene three

Elsinore. The Castle.

Enter KING, ROSENCRANTZ, and GUILDENSTERN.

KING
I like him not; nor stands it safe with us

3 **Commission will forthwith dispatch**   see that your warrant is prepared at once (i.e. the letter to the King of England about the unpaid taxes, mentioned in Act 3, scene 1, lines 181–2).

5 **terms of our estate**   authority of my position as king.

6 **near's**   near to us.

8 **provide**   prepare.

9 **Most holy and religious fear**   Guildenstern, following the doctrine that sovereigns are appointed by God, flatters Claudius by saying that it is his religious duty to keep himself safe.

10 **bodies**   people.

11 **live and feed**   depend.

12 **single and peculiar life**   life of an ordinary commoner.

14 **noyance**   harm.

15 **That spirit**   i.e. the sovereign.

weal   welfare.

16 **cease of majesty**   death of a monarch.

17 **gulf**   whirlpool.

18 **massy**   massive.

21 **mortis'd**   fixed, as in a carpenter's mortise join.

22 **annexment**   thing joined on.

23 **Attends**   shares in.

boist'rous ruin   noisy catastrophe.

24 **general groan**   everyone being upset.

25 **Arm you**   prepare yourselves.

26 **fetters**   shackles.

220

To let his madness range. Therefore prepare you;
I your commission will forthwith dispatch,
And he to England shall along with you.
The terms of our estate may not endure   5
Hazard so near's as doth hourly grow
Out of his brows.

GUILDENSTERN
We will ourselves provide.
Most holy and religious fear it is
To keep those many many bodies safe   10
That live and feed upon your Majesty.

ROSENCRANTZ
The single and peculiar life is bound
With all the strength and armour of the mind
To keep itself from noyance; but much more
That spirit upon whose weal depends and rests   15
The lives of many. The cease of majesty
Dies not alone, but like a gulf doth draw
What's near it with it. It is a massy wheel,
Fix'd on the summit of the highest mount,
To whose huge spokes ten thousand lesser things   20
Are mortis'd and adjoin'd; which when it falls,
Each small annexment, petty consequence,
Attends the boist'rous ruin. Never alone
Did the king sigh, but with a general groan.

KING
Arm you, I pray you, to this speedy voyage;   25
For we will fetters put about this fear,
Which now goes too free-footed.

ROSENCRANTZ
We will haste us.
                    Exeunt ROSENCRANTZ *and* GUILDENSTERN

221

29 **closet** private room.

30 **convey** hide.

31 **process** conversation.

tax him home take him to task.

35 **of vantage** in addition.

40 **primal eldest curse** first and oldest curse. In the Bible (Genesis 4), Cain, Adam and Eve's son, murdered his brother Abel, and was cursed by God.

42 **inclination** desire to do so.

will determination.

44 **to double business bound** with two pressing tasks on hand.

49 **Whereto serves mercy** what is the purpose of mercy.

50 **confront the visage of offence** be brought face-to-face with sin.

52 **forestalled ere we come to fall** prevented from falling into sin.

53 **being down** i.e. having sinned.

Enter POLONIUS.

POLONIUS
My lord, he's going to his mother's closet.
Behind the arras I'll convey myself   30
To hear the process. I'll warrant she'll tax him
    home;
And, as you said, and wisely was it said,
'Tis meet that some more audience than a mother,
Since nature makes them partial, should o'erhear
The speech, of vantage. Fare you well, my liege.   35
I'll call upon you ere you go to bed,
And tell you what I know.

KING   *examen speeku.*
Thanks, dear my lord.

                                        Exit POLONIUS

O, my offence is rank, it smells to heaven;
It hath the primal eldest curse upon't –   40
A brother's murder! Pray can I not,
Though inclination be as sharp as will.
My stronger guilt defeats my strong intent,
And, like a man to double business bound,
I stand in pause where I shall first begin,   45
And both neglect. What if this cursed hand
Were thicker than itself with brother's blood,
Is there not rain enough in the sweet heavens
To wash it white as snow? Whereto serves mercy
But to confront the visage of offence?   50
And what's in prayer but this twofold force,
To be forestalled ere we come to fall,
Or pardon'd being down? Then I'll look up;
My fault is past. But, O, what form of prayer
Can serve my turn? 'Forgive me my foul murder'!   55

223

59 **retain th' offence**   keep possession of the benefits.

63 **above**   in heaven, when we face the judgement of God.

64 **shuffling**   trickery.

65 **his**   its.

66 **to the teeth and forehead**   i.e. we are brought face-to-face with.

67 **rests**   remains.

71 **limed**   snared, trapped (as a bird in bird lime).

72 **assay**   attempt.

76 **pat**   easily.

78 **would be scann'd**   must be carefully considered.

82 **hire and salary**   a reward for him.

83 **grossly, full of bread**   when he was unprepared for death, having indulged his appetite rather than having fasted.

That cannot be; since I am still possess'd
Of those effects for which I did the murder –
My crown, mine own ambition, and my queen.
May one be pardon'd and retain th' offence?
In the corrupted currents of this world   60
Offence's gilded hand may shove by justice;
And oft 'tis seen the wicked prize itself
Buys out the law. But 'tis not so above:
There is no shuffling; there the action lies
In his true nature; and we ourselves compell'd,   65
Even to the teeth and forehead of our faults,
To give in evidence. What then? What rests?
Try what repentance can. What can it not?
Yet what can it when one can not repent?
O wretched state! O bosom black as death!   70
O limed soul, that, struggling to be free,
Art more engag'd! Help, angels. Make assay:
Bow, stubborn knees; and, heart, with strings of
  steel,
Be soft as sinews of the new-born babe.
All may be well.   75

Retires and kneels.

Enter HAMLET.

HAMLET
  Now might I do it pat, now 'a is a-praying;
  And now I'll do't – and so 'a goes to heaven,
  And so am I reveng'd. That would be scann'd:
  A villain kills my father; and for that,
  I, his sole son, do this same villain send   80
  To heaven.
  Why, this is hire and salary, not revenge.
  'A took my father grossly, full of bread,

225

84 **broad blown** in full blossom.

flush as May as fresh as the leaves and flowers of May.

85 **how his audit stands** how he has been judged.

save except.

86 **our circumstance and course of thought** as far as we on earth are able to judge.

87 **'Tis heavy with him** the judgement on him has been harsh.

89 **fit and season'd for his passage** well prepared for death, having repented his sins.

91 **Up, sword. . .horrid hent** back into your scabbard, sword, and wait for a time when I grip you ('hent') with a more terrible ('horrid') purpose.

94 **At game** when gambling.

95 **relish** taste.

98 **stays** waits.

99 **This physic. . .sickly days** rhetorically addressed to Claudius, not intended to be heard. Claudius's prayers ('This physic') are like a medicine which only puts off his death a little and does not cure him.

straight soon.

Look you lay home to him make sure you talk severely to him.

2 **broad** unrestrained.

With all his crimes broad blown, as flush as May;
And how his audit stands who knows save heaven? 85
But in our circumstance and course of thought
'Tis heavy with him; and am I then reveng'd
To take him in the purging of his soul,
When he is fit and season'd for his passage?
No. *I should kill him when he's drunk* 90
Up, sword, and know thou a more horrid hent. *when he's*
When he is drunk asleep, or in his rage; *having sex*
Or in th' incestuous pleasure of his bed; *with his mot-*
At game, a-swearing, or about some act *her*
That has no relish of salvation in't – 95
Then trip him, that his heels may kick at heaven,
And that his soul may be as damn'd and black
As hell, whereto it goes. My mother stays.
This physic but prolongs thy sickly days.

he is finding more excuses he don't   *Exit*

KING *have to kill his uncle*

  (*Rising*) My words fly up, my thoughts remain
    below. 100
  Words without thoughts never to heaven go.

                                        Exit

Scene four

The Queen's closet.

Enter QUEEN *and* POLONIUS.

POLONIUS
  'A will come straight. Look you lay home to him;
  Tell him his pranks have been too broad to bear
    with,

5 **_round_** blunt, stern.

7 **_I'll warrant you_** I promise to do as you ask.

Fear me not do not doubt me.

10 **_father_** i.e Claudius.

11 **_father_** i.e. old Hamlet.

Hamlet wishes she was not his mother.

And that your Grace hath screen'd and stood
  between
Much heat and him. I'll silence me even here.
Pray you be round with him.   5

HAMLET
(*Within*) Mother, mother, mother!

QUEEN
I'll warrant you. Fear me not.
Withdraw, I hear him coming.

POLONIUS *goes behind the arras.*

Enter HAMLET.

HAMLET
Now, mother, what's the matter?

QUEEN
Hamlet, thou hast thy father much offended.   10

HAMLET
Mother, you have my father much offended.

QUEEN
Come, come, you answer with an idle tongue.

HAMLET
Go, go, you question with a wicked tongue.

QUEEN
Why, how now, Hamlet!

HAMLET
What's the matter now?   15

QUEEN
Have you forgot me?

229

17 **rood**   cross on which Christ was crucified.

20 **set**   send.

27 **rat**   spy, traitor.

28 **for a ducat dead**   I'll bet a ducat that he is dead.

s.d. **pass**   thrust of his sword or dagger.

HAMLET

No, by the rood, not so;
You are the Queen, your husband's brother's wife;
And – would it were not so! – you are my mother.

QUEEN

Nay then, I'll set those to you that can speak.   20

HAMLET

Come, come, and sit you down; you shall not
    budge.
You go not till I set you up a glass
Where you may see the inmost part of you.

QUEEN

What wilt thou do? Thou wilt not murder me?
Help, help, ho!   25

POLONIUS

(*Behind*) What, ho! help, help, help!

HAMLET

(*Draws*) How now! a rat?
Dead, for a ducat dead? (*Kills* POLONIUS *with a pass
through the arras.*)

POLONIUS

(*Behind*) O, I am slain!

QUEEN

O me, what hast thou done?   30

HAMLET

Nay, I know not:
Is it the King?

QUEEN

O, what a rash and bloody deed is this!

39 **thy better** i.e. Claudius.

Take thy fortune accept your fate.

40 **busy** nosey, meddling.

44 **damned custom** sinful habits.

braz'd hardened it (as brass).

45 **proof and bulwark** strengthened and fortified.

sense feeling.

48 **act** i.e. incest.

49 **blurs** stains.

50 **rose** symbol of pure, chaste love.

52 **blister** prostitutes were sometimes branded on the forehead.

54 **contraction** marriage vows.

56 **rhapsody** meaningless jumble.

glow blush.

57 **solidity and compound mass** i.e. the earth.

58 **as against the doom** as if in preparation for Doomsday.

59 **thought-sick at** made sick by thinking of.

You can't be in love with Claudius because you are too old and you're hormons do not work anymore, only your brains. Hamlet to his mother.

HAMLET

A bloody deed! – almost as bad, good mother,
As kill a king and marry with his brother.   35

QUEEN

As kill a king!

HAMLET   *→ He thought it was a king*

Ay, lady, it was my word. (*Parting the arras.*)
Thou wretched, rash, intruding fool, farewell!
I took thee for thy better. Take thy fortune;
Thou find'st to be too busy is some danger –   40
Leave wringing of your hands. Peace; sit you
   down.
And let me wring your heart; for so I shall,
If it be made of penetrable stuff;
If damned custom have not braz'd it so
That it be proof and bulwark against sense.   45

QUEEN

What have I done that thou dar'st wag thy tongue
In noise so rude against me?

HAMLET

Such an act
That blurs the grace and blush of modesty;
Calls virtue hypocrite; takes off the rose   50
From the fair forehead of an innocent love,
And sets a blister there; makes marriage-vows
As false as dicers' oaths. O, such a deed
As from the body of contraction plucks
The very soul, and sweet religion makes   55
A rhapsody of words. Heaven's face does glow
O'er this solidity and compound mass
With heated visage, as against the doom –
Is thought-sick at the act.

233

61 **index** table of contents of a book (which is at the beginning). Gertrude is asking what the substance of Hamlet's accusation is, that he has introduced with such dramatic words.

63 **counterfeit presentment** likeness in pictures.

65 **Hyperion's curls** hair like the sun's (see note to Act 1, scene 2, line 142).

front of Jove forehead of Jupiter, king of the Roman gods.

66 **Mars** the Roman god of war.

67 **station** way of standing.

Mercury the Roman messenger god.

68 **lighted** landed.

69 **combination** i.e. a mixture of god-like attributes.

73 **ear** i.e. ear of corn.

74 **Blasting** infecting.

75 **leave to feed** cease feeding.

76 **batten on** grow fat by glutting yourself on.

78 **heyday in the blood** peak of sexual appetite.

79 **waits upon** takes its orders from.

80 **Sense** faculties of perception, your five senses.

81 **motion** the power of movement.

82 **apoplex'd** paralysed.

83 **ecstasy** madness.

thrall'd enslaved by bewitchment.

85 **difference** act of discrimination or comparison.

86 **cozen'd** cheated.

hoodman-blind blind man's buff.

234

QUEEN

  Ay me, what act,   60
  That roars so loud and thunders in the index?

HAMLET

  Look here upon this picture and on this,
  The counterfeit presentment of two brothers.
  See what a grace was seated on this brow;
  Hyperion's curls; the front of Jove himself;   65
  An eye like Mars, to threaten and command;
  A station like the herald Mercury
  New lighted on a heaven-kissing hill –
  A combination and a form indeed
  Where every god did seem to set his seal,   70
  To give the world assurance of a man.
  This was your husband. Look you now what
    follows:
  Here is your husband, like a mildew'd ear
  Blasting his wholesome brother. Have you eyes?
  Could you on this fair mountain leave to feed,   75
  And batten on this moor? Ha! have you eyes?
  You cannot call it love; for at your age
  The heyday in the blood is tame, it's humble,
  And waits upon the judgment; and what judgment
  Would step from this to this? Sense, sure, you
    have,   80
  Else could you not have motion; but sure that
    sense
  Is apoplex'd; for madness would not err,
  Nor sense to ecstasy was ne'er so thrall'd
  But it reserv'd some quantity of choice
  To serve in such a difference. What devil was't   85
  That thus hath cozen'd you at hoodman-blind?
  Eyes without feeling, feeling without sight,

88 *sans*   without.

90 *so mope*   act so foolishly.

92 *mutine*   mutiny, stir up trouble.

93–4 *To flaming youth . . .her own fire*   let virtue melt like wax in the fire of
youth's sexual passion.

95 *compulsive ardour*   compelling demands of lust.

charge   orders.

96 *frost itself*   i.e. older 'matrons' like Gertrude.

97 *reason panders will*   reason acts as a procurer for the satisfaction of sexual
appetites.

100 *grained*   ingrained.

101 *will not leave their tinct*   whose stain ('tinct') cannot be cleaned away.

103 *enseamed*   greasy.

104 *Stew'd*   soaked (with a further reference to 'stews' or brothels).

105 *sty*   pig-sty.

110 *tithe*   tenth part.

111 *precedent lord*   previous husband.

vice   probably a king like the figure of Vice from an old morality play, hence
a clown or buffoon.

112 *cutpurse*   thief.

113 *diadem*   crown.

Ears without hands or eyes, smelling sans all,
Or but a sickly part of one true sense
Could not so mope. O shame! where is thy
   blush?   90
Rebellious hell,
If thou canst mutine in a matron's bones,
To flaming youth let virtue be as wax
And melt in her own fire; proclaim no shame
When the compulsive ardour gives the charge,   95
Since frost itself as actively doth burn,
And reason panders will.

QUEEN
   O Hamlet, speak no more!
   Thou turn'st my eyes into my very soul;
   And there I see such black and grained spots   100
   As will not leave their tinct.

HAMLET
   Nay, but to live
   In the rank sweat of an enseamed bed,
   Stew'd in corruption, honeying and making love
   Over the nasty sty!   105

QUEEN
   O, speak to me no more!
   These words like daggers enter in my ears;
   No more, sweet Hamlet.

HAMLET
   A murderer and a villain!
   A slave that is not twentieth part the tithe   110
   Of your precedent lord; a vice of kings;
   A cutpurse of the empire and the rule,
   That from a shelf the precious diadem stole
   And put it in his pocket!

116 **shreds and patches**   tatters, referring to the costume worn by Vice in a morality play (see note to line 111).

120 **tardy**   slow, procrastinating.

121 **laps'd in time and passion**   having delayed, and thus cooled in ardour and resolution.

    lets go by   neglects.

126 **amazement**   bewilderment.

128 **Conceit**   imagination.

132 **vacancy**   an empty space. Gertrude cannot see the ghost, and therefore thinks she is witnessing further proof of Hamlet's madness.

133 **incorporal**   without body.

QUEEN
No more!   115

Enter Ghost.

HAMLET
A king of shreds and patches –
Save me, and hover o'er me with your wings,
You heavenly guards! What would your gracious
   figure?

QUEEN
Alas, he's mad!

HAMLET
Do you not come your tardy son to chide,   120
That, laps'd in time and passion, lets go by
Th' important acting of your dread command?
O, say!

GHOST
Do not forget; this visitation
Is but to whet thy almost blunted purpose.   125
But look, amazement on thy mother sits.
O, step between her and her fighting soul!
Conceit in weakest bodies strongest works.
Speak to her, Hamlet.

HAMLET
How is it with you, lady?   130

QUEEN
Alas, how is't with you,
That you do bend your eye on vacancy,
And with th' incorporal air do hold discourse?
Forth at your eyes your spirits wildly peep;
And, as the sleeping soldiers in th' alarm,   135

you speak with the air.

To who spoke you? I didn't see or hear anything.

239

136 **bedded hairs** hairs which usually lie flat.

like life in excrements as if they were living parts of your body.

137 **an** on

138 **distemper** illness.

141–2 **His form and cause. . .capable** his ghostly figure and just purpose would make stones capable of action if he preached to them.

144 **effects** intentions.

145 **Will want true colour** will lack suitable determination.

152 **habit** clothes.

153 **portal** doorway.

154 **very coinage** creation.

Your bedded hairs like life in excrements
Start up and stand an end. O gentle son,
Upon the heat and flame of thy distemper
Sprinkle cool patience! Whereon do you look?

HAMLET

On him, on him! Look you how pale he glares.   140
His form and cause conjoin'd, preaching to stones,
Would make them capable. – Do not look upon
  me,
Lest with this piteous action you convert
My stern effects; then what I have to do
Will want true colour – tears perchance for blood. 145

QUEEN

To whom do you speak this?

HAMLET

Do you see nothing there?

QUEEN

Nothing at all; yet all that is I see.

HAMLET

Nor did you nothing hear?

QUEEN

No, nothing but ourselves.   150

HAMLET

Why, look you there. Look how it steals away.
My father, in his habit as he liv'd!
Look where he goes even now out at the portal.

Exit Ghost

QUEEN

This is the very coinage of your brain.

241

155–6 **This bodiless creation. . .cunning in**   madness ('ecstasy') is very skilled ('cunning') in the creation of these hallucinations ('bodiless creation').

161 **the matter will re-word**   repeat what has just happened.

162 **gambol**   shy away.

163 **Lay not**   do not apply.

flattering unction   soothing ointment.

165 **skin and film**   form a thin film over.

166 **mining**   undermining.

170 **virtue**   judgemental tone.

171 **pursy**   swollen like a fat purse, i.e. grossly self-indulgent.

173 **curb**   bow.

178 **Assume**   act as if you have.

179–80 **who all sense. . .evil**   takes away all our consciousness that we have slipped into evil habits.

182 **livery**   uniform.

183 **aptly**   easily.

This bodiless creation ecstasy   155
Is very cunning in.

HAMLET

Ecstasy!
My pulse as yours doth temperately keep time,
And makes as healthful music. It is not madness
That I have utt'red. Bring me to the test,   160
And I the matter will re-word which madness
Would gambol from. Mother, for love of grace,
Lay not that flattering unction to your soul,
That not your trepass but my madness speaks:
It will but skin and film the ulcerous place,   165
Whiles rank corruption, mining all within,
Infects unseen. Confess yourself to heaven;
Repent what's past; avoid what is to come;
And do not spread the compost on the weeds,
To make them ranker. Forgive me this my virtue; 170
For in the fatness of these pursy times
Virtue itself of vice must pardon beg,
Yea, curb and woo for leave to do him good.

QUEEN

O Hamlet, thou hast cleft my heart in twain.

HAMLET

O, throw away the worser part of it,   175
And live the purer with the other half.
Good night – but go not to my uncle's bed;
Assume a virtue, if you have it not.
That monster custom, who all sense doth eat,
Of habits evil, is angel yet in this,   180
That to the use of actions fair and good
He likewise gives a frock or livery
That aptly is put on. Refrain to-night;

186 **use** habit.

stamp of nature inherited behaviour patterns.

190 **same lord** i.e. Polonius.

193 **their scourge and minister** heaven's instrument of punishment.

194 **bestow** dispose of.

answer well be ready to account for my actions.

197 **remains behind** is still to come.

201 **bloat** bloated.

203 **reechy** filthy.

204 **paddling** caressing.

205 **ravel all this matter out** explain by disentangling all this affair (of my madness).

206 **essentially** in my true, essential nature.

207 **craft** pretence.

209 **paddock** toad.

gib tom-cat.

210 **dear concernings** important matters.

211 **in despite of** in spite of.

212–5 **Unpeg the basket. . .neck down** the meaning of these lines is uncertain, because they refer to a story that has been lost. It presumably concerns an ape, which stole a basket full of birds, and took them up to the roof of a house. The ape then let the birds go, and concluded that they could fly because they came from the basket. The ape then got into the basket and jumped out, thinking it too would be able to fly, and broke its neck. The story's moral to Gertrude would be that if she let Hamlet's secrets go, as the ape released the birds, it would lead to her downfall.

And that shall lend a kind of easiness
To the next abstinence; the next more easy;   185
For use almost can change the stamp of nature,
And either curb the devil, or throw him out,
With wondrous potency. Once more, good night;
And when you are desirous to be blest,
I'll blessing beg of you. For this same lord   190
I do repent; but Heaven hath pleas'd it so,
To punish me with this, and this with me,
That I must be their scourge and minister.
I will bestow him, and will answer well
The death I gave him. So, again, good night.   195
I must be cruel only to be kind;
Thus bad begins and worse remains behind.
One word more, good lady.

QUEEN
    What shall I do?

HAMLET   _don't sleep with the king_
    Not this, by no means, that I bid you do;   200
Let the bloat King tempt you again to bed;
Pinch wanton on your cheek; call you his mouse;
And let him, for a pair of reechy kisses,
Or paddling in your neck with his damn'd fingers,
Make you to ravel all this matter out,   205
That I essentially am not in madness,
But mad in craft. 'Twere good you let him know;
For who that's but a queen, fair, sober, wise,
Would from a paddock, from a bat, a gib,
Such dear concernings hide? Who would do so?   210
No, in despite of sense and secrecy,
Unpeg the basket on the house's top,
Let the birds fly, and, like the famous ape,

believe his pretend madness?

Not sure, but she understand it

220 *concluded on*   decided.

223 *mandate*   royal commission.

sweep my way   clear my path.

224 *marshal me to knavery*   lead me into a trap.

225 *enginer*   military engineer, bomb-maker.

226 **Hoist with his own petar**   blown up by his own bomb.

and't shall go hard   and it will be the worse for me.

227 **But I will delve**   if I do not dig.

229 *in one line two crafts directly meet*   one plot can be used to counter another.

230 **This man**   i.e. Polonius. His death will cause Claudius to send Hamlet 'packing'.

231 *guts*   i.e. the corpse.

235 *draw toward an end*   pun on 'draw': meaning, conclude the interview, and also finally drag you off.

To try conclusions, in the basket creep
And break your own neck down.   215

QUEEN

Be thou assur'd, if words be made of breath
And breath of life, I have no life to breathe
What thou hast said to me.

HAMLET

I must to England; you know that?

QUEEN

Alack, I had forgot. 'Tis so concluded on.   220

HAMLET

There's letters seal'd; and my two school-fellows,
Whom I will trust as I will adders fang'd –
They bear the mandate; they must sweep my way
And marshal me to knavery. Let it work;
For 'tis the sport to have the enginer   225
Hoist with his own petar; and't shall go hard
But I will delve one yard below their mines
And blow them at the moon. O, 'tis most sweet
When in one line two crafts directly meet.
This man shall set me packing.   230
I'll lug the guts into the neighbour room.
Mother, good night. Indeed, this counsellor
Is now most still, most secret, and most grave,
Who was in life a foolish prating knave.
Come, sir, to draw toward an end with you.   235
Good night, mother.

Exeunt severally; HAMLET *tugging in* POLONIUS

Ophelia (Frances Barber): Royal Shakespeare Company, 1984–85.

Act 4: summary

Gertrude tells Claudius that Hamlet has killed Polonius. Claudius fears the blame will fall on him, for allowing the mad Hamlet his liberty for so long. Claudius tells Hamlet that he is to be sent away for his own safety. However, when Hamlet leaves, Claudius reveals his plan to have him killed on his arrival in England.

Hamlet watches Fortinbras marching with his army on their way to fight the Poles. He again condemns himself for his inaction and vows that from now on he will think only of revenge.

Gertrude is told that Ophelia has gone mad. Ophelia enters, and Claudius also witnesses her distracted singing. There is the sound of a mob outside, shouting that Laertes should be made king. Laertes storms in, demanding an explanation for the death of his father. Claudius placates him, but then the mad Ophelia re-appears, and Laertes breaks down in grief. Claudius tells him that he will help him gain revenge on whoever is guilty for these crimes against his family.

Horatio receives a letter from Hamlet, which tells him that his ship was attacked by pirates on the way to England. In the fight, Hamlet boarded their ship, and was brought back to Denmark. Rosencrantz and Guildenstern continued on their way.

Claudius has now told Laertes of Hamlet's involvement in Polonius's death and Ophelia's madness. A letter arrives from Hamlet telling Claudius that he is back in Denmark. Claudius and Laertes hatch a plot to kill Hamlet as if by accident with a poisoned sword in a fencing match. Claudius also plans to offer Hamlet a poisoned drink during the bout.

Gertrude enters with news that Ophelia has drowned. Collecting flowers, she fell into a brook, and let herself be pulled under by the weight of her clothes.

1 *matter* meaning.

  profound heaves deep sighs.

2 *translate* make clear the meaning of.

4 *Bestow this place* i.e. leave us alone.

11 *brainish apprehension* mad fit of imagination.

14 *us* i.e. me.

Act Four

The King realises that he's in danger because he could have been Polonius.

Scene one

Elsinore. The Castle.

Enter KING, QUEEN, ROSENCRANTZ, *and* GUILDENSTERN.

KING

There's matter in these sighs, these profound
  heaves,
You must translate; 'tis fit we understand them.
Where is your son?

QUEEN

Bestow this place on us a little while.

Exeunt ROSENCRANTZ *and* GUILDENSTERN

Ah, mine own lord, what have I seen to-night!   5

KING

What, Gertrude? How does Hamlet?

QUEEN

Mad as the sea and wind, when both contend
Which is the mightier. In his lawless fit,
Behind the arras hearing something stir,
Whips out his rapier, cries 'A rat, a rat!'   10
And in this brainish apprehension kills
The unseen good old man.

KING

O heavy deed!
It had been so with us had we been there.
His liberty is full of threats to all –   15
To you yourself, to us, to every one.

17 *answer'd*   accounted for.

18 *laid*   blamed.

   providence   foresight.

19 *kept short*   kept under control, on a short leash.

   out of haunt   out of circulation.

23 *divulging*   being divulged.

26 *ore*   gold.

33 *countenance*   tolerate.

[handwritten: he's angry. I should have acted to Hamlet in a more cruel way instead of using way.]

Alas, how shall this bloody deed be answer'd?
It will be laid to us, whose providence
Should have kept short, restrain'd, and out of
    haunt,
This mad young man. But so much was our love,   20
We would not understand what was most fit;
But, like the owner of a foul disease,
To keep it from divulging, let it feed
Even on the pith of life. Where is he gone?

[handwritten: to tell people, to explain, he didn't reveal, to make public.]

QUEEN
    To draw apart the body he hath kill'd;   25
    O'er whom his very madness, like some ore
    Among a mineral of metals base,
    Shows itself pure: 'a weeps for what is done.

KING
    O Gertrude, come away!   30
    The sun no sooner shall the mountains touch
    But we will ship him hence; and this vile deed
    We must with all our majesty and skill
    Both countenance and excuse. Ho, Guildenstern!

[handwritten: It's oke, now we must do something. He doesn't believe that Hamlet's really mad..]

Re-enter ROSENCRANTZ *and* GUILDENSTERN.

    Friends, both go join you with some further aid:
    Hamlet in madness hath Polonius slain,   35
    And from his mother's closet hath he dragg'd him;
    Go seek him out; speak fair, and bring the body
    Into the chapel. I pray you haste in this.

                Exeunt ROSENCRANTZ *and* GUILDENSTERN

    Come, Gertrude, we'll call up our wisest friends
    And let them know both what we mean to do   40
    And what's untimely done; so haply slander –
    Whose whisper o'er the world's diameter,

43–4 **level as the cannon. . .shot**   hits the target ('blank') as directly ('level') as a
cannon.

45 **woundless**   impossible to wound.

1 **Safely stow'd**   i.e. the body of Polonius has been safely disposed of.

6 **Compounded**   blended.

[handwritten: How do we prevent ooze?]

As level as the cannon to his blank,
Transport his pois'ned shot – may miss our name,
And hit the woundless air. O, come away!   45
My soul is full of discord and dismay.

[handwritten: He doesn't know what to do.]   *Exeunt*

Scene two

Elsinore. The Castle.

Enter HAMLET.

HAMLET

Safely stow'd.

GENTLEMEN

(*Within*) Hamlet! Lord Hamlet!

HAMLET

But soft! What noise? Who calls on Hamlet? O,
here they come!

Enter ROSENCRANTZ *and* GUILDENSTERN.

ROSENCRANTZ

What have you done, my lord, with the dead body?   5

HAMLET

Compounded it with dust, whereto 'tis kin.

ROSENCRANTZ

Tell us where 'tis, that we may take it thence
And bear it to the chapel.

HAMLET

Do not believe it.

255

11 *counsel*   secrets.

12 *demanded of*   asked questions by.

   sponge   i.e. someone ready to soak up any information.

13 *replication*   reply.

15 *soaks up the King's countenance*   cannot get enough of the king's favour.

16 *authorities*   positions of authority (and therefore profit).

23–4 *a knavish speech. . .ear*   insulting words are not understood by fools.

ROSENCRANTZ

Believe what? 10

HAMLET

That I can keep your counsel, and not mine own.
Besides, to be demanded of a sponge – what
replication should be made by the son of a king?

ROSENCRANTZ

Take you me for a sponge, my lord?

HAMLET

Ay, sir; that soaks up the King's countenance, his 15
rewards, his authorities. But such officers do the
King best service in the end: he keeps them, like
an ape an apple in the corner of his jaw; first
mouth'd, to be last swallowed; when he needs what
you have glean'd, it is but squeezing you and, 20
sponge, you shall be dry again.

ROSENCRANTZ

I understand you not, my lord.

HAMLET

I am glad of it; a knavish speech sleeps in a foolish
ear.

ROSENCRANTZ

My lord, you must tell us where the body is, and 25
go with us to the King.

HAMLET

The body is with the King, but the King is not
with the body. The King is a thing –

GUILDENSTERN

A thing, my lord!

30–1 **Hide fox, and all after**   probably deliberate nonsense, or alluding to a
version of hide and seek, where the person hiding is the 'fox'.

1 **sent to seek him**   i.e. sent someone to seek him.
4 **of**   by.

distracted multitude   confused population of Denmark.
5 **Who like not. . .their eyes**   who form their opinions by appearances rather
than reason.
6 **scourge is weigh'd**   punishment is considered.
7 **To bear all smooth and even**   to give the appearance of authority and
judiciousness.
9 **Deliberate pause**   the result of careful consideration.
10 **appliance**   remedy.

HAMLET

Of nothing. Bring me to him. Hide fox, and all 30
after.

Exeunt

Scene three

Elsinore. The Castle.

Enter KING, *attended.*

KING

I have sent to seek him, and to find the body.
How dangerous is it that this man goes loose!
Yet must not we put the strong law on him:
He's lov'd of the distracted multitude,
Who like not in their judgment but their eyes;   5
And where 'tis so, th' offender's scourge is weigh'd,
But never the offence. To bear all smooth and
even,
This sudden sending him away must seem
Deliberate pause. Diseases desperate grown
By desperate appliance are reliev'd,   10
Or not at all.

Enter ROSENCRANTZ.

How now! what hath befall'n?

ROSENCRANTZ

Where the dead body is bestow'd, my lord.
We cannot get from him.

KING

But where is he?   15

16 **Without** outside.

23 **convocation** assembly.

politic politically-minded.

e'en even now.

24 **only emperor for diet** punningly referring to the Diet of Worms, a gathering called by Emperor Charles V in 1521 to hear Martin Luther's defence of Protestantism.

fat fatten.

27 **variable service** different varieties of food.

ROSENCRANTZ

Without, my lord; guarded, to know your pleasure.

KING

Bring him before us.

ROSENCRANTZ

Ho, Guildenstern! bring in the lord.

Enter HAMLET *and* GUILDENSTERN.

KING

Now, Hamlet, where's Polonius?

HAMLET

At supper.   20

KING

At supper! Where?

HAMLET

Not where he eats, but where 'a is eaten; a certain
convocation of politic worms are e'en at him. Your
worm is your only emperor for diet: we fat all creatures else to fat us, and we fat ourselves for   25
maggots; your fat king and your lean beggar is but
variable service – two dishes, but to one table.
That's the end.

KING

Alas, alas!

HAMLET

A man may fish with the worm that hath eat of   30
a king, and eat of the fish that hath fed of that
worm.

KING

What dost thou mean by this?

35 **progress**   formal state journey made by a king around his kingdom.

38 **other place**   i.e. hell.

40 **nose**   smell.

45 **tender**   care for.

48 **bark**   ship.

   at help   blowing from a helpful direction.

49 **Th' associates tend**   your friends await.

   bent   directed towards.

HAMLET

Nothing but to show you how a king may go a
progress through the guts of a beggar.   35

KING

Where is Polonius?

HAMLET

In heaven; send thither to see; if your messenger
find him not there, seek him i' th' other place yourself. But if, indeed, you find him not within this
month, you shall nose him as you go up the stairs   40
into the lobby.

KING

(*To* Attendants) Go seek him there.

HAMLET

'A will stay till you come.

Exeunt Attendants

KING

Hamlet, this deed, for thine especial safety –
Which we do tender, as we dearly grieve   45
For that which thou hast done – must send thee
      hence
With fiery quickness. Therefore prepare thyself;
The bark is ready, and the wind at help,
Th' associates tend, and everything is bent
For England.   50

HAMLET

For England!

KING

Ay, Hamlet.

55 **cherub**   an order of angels who were thought to be well-informed about the secrets of humans.

61 **at foot**   hard on his heels.

64 **leans on th' affair**   relates to the matter.

65 **England**   i.e. the king of England.

   hold'st at aught   value for anything.

66 **my great power. . .sense**   my great military power may suggest to you the need to value it.

67 **cicatrice**   scar.

68 **free**   voluntary.

69–70 **thou mayst not. . .process**   you may not coolly disregard my royal command.

70 **imports at full**   commands in detail.

71 **letters congruing to that effect**   documents agreeing to that outcome.

72 **present**   immediate.

73 **hectic**   fever.

HAMLET

Good!

KING

So is it, if thou knew'st our purposes.

he knows what the king wants to do with him. He has already got a plan

HAMLET

I see a cherub that sees them. But, come; for   55
England! Farewell dear mother.

to save himself

KING

Thy loving father, Hamlet.

HAMLET

My mother: father and mother is man and wife;
man and wife is one flesh; and so, my mother.
Come, for England.   60

Exit

KING

Follow him at foot; tempt him with speed aboard;
Delay it not; I'll have him hence to-night.
Away! for everything is seal'd and done
That else leans on th' affair. Pray you make haste.

Exeunt all but the KING

And, England, if my love thou hold'st at aught –   65
As my great power thereof may give thee sense,
Since yet thy cicatrice looks raw and red
After the Danish sword, and thy free awe
Pays homage to us – thou mayst not coldly set
Our sovereign process; which imports at full,   70
By letters congruing to that effect,
The present death of Hamlet. Do it, England:
For like the hectic in my blood he rages,

he're the king admits he's being killed in England. The imagination yells it out.

75 **Howe'er my haps**   whatever else happens to me.

2 **licence**   permission. See Act 2, scene 2, lines 81–5.

3 **conveyance**   fulfilment of the promise.

5 **would aught with us**   wishes to say anything to us.

6 **in his eye**   to his face.

10 **powers**   troops.

12 **How purpos'd**   what is the object or purpose of their expedition?

And thou must cure me. Till I know 'tis done,
Howe'er my haps, my joys were ne'er begun.   75

Exit

Scene four

A plain in Denmark.

Enter FORTINBRAS *with his* Army *over the stage.*

FORTINBRAS
    Go, Captain, from me greet the Danish king.
    Tell him that by his licence Fortinbras
    Craves the conveyance of a promis'd march
    Over his kingdom. You know the rendezvous.
    If that his Majesty would aught with us,   5
    We shall express our duty in his eye;
    And let him know so.

CAPTAIN
    I will do't, my lord.

FORTINBRAS
    Go softly on.

Exeunt all but the CAPTAIN

Enter HAMLET, ROSENCRANTZ, GUILDENSTERN, *and* Others.

HAMLET
    Good sir, whose powers are these?   10

CAPTAIN
    They are of Norway, sir.

HAMLET
    How purpos'd, sir, I pray you?

15 **old Norway**   the elderly king of Norway.

16 **main**   main area of the country.

17 **frontier**   remote, outlying part.

18 **with no addition**   without dressing it up in fine words.

21 **five ducats**   i.e. a paltry sum of money.

   farm   rent.

23 **ranker rate**   higher price.

   in fee   freehold.

27 **debate the question of this straw**   bring to a conclusion the dispute over this trifle.

28 **imposthume**   ulcer, abscess.

29 **inward breaks**   erupts inside the body.

   without   outside the body.

CAPTAIN

Against some part of Poland.

HAMLET

Who commands them, sir?

CAPTAIN

The nephew to old Norway, Fortinbras.   15

HAMLET

Goes it against the main of Poland, sir,
Or for some frontier?

CAPTAIN

Truly to speak, and with no addition,
We go to gain a little patch of ground
That hath in it no profit but the name.   20
To pay five ducats, five, I would not farm it;
Nor will it yield to Norway or the Pole
A ranker rate should it be sold in fee.

HAMLET

Why, then the Polack never will defend it.

CAPTAIN

Yes, it is already garrison'd.   25

HAMLET

Two thousand souls and twenty thousand ducats
Will not debate the question of this straw.
This is th' imposthume of much wealth and peace,
That inward breaks, and shows no cause without
Why the man dies. I humbly thank you, sir.   30

CAPTAIN

God buy you, sir.

Exit

34 *all occasions*   every chance event.

inform against   bring charges against.

36 *chief good and market*   main use and business.

38 *he*   i.e. God.

large discourse   wide-ranging intellect.

39 *Looking before and after*   looking into the future and past.

41 *fust*   grow mouldy.

42 *Bestial oblivion*   animal-like forgetfulness.

craven scruple   cowardly misgiving.

43 *too precisely*   too exactly and fastidiously.

th' event   the matter.

47 *Sith*   since.

48 *gross*   obvious.

49 *mass and charge*   size and cost.

50 *delicate*   well brought up.

tender   young.

52 *Makes mouths at*   mocks.

invisible event   unseen future outcome.

55 *egg-shell*   trifle (i.e. the 'little patch of ground' mentioned by the Captain in line 19).

Rightly to be great   to be truly great.

56 *Is not to stir without great argument*   is not to take action without good reason for doing so.

57–8 *But greatly to find. . .the stake*   but nobly to find reasons for fighting for insignificant things when honour *is* at stake.

ROSENCRANTZ

    Will't please you go, my lord?

HAMLET

    I'll be with you straight. Go a little before.

                              Exeunt all but HAMLET

How all occasions do inform against me,
And spur my dull revenge! What is a man,   35
If his chief good and market of his time
Be but to sleep and feed? A beast, no more!
Sure he that made us with such large discourse,
Looking before and after, gave us not
That capability and godlike reason   40
To fust in us unus'd. Now, whether it be
Bestial oblivion, or some craven scruple
Of thinking too precisely on th' event –
A thought which, quarter'd, hath but one part
    wisdom
And ever three parts coward – I do not know   45
Why yet I live to say 'This thing's to do',
Sith I have cause, and will, and strength, and
    means,
To do't. Examples gross as earth exhort me:
Witness this army, of such mass and charge,
Led by a delicate and tender prince,   50
Whose spirit, with divine ambition puff'd,
Makes mouths at the invisible event,
Exposing what is mortal and unsure
To all that fortune, death, and danger, dare,
Even for an egg-shell. Rightly to be great   55
Is not to stir without great argument,
But greatly to find quarrel in a straw,
When honour's at the stake. How stand I, then,

59 **stain'd**   dishonoured.

60 **Excitements**   spurrings on.

    blood   emotions.

63 **fantasy and trick of fame**   illusion, imaginary point of honour.

65 **Whereon the numbers cannot try the cause**   which is not big enough to hold all the soldiers who are fighting over it.

66 **continent**   container.

2 **distract**   distracted, mad.

3 **will needs**   must be.

6 **hems**   sound made by clearing the throat.

7 **Spurns enviously at straws**   kicks out aggressively at the most trivial things.

8 **nothing**   nonsense.

9 **unshaped use**   random, unformed manner.

he compares himself
with Hamlet? or Laertes   *she had sex with*
That have a father kill'd, a mother stain'd,   *true man*
Excitements of my reason and my blood,   60
And let all sleep, while to my shame I see
The imminent death of twenty thousand men
That, for a fantasy and trick of fame,
Go to their graves like beds, fight for a plot
Whereon the numbers cannot try the cause,   65
Which is not tomb enough and continent
To hide the slain? O, from this time forth,
My thoughts be bloody, or be nothing worth!

Exit

The grave will not be big enough.
Good opinion?

Scene five

Elsinore. The Castle.

Enter QUEEN, HORATIO, *and a* Gentleman.

QUEEN

I will not speak with her.

GENTLEMAN

She is importunate, indeed distract.
Her mood will needs be pitied.

QUEEN

What would she have?

GENTLEMAN

She speaks much of her father; says she hears   5
There's tricks i' th' world, and hems, and beats her
heart;
Spurns enviously at straws; speaks things in doubt,
That carry but half sense. Her speech is nothing,
Yet the unshaped use of it doth move

273

10 **collection** collect her words to try to make sense of them.

    yawn gape (with astonishment).

11 **fit to their own thoughts** make their own meanings from it.

12 **yield** deliver.

14 **unhappily** i.e. the hearers cannot discern the meaning of Ophelia's words, although they realise they spring from unhappiness.

15 **'Twere good she were** it would be a good thing if she were.

16 **ill-breeding minds** minds which conceive evil thoughts.

19 **toy** trifle.

    great amiss disaster.

20 **artless jealousy** uncontrollable suspicion.

21 **spills itself in fearing to be spilt** gives itself away in trying to hide itself.

26–7 **By his cockle hat. . .shoon** by his pilgrim's appearance.

26 **cockle hat** a hat with a cockle shell in it signified that the wearer had been on a pilgrimage overseas.

27 **shoon** shoes.

The hearers to collection; they yawn at it,   10
And botch the words up fit to their own.
   thoughts;
Which, as her winks and nods and gestures yield
   them,
Indeed would make one think there might be
   thought,
Though nothing sure, yet much unhappily.

HORATIO

'Twere good she were spoken with; for she may
   strew   15
Dangerous conjectures in ill-breeding minds.

QUEEN

Let her come in.

Exit Gentleman

(*Aside*) To my sick soul, as sin's true nature is,
Each toy seems prologue to some great amiss.
So full of artless jealousy is guilt,   20
It spills itself in fearing to be spilt.

Enter OPHELIA *distracted.*

OPHELIA

Where is the beautous Majesty of Denmark?

QUEEN

How now, Ophelia!

OPHELIA

(*Sings*)
How should I your true love know
   From another one?   25
By his cockle hat and staff,
   And his sandal shoon.

275

28 **imports**   is the meaning of.

29 **Say you?**   what did you say?

39 **Larded**   strewn.

40 **bewept**   wept over.

41 **true-love showers**   tears of true love.

43 **God 'dild you!**   thank you (i.e. may God yield to you).

43–4 **They say the owl was a baker's daughter**   an obscure remark, which editors have many diverse theories about. Ophelia is mad, so we must not expect everything she says to make sense!

45 **God be at your table!**   a form of grace said before a meal.

46 **Conceit upon her father**   these are far-fetched thoughts about her father.

QUEEN

Alas, sweet lady, what imports this song?

OPHELIA

Say you? Nay, pray you mark.
(*Sings*) He is dead and gone, lady,   30
   He is dead and gone;
At his head a grass-green turf,
   At his heels a stone.
O, ho!

QUEEN

Nay, but, Ophelia –   35

OPHELIA

Pray you mark.
(*Sings*) White his shroud as the mountain snow –

Enter KING.

QUEEN

Alas, look here, my lord.

OPHELIA

   Larded with sweet flowers;
Which bewept to the grave did not go   40
   With true-love showers.

KING

How do you, pretty lady?

OPHELIA

Well, God 'dild you! They say the owl was a
baker's daughter. Lord, we know what we are, but
know not what we may be. God be at your table!   45

KING

Conceit upon her father.

49 **Saint Valentine's day** 14 February, when traditionally birds were thought to choose their mates, and when the first person of the opposite sex one met would become one's sweetheart.

50 **betime** early.

54 **dupp'd** opened.

55–6 **that out a maid. . .more** i.e. by the time she left the room she was no longer a virgin.

58 **without an oath** avoiding blasphemy (as she does by singing 'Gis' for Jesus and 'Cock' for God).

59 **Gis** Jesus.

Saint Charity not a human being, but the saintly quality of charity.

61 **do't** i.e. have sexual intercourse.

62 **Cock** God, but also slang for a penis.

63 **tumbled me** had sex with me.

67 **An** if.

OPHELIA

Pray let's have no words of this; but when they ask
you what it means, say you this:
(*Sings*) To-morrow is Saint Valentine's day,
   All in the morning betime,   50
And I a maid at your window,
   To be your Valentine.

Then up he rose, and donn'd his clothes,
   And dupp'd the chamber-door;
Let in the maid, that out a maid   55
   Never departed more.

KING

Pretty Ophelia!

OPHELIA

Indeed, la, without an oath, I'll make an end on't.

(*Sings*) By Gis and by Saint Charity,
   Alack, and fie for shame!   60
Young men will do't, if they come to't;
   By Cock, they are to blame.

Quoth she 'Before you tumbled me,
   You promis'd me to wed'.

He answers: 65

'So would I 'a done, by yonder sun,
An thou hadst not come to my bed'.

KING

How long hath she been thus?

OPHELIA

I hope all will be well. We must be patient; but
I cannot choose but weep to think they would lay 70

71 *him*   i.e. Polonius.

75 *close*   closely.

79 *single spies*   individual scouts.

81 *author*   cause.

82 *remove*   removal.

   muddied   stirred up.

84 *greenly*   unskilfully, as if inexperienced.

85 *hugger-mugger*   secret.

87 *pictures*   things with only the appearance and not the substance of people.

88 *as much containing*   containing as much potential trouble.

90 *Feeds on his wonder*   broods on the mystery of his father's death.

   keeps himself in clouds   hides away.

91 *wants not*   has plenty of.

   buzzers   rumour-mongers.

93 *Wherein necessity*   where of necessity.

   of matter beggar'd   because they have no hard facts to go on.

94 *Will nothing stick*   will stick at nothing.

   our person to arraign   to slander me.

96 *murd'ring piece*   small cannon which fires grape-shot, killing many soldiers at once.

97 *superfluous death*   more wounds than are needed to kill me.

him i' th' cold ground. My brother shall know of
it; and so I thank you for your good counsel.
Come, my coach! Good night, ladies; good night,
sweet ladies, good night, good night.

Exit

→ he gives a sort of summary

KING

Follow her close; give her good watch, I pray you.   75

Exeunt HORATIO *and* Gentleman

O, this is the poison of deep grief; it springs
All from her father's death. And now behold –
O Gertrude, Gertrude!
When sorrows come, they come not single spies,
But in battalions! First, her father slain;   80
Next, your son gone, and he most violent author
Of his own just remove; the people muddied,
Thick and unwholesome in their thoughts and
   whispers → there is already gossip, the murder
For good Polonius' death; and we have done but
   greenly
In hugger-mugger to inter him; poor Ophelia   85
Divided from herself and her fair judgment, madness
Without the which we are pictures, or mere beasts; if we
Last, and as much containing as all these, can't think
Her brother is in secret come from France; we are beasts
Feeds on his wonder, keeps himself in clouds,   90
And wants not buzzers to infect his ear
With pestilent speeches of his father's death;
Wherein necessity, of matter beggar'd, → king realises
Will nothing stick our person to arraign   that he has been
In ear and ear. O my dear Gertrude, this,   not so careful
Like to a murd'ring piece, in many places   95
Gives me superfluous death.

Laertes has returned alone, he wants revenge

100 **Switzers**   bodyguard of Swiss soldiers.

103 **overpeering of his list**   rising above the shoreline.

104 **Eats not the flats**   does not flood the flat land.

   impitious   merciless.

105 **riotous head**   rebellion.

109 **ratifiers and props**   things which give authority and support.

113 **false trail**   like a pack of hounds on the wrong scent (because Claudius is not responsible for the death of Polonius).

114 **counter**   following the scent in the wrong direction, away from rather than towards the quarry.

A noise within.

QUEEN
Alack, what noise is this?

KING
Attend!

Enter a Gentleman.

Where are my Switzers? Let them guard the door. 100
What is the matter?

GENTLEMAN
Save yourself, my lord:
The ocean, overpeering of his list,
Eats not the flats with more impitious haste
Than young Laertes, in a riotous head,   105
O'erbears your officers. The rabble call him lord;
And, as the world were now but to begin,
Antiquity forgot, custom not known,
The ratifiers and props of every word,
They cry 'Choose we; Laertes shall be king'.   110
Caps, hands, and tongues, applaud it to the
    clouds.
'Laertes shall be king, Laertes king'.

QUEEN
How cheerfully on the false trail they cry!

Noise within.

O, this is counter, you false Danish dogs!

KING
The doors are broke.   115

Enter LAERTES, *with* Others, *in arms.*

283

120 **Keep** guard.

124 **cuckold** a husband whose wife has been unfaithful.

125 **unsmirched brow** smooth and clean forehead. (Prostitutes were sometimes branded on the forehead.)

128 **giant-like** large and threatening.

129 **fear our person** fear for my personal safety.

130 **divinity** heavenly power (referring to the belief that kings were God's representatives on earth, and enjoyed His protection).

hedge protect.

131 **but peep to what it would** only just peep at what it wants to overthrow.

132 **Acts little of his will** performing little of what it wants to do.

LAERTES

Where is this king? – Sirs, stand you all without.

ALL

No, let's come in.

LAERTES

I pray you give me leave.

ALL

We will, we will.

Exeunt

LAERTES

I thank you. Keep the door. – O thou vile king,   120
Give me my father!

QUEEN

Calmly, good Laertes.

LAERTES

That drop of blood that's calm proclaims me
    bastard;
Cries cuckold to my father; brands the harlot
Even here, between the chaste unsmirched brow   125
Of my true mother.

KING

What is the cause, Laertes,
That thy rebellion looks so giant-like?
Let him go, Gertrude; do not fear our person:
There's such divinity doth hedge a king   130
That treason can but peep to what it would,
Acts little of his will. Tell me, Laertes,
Why thou art thus incens'd. Let him go, Gertrude.
Speak, man.

139 *juggled with*   deceived.

140 *allegiance*   loyalty to the king.

141 *grace*   the grace of God. Laertes is aware that rebellion against the king is contrary to the will of God (see note to line 130) but is still persisting in it. This would be very shocking to Shakespeare's audiences.

142 *To this point I stand*   I will not be moved from this position.

143 *both the worlds*   i.e. this world, and the life to come.

145 *throughly*   thoroughly.

146 *stay*   stop.

147 *My will, not all the world's*   my own decision, not any outside pressure.

148 *means*   resources.

    husband   eke out, use economically.

153 *swoopstake*   indiscriminately, like a sweepstake where one wins all or nothing.

    draw   flush out and pursue.

LAERTES
Where is my father?   135

KING
Dead.

QUEEN
But not by him.

KING
Let him demand his fill.

LAERTES
How came he dead? I'll not be juggled with.
To hell, allegiance! Vows, to the blackest devil!   140
Conscience and grace, to the profoundest pit!
I dare damnation. To this point I stand,
That both the worlds I give to negligence,
Let come what comes; only I'll be reveng'd
Most throughly for my father.   145

KING
Who shall stay you?

LAERTES
My will, not all the world's.
And for my means, I'll husband them so well
They shall go far with little.

KING
Good Laertes,   150
If you desire to know the certainty
Of your dear father, is't writ in your revenge
That, swoopstake, you will draw both friend and foe,
Winner and loser?

LAERTES
None but his enemies.   155

157 **ope**   open.

158 **pelican**   reference to the legend that pelicans feed ('repast'') their young with blood from their own breasts.

163 **sensibly**   feelingly.

164 **level**   plain.

   'pear   appear.

167 **heat**   anger.

168 **sense and virtue**   feeling and power (of vision).

169 **paid with weight**   revenged in full measure.

170 **Till our scale turn the beam**   until our revenge outweighs the original offence.

174–6 **Nature is fine. . .thing it loves**   human nature is pure and refined ('fine') when in love, and in this state it sends to the object of its love (Polonius) a precious token ('instance') of itself (Ophelia's sanity).

KING

Will you know them, then?

LAERTES

To his good friends thus wide I'll ope my arms.
And, like the kind life-rend'ring pelican,
Repast them with my blood.

KING

Why, now you speak   160
Like a good child and a true gentleman.
That I am guiltless of your father's death,
And am most sensibly in grief for it,
It shall as level to your judgment 'pear
As day does to your eye. (*A noise within*) 'Let her
    come in.'   165

LAERTES

How now! What noise is that?

Re-enter OPHELIA.

O, heat dry up my brains! tears seven times salt
Burn out the sense and virtue of mine eye!
By heaven, thy madness shall be paid with
    weight
Till our scale turn the beam. O rose of May!   170
Dear maid, kind sister, sweet Ophelia!
O heavens! is't possible a young maid's wits
Should be as mortal as an old man's life?
Nature is fine in love; and where 'tis fine
It sends some precious instance of itself   175
After the thing it loves.

OPHELIA

(*Sings*)   They bore him barefac'd on the bier;
             Hey non nonny, nonny, hey nonny;

181 **persuade**   convince me rationally.

182 **move**   incite.

183 **an**   if.

184 **wheel**   refrain of the ballad.

185 **false steward**   presumably a reference to a ballad, now lost.

186 **This nothing's more than matter**   this nonsense is more than significant.

187 **rosemary**   all the flowers that Ophelia distributes have meanings, in the
language of flowers. It is not always clear to whom the flowers are given.
Rosemary, as she says, stands for remembrance.

190 **document**   lesson.

191 **fitted**   i.e. given to appropriate people.

192 **fennel**   associated with flattery.

columbines   associated with cuckoldry or unfaithfulness in love.

193 **rue**   associated with sorrow and repentance.

194 **herb of grace**   alternative name for rue.

195 **daisy**   associated with deception.

196 **violets**   associated with faithful love.

198 **For bonny sweet Robin. . .**   line of a popular song.

199 **Thought**   sorrow.

passion   suffering.

And in his grave rain'd many a tear –

Fare you well, my dove! 180

LAERTES

Hadst thou thy wits, and didst persuade revenge,
It could not move thus.

OPHELIA

You must sing 'A-down, a-down', an you call him
a-down-a. O, how the wheel becomes it! It is the
false steward, that stole his master's daughter. 185

LAERTES

This nothing's more than matter.

OPHELIA

There's rosemary, that's for remembrance; pray
you, love, remember. And there is pansies, that's
for thoughts.

LAERTES

A document in madness – thoughts and remem-190
brance fitted.

OPHELIA

There's fennel for you, and columbines. There's
rue for you; and here's some for me. We may call
it herb of grace a Sundays. O, you must wear your
rue with a difference. There's a daisy. I would give 195
you some violets, but they wither'd all when my
father died. They say 'a made a good end.

(*Sings*) For bonny sweet Robin is all my joy.

LAERTES

Thought and affliction, passion, hell itself,
She turns to favour and to prettiness. 200

207 **All flaxen was his poll**   his head was white.

209 **cast away moan**   uselessly mourn.

213 **commune**   share.

214 **deny me right**   deny me what is rightfully mine.

217 **collateral hand**   the action of an agent.

218 **They find us touch'd**   they find me implicated in guilt.

225 **means**   cause.

   obscure   hidden, secret.

Se koning van Laertes begrypen dat hij zich
op de dader wil wreken. Dat kan echter niet
want Hamlet is in England.

L7 clever!

OPHELIA

(*Sings*) And will 'a not come again?
And will 'a not come again?
 No, no, he is dead,
 Go to thy death-bed,
He never will come again.   205
His beard was as white as snow,

All flaxen was his poll;
 He is gone, he is gone,
 And we cast away moan:
God-a-mercy on his soul!   210

And of all Christian souls, I pray God. God buy
 you.

Exit

LAERTES

Do you see this, O God?

KING

Laertes, I must commune with your grief,
Or you deny me right. Go but apart,
Make choice of whom your wisest friends you will, 215
And they shall hear and judge 'twixt you and me.
If by direct or by collateral hand
They find us touch'd, we will our kingdom give,
Our crown, our life, and all that we call ours,
To you in satisfaction; but if not,   220
Be you content to lend your patience to us,
And we shall jointly labour with your soul
To give it due content.

LAERTES

Let this be so.
His means of death, his obscure funeral –   225

293

226 **trophy, sword, nor hatchment** noblemen would usually have their graves marked by a memorial of armour ('trophy'), their sword, and a painted coat of arms ('hatchment').

227 **ostentation** ceremony.

229 **call't in question** demand an explanation.

231 **great axe** presumably the executioner's.

6 **greeted** addressed in a letter.

No trophy, sword, nor hatchment, o'er his bones,
No noble rite nor formal ostentation –
Cry to be heard, as 'twere from heaven to earth,
That I must call't in question.

KING
So you shall;   230
And where th' offence is, let the great axe fall.
I pray you go with me.

Exeunt

Scene six

Elsinore. The Castle.

Enter HORATIO *with an* Attendant.

HORATIO
What are they that would speak with me?

ATTENDANT
Sea-faring men, sir; they say they have letters for
you.

HORATIO
Let them come in.

Exit Attendant

I do not know from what part of the world I   5
should be greeted, if not from Lord Hamlet.

Enter Sailors.

SAILORS
God bless you, sir.

295

13 **overlook'd** looked over, read.

14 **means** method of access.

16 **of very warlike appointment** very well-equipped for fighting.

18 **put on a compelled valour** had no choice but to be brave.

grapple i.e. when the ships were alongside.

21 **thieves of mercy** merciful thieves.

26–7 **much too light for the bore of the matter** inadequate to express the gravity of the subject.

32 **give you way** provide you with access (to the king).

HORATIO

Let Him bless thee too.

SAILORS

'A shall, sir, an't please Him. There's a letter for
you, sir; it came from th' ambassador that was   10
bound for England – if your name be Horatio, as
I am let to know it is.

HORATIO

(*Reads*) 'Horatio, when thou shalt have overlook'd
this, give these fellows some means to the King:
they have letters for him. Ere we were two days   15
old at sea, a pirate of very warlike appointment
gave us chase. Finding ourselves too slow of sail,
we put on a compelled valour; and in the grapple
I boarded them. On the instant they got clear of
our ship; so I alone became their prisoner. They   20
have dealt with me like thieves of mercy; but they
knew what they did: I am to do a good turn for
them. Let the King have the letters I have sent;
and repair thou to me with as much speed as thou
wouldst fly death. I have words to speak in thine   25
ear will make thee dumb; yet are they much too
light for the bore of the matter. These good fellows
will bring thee where I am. Rosencrantz and Guildenstern hold their course for England; of them I
have much to tell thee. Farewell.   30

He that thou knowest thine, HAMLET.'
Come, I will give you way for these your letters,
And do't the speedier that you may direct me
To him from whom you brought them.

Exeunt

297

1 *my acquittance seal* confirm my innocence.

3 *knowing* intelligent.

7 *feats* misdeeds.

8 *capital* deserving punishment by death.

10 *mainly* strongly.

12 *unsinew'd* weak, without sinews.

16 *conjunctive* united.

17 *sphere* orbit. It was believed that stars were fixed to transparent, hollow globes which rotated around the earth.

18 *I could not but by her* I could not do anything without her.

19 *count* reckoning, accusation.

20 *general gender* people of Denmark.

22 **Work like the spring. . .stone** have an effect like a spring in a region of limestone, which forms a coating of stone over pieces of wood left in it.

De koning weet dat Hamlet hem wil vermoorden omdat hij erachter is gekomen dat hij hem had willen doden.

→ vieze trick

he's got an angry Laertes before him and makes a plan with him.

↳ this plan fails because it has too many ejsles in the end.

! reason ① his mother

why he ② everybody loves him, the population would turn against him

didn't did anything

with Hamlet.

Scene seven

Elsinore. The Castle.

Enter KING *and* LAERTES.

KING

    Now must your conscience my acquittance seal,
    And you must put me in your heart for friend,
    Sith you have heard, and with a knowing ear,
    That he which hath your noble father slain
    Pursu'd my life.   5

LAERTES

    It well appears. But tell me
    Why you proceeded not against these feats,
    So crimeful and so capital in nature,
    As by your safety, wisdom, all things else,
    You mainly were stirr'd up.   10

KING

    O, for two special reasons,
    Which may to you, perhaps, seem much
      unsinew'd,
    But yet to me th'are strong. The Queen his
      mother
    Lives almost by his looks; and for myself,
    My virtue or my plague, be it either which –   15
    She is so conjunctive to my life and soul
    That, as the star moves not but in his sphere,
    I could not but by her. The other motive,
    Why to a public count I might not go,
    Is the great love the general gender bear him;   20
    Who, dipping all his faults in their affection,
    Work like the spring that turneth wood to
      stone,

23 **gyves**   shackles.

    graces   marks of distinction.

24 **Too slightly timber'd**   with shafts that are too light.

    for so loud a wind   for such a strong wind of public opinion.

25 **reverted**   returned.

28 **desp'rate terms**   utmost desperation, madness.

29 **may go back again**   may refer to her previous condition.

30–1 **Stood challenger. . .perfections**   stood as an outstanding example of
      perfection, which challenged anyone of our times to match.

32 **Break not your sleeps for that**   do not loose any sleep over that.

35 **with**   by.

36 **think it pastime**   think that it is amusing.

Convert his gyves to graces; so that my arrows,
Too slightly timber'd for so loud a wind,
Would have reverted to my bow again,   25
But not where I have aim'd them.

LAERTES

And so have I a noble father lost;
A sister driven into desp'rate terms,
Whose worth, if praises may go back again,
Stood challenger on mount of all the age   30
For her perfections. But my revenge will come.

KING

Break not your sleeps for that.
You must not think
That we are made of stuff so flat and duil
That we can let our beard be shook with danger,   35
And think it pastime. You shortly shall hear
    more.
I lov'd your father, and we love our self;
And that, I hope, will teach you to imagine –

Enter a Messenger *with letters.*

How now! What news?

MESSENGER

Letters, my lord, from Hamlet: 40
These to your Majesty; this to the Queen.

KING

From Hamlet! Who brought them?

MESSENGER

Sailors, my lord, they say; I saw them not.
They were given me by Claudio; he receiv'd them
Of him that brought them.   45

301

49 *naked* destitute.

54 *all the rest* i.e. the rest of Hamlet's company.

55 *abuse* deceit.

56 *hand* handwriting.

57 *character* handwriting.

59 *devise* advise.

60 *lost in it* bewildered by it.

63 *'Thus didest thou'* i.e. 'You killed my father in the same way that I am killing you.'

66 *rul'd* governed, advised.

KING

Laertes, you shall hear them.
Leave us.

Exit Messenger

(*Reads*) 'High and Mighty. You shall know I am set
naked on your kingdom. Tomorrow shall I beg
leave to see your kingly eyes; when I shall, first 50
asking your pardon, thereunto recount the
occasion of my sudden and more strange return.

HAMLET.'?

What should this mean? Are all the rest come
back?
Or is it some abuse, and no such thing? 55

LAERTES

Know you the hand?

KING

'Tis Hamlet's character. 'Naked'!
And in a postscript here, he says 'alone'.
Can you devise me?

LAERTES *would kill him*

I am lost in it, my lord. But let him come; 60
It warms the very sickness in my heart
That I shall live and tell him to his teeth
'Thus didest thou'.

KING

If it be so, Laertes –
As how should it be so, how otherwise? – 65
Will you be rul'd by me?

LAERTES

Ay, my lord;

303

68 **So you will not. . .peace**   so long as you do not order me to reach a peaceful solution.

69 **To thine own peace**   i.e. I will give you peace of mind (by letting you have your revenge).

70 **checking at**   backing off from.

71 **work him**   manoeuvre him into.

72 **an exploit now ripe in my device**   to a scheme that I have now perfectly worked out.

75 **uncharge the practice**   not suspect the stratagem.

79 **organ**   agent (of Hamlet's destruction).

80 **It falls right**   it has turned out fortunately for us.

83 **sum of parts**   the sum total of all your abilities.

86 **unworthiest siege**   lowest rank, least important.

88 **A very riband**   a mere scrap of decoration.

89 **needful**   necessary.

   no less becomes   is not less suited by.

90 **livery**   clothing.

91 **sables and his weeds**   furs and dark-coloured clothes.

92 **Importing health**   signifying prosperity.

So you will not o'errule me to a peace.

KING

To thine own peace. If he be now return'd,
As checking at his voyage, and that he means   70
No more to undertake it, I will work him
To an exploit now ripe in my device,
Under the which he shall not choose but fall;
And for his death, no wind of blame shall breathe;
But even his mother shall uncharge the practice   75
And call it accident.

LAERTES

My lord, I will be rul'd
The rather, if you could devise it so
That I might be the organ.

KING

It falls right.   80
You have been talk'd of since your travel much,
And that in Hamlet's hearing, for a quality
Wherein they say you shine. Your sum of parts
Did not together pluck such envy from him
As did that one; and that, in my regard,   85
Of the unworthiest siege.

LAERTES

What part is that, my lord?

KING

A very riband in the cap of youth,
Yet needful too; for youth no less becomes
The light and careless livery that it wears   90
Than settled age his sables and his weeds,
Importing health and graveness. Two months
   since

305

95 *can well*   are skilful.

96 *unto his seat*   into his saddle.

98 *As*   as if.

incorps'd and demi-natur'd   shared a single body and spirit.

99 *topp'd my thought*   surpassed my imagination.

100 *in forgery of shapes and tricks*   when imagining manoeuvres ('shapes') and feats of skill ('tricks').

106–7 *brooch indeed And gem*   outstanding ornament.

108 *made confession of you*   admitted that he knew you.

109 *masterly report*   report saying that you were a master.

113 *scrimers*   fencers.

114 *motion*   trained movement of the body.

Here was a gentleman of Normandy –
I have seen myself, and serv'd against, the French,
And they can well on horseback; but this gallant   95
Had witchcraft in't; he grew unto his seat,
And to such wondrous doing brought his horse,
As had he been incorps'd and demi-natur'd
With the brave beast. So far he topp'd my thought,
That I, in forgery of shapes and tricks,   100
Come short of what he did.

LAERTES
A Norman was't?

KING
A Norman.

LAERTES
Upon my life, Lamord.

KING
The very same.   105

LAERTES
I know him well. He is the brooch indeed
And gem of all the nation.

KING
He made confession of you;
And gave you such a masterly report
For art and exercise in your defence,   110
And for your rapier most especial,
That he cried out 'twould be a sight indeed
If one could match you. The scrimers of their
    nation
He swore had neither motion, guard, nor eye,
If you oppos'd them. Sir, this report of his   115
Did Hamlet so envenom with his envy

307

118 **play** fence.

127 **passages of proof** events which confirm my views.

128 **qualifies** moderates.

131 **nothing is at a like goodness still** nothing remains as good for ever.

132 **pleurisy** excess.

133 **That** that which.

135 **abatements** reductions.

137–8 **spendthrift's sigh. . .easing** in Shakespeare's day it was thought that sighing damaged one's health, by drawing blood from the heart. Thus, a spendthrift's sigh gives short-term relief to a bad conscience, but is harmful in the longer term.

138 **quick of th' ulcer** heart of the problem.

That he could nothing do but wish and beg
Your sudden coming o'er, to play with you.
Now, out of this –

LAERTES

What out of this, my lord? *like Hamlet* 120

KING

Laertes, was your father dear to you?
Or are you like the painting of a sorrow, *said about*
A face without a heart? *your father?*

Are you pretending, or are you really

LAERTES

Why ask you this?

KING

Not that I think you did not love your father;   125
But that I know love is begun by time,
And that I see, in passages of proof,
Time qualifies the spark and fire of it.
There lives within the very flame of love
A kind of wick or snuff that will abate it;   130
And nothing is at a like goodness still;
For goodness, growing to a pleurisy,
Dies in his own too much. That we would do,
We should do when we would; for this 'would'
    changes,
wat jij moet doen, moet
And hath abatements and delays as many *je nu*   135
As there are tongues, are hands, are accidents;
And then this 'should' is like a spendthrift's sigh
That hurts by easing. But to the quick of th'
    ulcer:
Hamlet comes back; what would you undertake
To show yourself in deed your father's son   140
More than in words?

143 **should murder sanctuarize**   provide a sanctuary for a murderer.

145 **this**   what I am about to tell you.

147 **put on**   set up.

149 **in fine**   finally.

150 **wager on your heads**   make bets about which of you will win.

      remiss   careless.

151 **generous**   noble-minded.

      free from all contriving   without any suspicion of trickery.

152 **peruse the foils**   examine the fencing swords.

154 **unbated**   not blunted. Swords used for practice were usually made blunt for safety's sake.

      pass of practice   treacherous thrust.

158 **unction**   ointment, potion.

      mountebank   unlicensed quack doctor.

160 **cataplasm**   poultice.

161 **simples that have virtue**   herbs that have medicinal qualities.

162 **Under the moon**   herbs were believed to be more powerful if gathered by night.

164 **contagion**   poison.

      gall   wound.

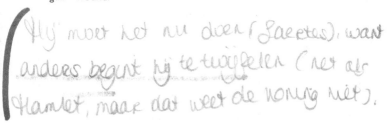

Hij moet het nu doen (Laertes), want anders begint hij te twijfelen (net als Hamlet, maar dat weet de koning niet).

LAERTES

To cut his throat i' th' church.

KING

No place, indeed, should murder sanctuarize;
Revenge should have no bounds. But, good
   Laertes,
Will you do this? Keep close within your chamber. 145
Hamlet return'd shall know you are come home.
We'll put on those shall praise your excellence,
And set a double varnish on the fame
The Frenchman gave you; bring you, in fine,
   together,
And wager on your heads. He, being remiss,   150
Most generous, and free from all contriving,
Will not peruse the foils; so that with ease
Or with a little shuffling, you may choose
A sword unbated, and, in a pass of practice,
Requite him for your father.   155

LAERTES

I will do't;
And for that purpose I'll anoint my sword.
I bought an unction of a mountebank,
So mortal that but dip a knife in it,
Where it draws blood no cataplasm so rare,   160
Collected from all simples that have virtue
Under the moon, can save the thing from death
This is but scratch'd withal. I'll touch my point
With this contagion, that, if I gall him slightly,
It may be death.   165

KING

Let's further think of this;
Weight what convenience both of time and means

311

168 **to our shape**   for the part we intend to play.

169 **drift**   scheme.

   look through our bad performance   becomes obvious because of our inability to play our parts.

170 **assay'd**   attempted.

171 **back or second**   a reserve plan.

   hold   work.

172 **blast in proof**   go wrong when put into execution.

173 **cunnings**   respective skills.

175 **in your motion**   from your exertions.

177 **preferr'd**   offered to.

178 **for the nonce**   for the occasion.

179 **venom'd stuck**   poisoned thrust.

184 **aslant**   slanting over.

185 **hoar**   grey. (The undersides of willow leaves are silvery-grey.)

187 **crowflowers**   crowfoot, sometimes called Fair Maid of France.

   long purples   a kind of orchid. The language of flowers symbolism here is the fair maid ('crowflowers') is stung ('nettles') in her prime of beauty ('daisies') by the cold fingers of death ('long purples').

188 **liberal**   less inhibited about what they say.

   grosser   more obscene.

189 **cold**   virginal.

190 **pendent**   hanging.

   coronet weeds   crown of wild flowers.

191 **envious sliver**   malicious twig.

May fit us to our shape. If this should fail,
And that our drift look through our bad
   performance,
'Twere better not assay'd. Therefore this project 170
Should have a back or second, that might hold
If this did blast in proof. Soft! let me see.
We'll make a solemn wager on your cunnings –
I ha't.
When in your motion you are hot and dry –   175
As make your bouts more violent to that end –
And that he calls for drink, I'll have preferr'd him
A chalice for the nonce; whereon but sipping,
If he by chance escape your venom'd stuck,
Our purpose may hold there. But stay;
   what noise?   180

Enter QUEEN.

QUEEN
One woe doth tread upon another's heel,
So fast they follow. Your sister's drown'd, Laertes.

LAERTES
   Drown'd! O, where?

QUEEN
   There is a willow grows aslant the brook
   That shows his hoar leaves in the glassy stream; 185
   Therewith fantastic garlands did she make
   Of crowflowers, nettles, daisies, and long purples
   That liberal shepherds give a grosser name,
   But our cold maids do dead men's fingers call
      them.
   There, on the pendent boughs her coronet weeds 190
   Clamb'ring to hang, an envious sliver broke;
   When down her weedy trophies and herself

196 *incapable*   i.e. unable to understand.

197–8 *indued Unto*   equipped for.

200 *lay*   song.

206 *trick*   habit.

207 *these*   i.e. his tears.

208 **The woman will be out**   the womanly side of my character will have left me.

210 *this folly*   i.e. his tears.

douts   extinguishes.

[handwritten: first she was seated, then she was carried away]

Fell in the weeping brook. Her clothes spread wide *[handwritten: with the steam...]*
And, mermaid-like, awhile they bore her up;
Which time she chanted snatches of old tunes,   195
As one incapable of her own distress, *[handwritten: ...ing of the water.]*
Or like a creature native and indued
Unto that element; but long it could not be
Till that her garments, heavy with their drink,
Pull'd the poor wretch from her melodious lay   200
To muddy death. *[handwritten: It is a suicide, but the]*

[handwritten: Queen explains it as an accident.]

LAERTES

Alas, then she is drown'd!

QUEEN

Drown'd, drown'd.

LAERTES

Too much of water hast thou, poor Ophelia,
And therefore I forbid my tears; but yet   205
It is our trick; nature her custom holds,
Let shame say what it will. When these are gone,
The woman will be out. Adieu, my lord.
I have a speech o' fire that fain would blaze
But that this folly douts it.   210

Exit

KING

Let's follow, Gertrude.
How much I had to do to calm his rage!
Now fear I this will give it start again;
Therefore let's follow.

Exeunt

[handwritten: Queen → has having her doubts for the first time]

[handwritten: → separation, she doesn't follow the king.]

Hamlet (Roger Rees): Royal Shakespeare Company, 1984–85.

Two gravediggers are at work, watched by Hamlet and Horatio. As skulls are unearthed, Hamlet reflects on death and that whatever glories we have in life, in the grave we are all equal. The king, queen, and Laertes enter with the court in Ophelia's funeral procession and Hamlet and Horatio hide. Laertes' grief is so acute that he leaps into the grave to embrace his sister's body. Hamlet, angered by this, jumps into the grave too, where he struggles with Laertes. They are parted, and Hamlet vows to fight Laertes later.

Hamlet tells Horatio that on board ship he discovered papers from Claudius ordering his execution when he arrived in England. He forged a document ordering the same fate for Rosencrantz and Guildenstern, who are now sailing unsuspecting to their deaths.

Osric delivers a challenge to a fencing match from Laertes. Hamlet accepts the challenge. The contest begins and Hamlet wins the first two passes. Gertrude drinks from the poisoned chalice before Claudius can stop her. The third bout is indecisive, but when Hamlet turns away, Laertes wounds him with the poisoned sword. They now fight in earnest. In the struggle they exchange swords, and Hamlet wounds Laertes. Gertrude collapses from the effects of the poison, and before she dies, warns Hamlet not to drink. Laertes, fatally wounded, confesses the plot, telling Hamlet that he is sure to die from the effect of the poison. Hamlet stabs Claudius with the poisoned sword, and forces him to drink the dregs from the poisoned chalice. Claudius dies, as does Laertes shortly afterwards. Hamlet tells Horatio to tell the story of these terrible happenings. Hamlet's dying wish is that Fortinbras should be the next King of Denmark. Fortinbras arrives and claims the throne. He orders that the body of Hamlet be borne off with military ceremony.

s.d. **Clowns** simple country men. They are gravediggers, and are often referred to as such in writings on the play.

1 *in Christian burial* i.e. in consecrated ground and with a full funeral service (both of which were denied suicides).

2 *seeks her own salvation* euphemism for 'kills herself'.

3 *straight* immediately.

4 *crowner hath sat on her* coroner has judged her case.

9 *'se offendendo'* the gravedigger half-remembers the legal phrase in Latin 'se defendendo'. This is the form of words used where a plea of self-defence is being offered in a case of homicide.

10 *wittingly* on purpose.

12 *argal* a mistaken version of 'ergo', the Latin for therefore. The first gravedigger is self-important and is not as learned as he thinks he is, like many of Shakespeare's comic characters.

14 *Delver* to 'delve' means to dig.

Act Five

Scene one

Elsinore. A churchyard.

Enter two Clowns *with spades and picks.*

1 CLOWN

Is she to be buried in <u>Christian burial</u> when she
wilfully seeks her own salvation?

2 CLOWN

I tell thee she is; therefore make her grave straight.
The crowner hath sat on her, and finds it Christian
burial.   5

1 CLOWN

How can that be, unless she drown'd herself in her
own defence?

2 CLOWN

Why, 'tis found so.

1 CLOWN

It must be 'se offendendo'; it cannot be else. For
here lies the point: if I drown myself wittingly, it   10
argues an act; and an act hath three branches –
it is to act, to do, to perform; argal, she drown'd
herself wittingly.

2 CLOWN

Nay, but hear you, Goodman Delver.

1 CLOWN

Give me leave. Here lies the water; good. Here   15
stands the man; good. If the man go to this water

17 **will he, nill he** whether he likes it or not (the origin of the modern phrase willy nilly).

23 **crowner's quest** coroner's inquest.

24 **ha** have.

25 **out a** without a.

28 **count'nance** special permission.

29–30 **even Christen** fellow Christians.

30–1 **ancient gentlemen** gentlemen of old-established families. The joke that follows relies on the fact that only gentlemen had coats-of-arms.

and drown himself, it is, will he, nill he, he goes
– mark you that; but if the water come to him and
drown him, he drowns not himself. Argal, he that
is not guilty of his own death shortens not his own   20
life.

2 CLOWN
But is this law?

1 CLOWN
Ay, marry, is't; crowner's quest law.

2 CLOWN
Will you ha the truth on't? If this had not been a
gentlewoman, she should have been buried out a   25
Christian burial.

1 CLOWN
Why, there thou say'st; and the more pity that
great folk should have count'nance in this world
to drown or hang themselves more than their even
Christen. Come, my spade. There is no ancient   30
gentlemen but gard'ners, ditchers, and grave-
makers; they hold up Adam's profession.

2 CLOWN
Was he a gentleman?

1 CLOWN
'A was the first that ever bore arms.

2 CLOWN
Why, he had none.   35

1 CLOWN
What, art a heathen? How dost thou understand
the Scripture? The Scripture says Adam digg'd.
Could he dig without arms? I'll put another

40 **confess thyself** confess your sins to a priest. The phrase usually continues 'and be hanged', but the second gravedigger interrupts.

41 **Go to** an exclamation signifying doubt and impatience.

53 **unyoke** i.e. your work will then be done.

56 **Mass** (mild oath) by the Holy Mass.

question to thee. If thou answerest me not to the
purpose, confess thyself –   40

2 CLOWN
Go to.

1 CLOWN
What is he that builds stronger than either the
mason, the shipwright, or the carpenter?

2 CLOWN
The gallows-maker; for that frame outlives a thousand tenants.   45

1 CLOWN
I like thy wit well; in good faith the gallows does
well; but how does it well? It does well to those
that do ill. Now thou dost ill to say the gallows is
built stronger than the church; argal, the gallows
may do well to thee. To 't again, come.   50

2 CLOWN
Who builds stronger than a mason, a shipwright,
or a carpenter?

1 CLOWN
Ay, tell me that, and unyoke.

2 CLOWN
Marry, now I can tell.

1 CLOWN
To 't.   55

2 CLOWN
Mass, I cannot tell.

Enter HAMLET *and* HORATIO, *afar off.*

61 **Yaughan** presumably the name of a local publican.

63–6 **In youth. . .nothing a-meet** the gravedigger's song is a half-remembered song, identified as one in Totten's **Miscellany** (1557). It is hard to make sense of, because he muddles the words. The original song is that of an old man, sadly thinking about his declining strength and vigour.

70 **the hand of little employment** i.e. those who do not have to work very hard.

71 **daintier sense** more delicate feelings.

77 **jowls** hurls, but also a pun, because 'jowls' are jaw-bones.

78 **Cain's jawbone** according to legend, Cain, the son of Adam and Eve, murdered his brother Abel by hitting him with the jawbone of an ass.

1 CLOWN

Cudgel thy brains no more about it, for your dull
ass will not mend his pace with beating; and when
you are ask'd this question next, say 'a grave-
maker': the houses he makes lasts till doomsday. 60
Go, get thee to Yaughan; fetch me a stoup of
liquor.

Exit Second Clown

(*Digs and sings*) In youth, when I did love, did love,
    Methought it was very sweet,
To contract-o-the time for-a my behove,   65
    O, methought there-a-was nothing-a meet.

HAMLET

Has this fellow no feeling of his business, that 'a
sings in grave-making?

HORATIO

Custom hath made it in him a property of easiness.

HAMLET

'Tis e'en so; the hand of little employment hath the 70
daintier sense.

1 CLOWN

(*Sings*) But age, with his stealing steps,
    Hath clawed me in his clutch,
And hath shipped me intil the land,
    As if I had never been such.   75

Throws up a skull.

HAMLET

That skull had a tongue in it, and could sing
once. How the knave jowls it to the ground, as if
'twere Cain's jawbone, that did the first murder!

325

79 *pate*   head.

  politician   schemer, plotter. The word had an even more negative flavour in Shakespeare's day.

80 *o'er-reaches*   reaches over, and also gets the advantage over.

  circumvent   outwit.

89 *chapless*   without his lower jawbone.

90 *mazard*   head.

91 *an*   if.

92 *cost no more the breeding*   cost so little to breed that all they are worth is.

93 *loggats*   a game played by trying to throw 'loggats' (pieces of wood) as close as possible to a stake.

100–1 *quiddities now, his quillets*   'quiddities' and 'quillets' are both fine and subtle differentiations of meaning such as a lawyer needs to be able to make.

101 *tenures*   cases about property leases.

This might be the pate of a politician, which this
ass now o'er-reaches; one that would circumvent 80
God, might it not?

HORATIO

It might, my lord.

HAMLET

Or of a courtier; which could say 'Good morrow,
sweet lord! How dost thou, sweet lord?' This might
be my Lord Such-a-one, that praised my Lord 85
Such-a-one's horse, when 'a meant to beg it –
might it not?

HORATIO

Ay, my lord.

HAMLET

Why, e'en so; and now my Lady Worm's, chapless,
and knock'd about the mazard with a sexton's 90
spade. Here's fine revolution, an we had the trick
to see't. Did these bones cost no more the breeding
but to play at loggats with them? Mine ache to
think on't.

1 CLOWN

(*Sings*) A pick-axe and a spade, a spade, 95
    For and a shrouding sheet:
O, a pit of clay for to be made
    For such a guest is meet.

Throws up another skull.

HAMLET

There's another. Why may not that be the skull
of a lawyer? Where be his quiddities now, his quil- 100
lets, his cases, his tenures, and his tricks? Why

327

102 **suffer**   allow.

103 **sconce**   head.

105 **in's**   in his.

106–7 **statutes. . .recognizances. . .fines. . .double vouchers. . .recoveries**   various legal terms to do with dealing in buildings and land.

107 **fine**   end result, sum total.

111–2 **length and breadth of a pair of indentures**   the area covered by two legal documents ('indentures'), i.e. the area of a grave.

113 **box**   i.e. coffin.

inheritor   the dead man. Hamlet is reflecting that all we inherit finally is our own grave.

118–9 **They are sheep. . .in that**   they are fools who set great store in property, and evidence of ownership in legal documents (because we end up with nothing but a grave).

does he suffer this rude knave now to knock him
about the sconce with a dirty shovel, and will not
tell him of his action of battery? Hum! This fellow
might be in's time a great buyer of land, with his 105
statutes, his recognizances, his fines, his double
vouchers, his recoveries. Is this the fine of his fines,
and the recovery of his recoveries, to have his fine
pate full of fine dirt? Will his vouchers vouch him
no more of his purchases, and double ones too, 110
than the length and breadth of a pair of indentures? The very conveyances of his lands will
scarcely lie in this box; and must th' inheritor
himself have no more, ha?

HORATIO

Not a jot more, my lord. 115

HAMLET

Is not parchment made of sheepskins?

HORATIO

Ay, my lord, and of calves' skins too.

HAMLET

They are sheep and calves which seek out assurance in that. I will speak to this fellow. Whose
grave's this, sirrah? 120

1 CLOWN

Mine, sir.
(*Sings*) O, a pit of clay for to be made
    For such a guest is meet.

HAMLET

I think it be thine indeed, for thou liest in't.

128 *quick*   living.

139 *absolute*   pedantic.

140 *equivocation*   ambiguity.

142 *picked*   pernickety.

1 CLOWN

You lie out on't, sir, and therefore 'tis not
yours. For my part, I do not lie in't, yet it is   125
mine.

HAMLET

Thou dost lie in't, to be in't and say it is thine;
'tis for the dead, not for the quick; therefore thou
liest.

1 CLOWN

'Tis a quick lie, sir; 'twill away again from me to 130
you.

HAMLET

What man dost thou dig it for?

1 CLOWN

For no man, sir.

HAMLET

What woman, then?

1 CLOWN

For none neither.   135

HAMLET

Who is to be buried in't?

1 CLOWN

One that was a woman, sir; but, rest her soul, she's
dead.

HAMLET

How absolute the knave is! We must speak by the
card, or equivocation will undo us. By the Lord, 140
Horatio, this three years I have took note of it: the
age is grown so picked that the toe of the peasant

143–4 **_galls his kibe_**   kicks his chilblain.

comes so near the heel of the courtier, he galls his
kibe. How long hast thou been a grave-maker?

1 CLOWN

Of all the days i' th' year, I came to't that day that 145
our last King Hamlet overcame Fortinbras.

HAMLET

How long is that since?

1 CLOWN

Cannot you tell that? Every fool can tell that: it
was that very day that young Hamlet was born –
he that is mad, and sent into England. 150

HAMLET

Ay, marry, why was he sent into England?

1 CLOWN

Why, because 'a was mad: 'a shall recover his wits
there; or, if 'a do not, 'tis no great matter there.

HAMLET

Why?

1 CLOWN

'Twill not be seen in him there: there the men are 155
as mad as he.

HAMLET

How came he mad?

1 CLOWN

Very strangely, they say.

HAMLET

How strangely?

161 **Upon what ground?** for what reason?

166 **pocky corses** bodies pock-marked by venereal diseases.

167 **hold the laying in** last the burial.

172 **whoreson** (swear word) son of a whore.

173 **lien** lain.

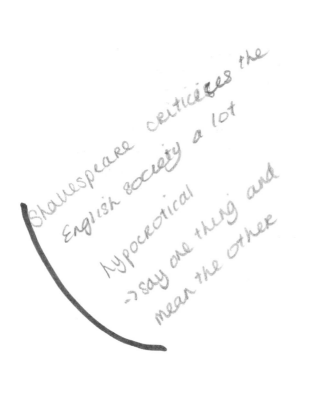

Shakespeare criticises the English society a lot
hypocritical
→ say one thing and mean the other

1 CLOWN

Faith, e'en with losing his wits.   160

HAMLET

Upon what ground?

1 CLOWN

Why, here in Denmark. I have been sexton here,
man and boy, thirty years.

HAMLET

How long will a man lie i' th' earth ere he rot?

1 CLOWN

Faith, if 'a be not rotten before 'a die – as we have 165
many pocky corses now-a-days that will scarce
hold the laying in – 'a will last you some eight year
or nine year. A tanner will last you nine year.

HAMLET

Why he more than another?

1 CLOWN

Why, sir, his hide is so tann'd with his trade that 170
'a will keep out water a great while; and your
water is a sore decayer of your whoreson dead
body. Here's a skull now; this skull has lien you
i' th' earth three and twenty years.

HAMLET

Whose was it?   175

1 CLOWN

A whoreson mad fellow's it was. Whose do you
think it was?

HAMLET

Nay, I know not.

180 **Rhenish**   wine from the Rhine region.

188 **My gorge rises**   I feel sick.

190 **gibes**   sarcastic jokes.

gambols   capers.

193 **chap-fall'n**   dispirited, and literally with the lower jaw hanging.

195 **favour**   appearance.

199 **Alexander**   Alexander the Great, King of Macedon and conqueror of most of the world known to him.

1 CLOWN

A pestilence on him for a mad rogue! 'A poured
a flagon of Rhenish on my head once. This same 180
skull, sir, was, sir, Yorick's skull, the King's jester.

HAMLET

This?

1 CLOWN

E'en that.

HAMLET

Let me see. (*Takes the skull*) Alas, poor Yorick! I
knew him, Horatio: a fellow of infinite jest, of most 185
excellent fancy; he hath borne me on his back a
thousand times. And now how abhorred in my
imagination it is! My gorge rises at it. Here hung
those lips that I have kiss'd I know not how oft.
Where be your gibes now, your gambols, your 190
songs, your flashes of merriment that were wont
to set the table on a roar? Not one now to mock
your own grinning – quite chap-fall'n? Now get
you to my lady's chamber, and tell her, let her
paint an inch thick, to this favour she must come; 195
make her laugh at that. Prithee, Horatio, tell me
one thing.

HORATIO

What's that, my lord?

HAMLET

Dost thou think Alexander look'd a this fashion i'
th' earth?   200

HORATIO

E'en so.

207   **too curiously**   too inquisitively or obsessively.

208   **follow him thither**   i.e. trace the progress of Alexander's body to the bung-hole.

209–10   **with modesty enough**   reasonably (not 'curiously').

212   **loam**   plaster made of clay and water.

217   **expel the winter's flaw**   keep out the winter wind.

220   **maimed rites**   incomplete funeral rites.

222   **Fordo it own life**   i.e. commit suicide.

       estate   rank, importance.

223   **Couch we awhile and mark**   let us keep down and watch.

HAMLET

And smelt so? Pah!

Throws down the skull.

HORATIO

E'en so, my lord.

HAMLET

To what base uses we may return, Horatio! Why
may not imagination trace the noble dust of Alex- 205
ander til 'a find it stopping a bung-hole?

HORATIO

'Twere to consider too curiously to consider so.

HAMLET

No, faith, not a jot; but to follow him thither with
modesty enough, and likelihood to lead it, as thus:
Alexander died, Alexander was buried, Alexander 210
returneth to dust; the dust is earth; of earth we
make loam; and why of that loam whereto he was
converted might they not stop a beer-barrel?
Imperious Caesar, dead and turn'd to clay,
Might stop a hole to keep the wind away.   215
O, that that earth which kept the world in awe
Should patch a wall t' expel the winter's flaw!
But soft! but soft! awhile. Here comes the King.

Enter the KING, QUEEN, LAERTES, *in funeral procession after the
coffin, with* Priest *and* Lords *attendant.*

The Queen, the courtiers. Who is this they follow?
And with such maimed rites? This doth betoken   220
The corse they follow did with desperate hand
Fordo it own life. 'Twas of some estate.
Couch we awhile and mark.

227 **obsequies**   funeral rites.

  enlarg'd   extended.

228 **warrantise**   justification.

  doubtful   questionable. He means that it is uncertain whether she killed
    herself or not.

229 **great command o'ersways the order**   i.e. the king's command has overruled
    the usual procedure. The priest is speaking as tactfully as he can.

231 **the last trumpet**   Judgement Day.

  for   instead of.

232 **Shards**   pieces of broken pottery.

233 **crants**   garlands.

234 **maiden strewments**   flowers symbolising her virginity, strewn over the coffin.

234–5 **bringing home. . .burial**   going to her final resting place ('bringing home')
    with a church bell tolling and a burial service.

239 **sage**   solemn.

240 **peace-parted souls**   souls who departed in peace (rather than by suicide).

243 **churlish**   uncharitable.

Retiring with HORATIO.

LAERTES
What ceremony else?

HAMLET
That is Laertes, a very noble youth. Mark.   225

LAERTES
What ceremony else?

PRIEST
Her obsequies have been as far enlarg'd
As we have warrantise. Her death was doubtful;
And, but that great command o'ersways the
     order,
She should in ground unsanctified have lodg'd   230
Till the last trumpet; for charitable prayers,
Shards, flints, and pebbles, should be thrown on
     her;
Yet here she is allow'd her virgin crants,
Her maiden strewments, and the bringing home
Of bell and burial.   235

LAERTES
Must there no more be done?

> blamed Hamlet because through his causes, Ophelia is now dead.

PRIEST
No more be done.
We should profane the service of the dead
To sing sage requiem and such rest to her
As to peace-parted souls.   240

LAERTES
Lay her i' th' earth;
And from her fair and unpolluted flesh
May violets spring! I tell thee, churlish priest,

244 *minist'ring*   charitable.

245 *howling*   i.e. in hell.

249 *deck'd*   decorated with flowers.

253 *ingenious sense*   reason, sanity.

258 *old Pelion*   a mountain in Thessaly, mentioned in classical literature.

259 *Olympus*   in classical mythology, the home of the gods.

262 *Conjures*   charms, bewitches.

    wand'ring stars   planets.

    stand   remain still.

263 *wonder-wounded*   struck motionless with astonishment.

    the Dane   i.e. the King of Denmark.

A minist'ring angel shall my sister be
When thou liest howling.   245

HAMLET

What, the fair Ophelia!

QUEEN

Sweets to the sweet; farewell!

Scattering flowers.

I hop'd thou shouldst have been my Hamlet's wife;
I thought thy bride-bed to have deck'd, sweet
    maid,
And not have strew'd thy grave.   250

LAERTES

O, treble woe
Fall ten times treble on that cursed head
Whose wicked deed thy most ingenious sense
Depriv'd thee of! Hold off the earth awhile,
Till I have caught her once more in mine arms.   255

Leaps into the grave.

Now pile your dust upon the quick and dead,
Till of this flat a mountain you have made
T' o'er-top old Pelion or the skyish head
Of blue Olympus.

HAMLET

(*Advancing*) What is he whose grief   260
Bears such an emphasis, whose phrase of sorrow
Conjures the wand'ring stars, and makes them
    stand
Like wonder-wounded hearers? This is I, Hamlet
    the Dane.

343

267 **splenitive** short-tempered.

275 **wag** open and shut; i.e. until he is dead.

Leaps into the grave.

LAERTES

The devil take thy soul!

Grappling with him.

HAMLET

Thou pray'st not well.   265
I prithee take thy fingers from my throat;
For, though I am not splenitive and rash,
Yet have I in me something dangerous,
Which let thy wiseness fear. Hold off thy hand.

KING

Pluck them asunder.   270

QUEEN

Hamlet! Hamlet!

ALL

Gentlemen!

HORATIO

Good my lord, be quiet.

The Attendants *part them, and they come out of the grave.*

HAMLET

Why, I will fight with him upon this theme.
Until my eyelids will no longer wag.   275

QUEEN

O my son, what theme?

HAMLET

I lov'd Ophelia: forty thousand brothers
Could not, with all their quantity of love,
Make up my sum. What wilt thou do for her?

345

281 **forbear**   have patience with.

282 **'Swounds**   (oath) by God's wounds.

283 **Woo't**   (colloquial) wilt.

284 **eisel**   vinegar.

289 **our ground**   i.e. the pile of earth heaped up on them.

290 **Singeing his pate. . .zone**   scorching his head against the burning sphere of the sun.

291 **Ossa**   Mount Ossa, another mountain mentioned in classical mythology.

   mouth   make a show of feeling by wild speeches.

296 **When that her. . .disclos'd**   when her two golden chicks have hatched.

299 **use**   treat.

KING

O, he is mad, Laertes.   280

QUEEN

For love of God, forbear him.

HAMLET

'Swounds, show me what thou'lt do:

Woo't weep, woo't fight, woo't fast, woo't tear
    thyself,
Woo't drink up eisel, eat a crocodile?
I'll do't. Dost come here to whine?   285
To outface me with leaping in her grave?
Be buried quick with her, and so will I;
And, if thou prate of mountains, let them throw
Millions of acres on us, till our ground,
Singeing his pate against the burning zone,   290
Make Ossa like a wart! Nay, an thou'lt mouth,
I'll rant as well as thou.

QUEEN

This is mere madness;
And thus awhile the fit will work on him;
Anon, as patient as the female dove   295
When that her golden couplets are disclos'd,
His silence will sit drooping.

HAMLET

Hear you, sir:
What is the reason that you use me thus?
I lov'd you ever. But it is no matter.   300
Let Hercules himself do what he may,
The cat will mew, and dog will have his day.

                                                          Exit

305 **to the present push**   into immediate execution.

307 **living**   permanent, enduring.

6 **mutines**   mutineers.

bilboes   shackles.

Rashly   hastily, without thought.

7 **know**   acknowledge.

9 **pall**   fail.

learn   teach.

KING

I pray thee, good Horatio, wait upon him.

Exit HORATIO

(*To* LAERTES) Strengthen your patience in our last
   night's speech;
We'll put the matter to the present push. –   305
Good Gertrude, set some watch over your son. –
This grave shall have a living monument.
An hour of quiet shortly shall we see;
Till then in patience our proceeding be.

Exeunt

Scene two

Elsinore. The Castle.

Enter HAMLET *and* HORATIO.

HAMLET

So much for this, sir; now shall you see the other.
You do remember all the circumstance?

HORATIO

Remember it, my lord!

HAMLET

Sir, in my heart there was a kind of fighting
That would not let me sleep. Methought I lay   5
Worse than the mutines in the bilboes. Rashly,
And prais'd be rashness for it – let us know,
Our indiscretion sometime serves us well,
When our deep plots do pall; and that should learn
   us

10 **ends**   destinies.

11 ***Rough-hew them how we will***   whatever crude attempts we make to control them.

14 ***scarf'd***   wrapped.

15 **them**   i.e. Rosencrantz and Guildenstern.

16 ***Finger'd***   stole.

   in fine   in conclusion.

21 **Larded**   padded out.

22 **Importing**   concerning.

23 **bugs and goblins**   imaginary terrors. The letter suggested that Hamlet was a very dangerous man, and that he should be killed before he could do any damage.

24 **on the supervise**   as soon as it had been read.

   no leisure bated   without delay.

25 ***stay***   wait for.

31 ***benetted***   trapped as if in a net.

32 ***Ere I could. . .brains***   before I could begin to think about it.

33 **They**   i.e. his brains.

34 ***fair***   clearly and neatly.

There's a divinity that shapes our ends,   10
Rough-hew them how we will.

HORATIO

That is most certain.

HAMLET

Up from my cabin,
My sea-gown scarf'd about me, in the dark
Grop'd I to find out them; had my desire;   15
Finger'd their packet, and in fine withdrew
To mine own room again, making so bold,
My fears forgetting manners, to unseal
Their grand commission; where I found, Horatio,
Ah, royal knavery! an exact command,   20
Larded with many several sorts of reasons,
Importing Denmark's health and England's too,
With, ho! such bugs and goblins in my life –
That, on the supervise, no leisure bated,
No, not to stay the grinding of the axe,   25
My head should be struck off.

HORATIO

Is't possible?

HAMLET

Here's the commission; read it at more leisure.
But wilt thou hear now how I did proceed?

HORATIO

I beseech you.   30

HAMLET

Being thus benetted round with villainies –
Ere I could make a prologue to my brains,
They had begun the play – I sat me down;
Devis'd a new commission; wrote it fair.

35 **hold**   believe.

statists   statesmen.

38 **yeoman's service**   good and faithful service.

41 **conjuration**   appeal.

45 **comma**   peace should stand between their friendships ('amities') like a comma between two words.

46 **as-es**   punning on the many important-sounding clauses in the document beginning 'as . . .' and 'asses', which also bear great 'charges' (loads).

50 **shriving-time**   time for them to confess their sins.

52 **ordinant**   directing matters.

56 **Subscrib'd**   signed.

impression   i.e. of the seal.

57 **changeling never known**   without Rosencrantz and Guildenstern being aware of the letters having been swapped.

58 **was sequent**   followed.

60 **go to't**   go to their deaths.

I once did hold it, as our statists do,   35
A baseness to write fair, and labour'd much
How to forget that learning; but, sir, now
It did me yeoman's service. Wilt thou know
Th' effect of what I wrote?

HORATIO

Ay, good my lord.   40

HAMLET

An earnest conjuration from the King,
As England was his faithful tributary,
As love between them like the palm might flourish,
As peace should still her wheaten garland wear
And stand a comma 'tween their amities,   45
And many such like as-es of great charge,
That, on the view and knowing of these contents,
Without debatement further more or less,
He should those bearers put to sudden death,
Not shriving-time allow'd.   50

HORATIO

How was this seal'd?

HAMLET

Why, even in that was heaven ordinant.
I had my father's signet in my purse,
Which was the model of that Danish seal;
Folded the writ up in the form of th' other;   55
Subscrib'd it, gave't th' impression, plac'd it safely,
The changeling never known. Now, the next day
Was our sea-fight; and what to this was sequent
Thou knowest already.

HORATIO

So Guildenstern and Rosencrantz go to't.   60

62–3 **their defeat. . .insinuation grow**   their downfall is a result of their having wheedled their way cunningly into their position.

64 **baser**   less noble.

65 **pass and fell incensed points**   thrusts and fiercely angry swords.

66 **opposites**   opponents (i.e. Claudius and Hamlet).

68 **stand me now upon**   fall to me to do.

70 **Popp'd in between. . .hopes**   thrust himself in before my own hopes of becoming king could be aired.

71 **angle**   hook.

proper   own.

72 **coz'nage**   trickery.

perfect conscience   in accord with a good conscience.

73 **quit**   repay (i.e. kill).

74 **canker**   cancerous growth.

74–5 **come In**   bring about.

79 **And a man's life's. . .'one'**   a man can be killed in the time that it takes to say 'one' (punning on the fact that a fencer says 'one' when claiming to have hit an opponent).

82–3 **by the image. . .of his**   by examining my grievance, I can see a likeness of his (i.e. both have had a father killed).

83 **court his favours**   seek his goodwill.

HAMLET

  Why, man, they did make love to this
     employment;
  They are not near my conscience; their defeat
  Does by their own insinuation grow:
  'Tis dangerous when the baser nature comes
  Between the pass and fell incensed points   65
  Of mighty opposites.

HORATIO

  Why, what a king is this!

HAMLET

  Does it not, think thee, stand me now upon –
  He that hath kill'd my king and whor'd my
     mother;
  Popp'd in between th' election and my hopes;   70
  Thrown out his angle for my proper life,
  And with such coz'nage – is't not perfect
     conscience
  To quit him with this arm? And is't not to be
     damn'd
  To let this canker of our nature come
  In further evil?   75

HORATIO

  It must be shortly known to him from England
  What is the issue of the business there.

HAMLET

  It will be short; the interim is mine,
  And a man's life's no more than to say 'one'.
  But I am very sorry, good Horatio,   80
  That to Laertes I forgot myself;
  For by the image of my cause I see
  The portraiture of his. I'll court his favours.

84 *bravery*   showiness.

89 *water-fly*   insignificant creature.

91 *Thy state*   i.e. of ignorance.

93–4 *Let a beast be. . .king's mess*   even a beast, if he is a landowner, is welcome to eat at the king's table.

94 *chough*   chattering jackdaw.

95 *spacious in the possession of dirt*   the owner of much land.

99 *'tis for the head*   Osric has evidently removed his hat as a sign of respect, and Hamlet tells him to replace it.

But sure the bravery of his grief did put me
Into a tow'ring passion.   85

HORATIO

Peace; who comes here?

Enter young OSRIC.

OSRIC

Your lordship is right welcome back to Denmark.

HAMLET

I humbly thank you, sir. (*Aside to* HORATIO) Dost
know this water-fly?

HORATIO

(*Aside to* HAMLET) No, my good lord.   90

HAMLET

(*Aside to* HORATIO) Thy state is the more gracious;
for 'tis a vice to know him. He hath much land,
and fertile. Let a beast be lord of beasts, and his
crib shall stand at the king's mess. 'Tis a chough;
but, as I say, spacious in the possession of dirt.   95

OSRIC

Sweet lord, if your lordship were at leisure, I
should impart a thing to you from his Majesty.

HAMLET

I will receive it, sir, with all diligence of spirit. Put
your bonnet to his right use; 'tis for the head.

OSRIC

I thank your lordship; it is very hot.   100

HAMLET

No, believe me, 'tis very cold; the wind is
northerly.

103 **indifferent**   fairly.

105 **complexion**   constitution.

110 **remember**   i.e. to replace your hat.

113 **absolute**   perfect.

113–4 **differences**   qualities which mark him out as exceptional.

114 **soft society**   pleasing manners.

great showing   impressive appearance.

115 **feelingly**   sincerely.

115–6 **card or calendar**   model or perfect example. Literally, a 'card' is a map, and a 'calendar', a directory.

117 **continent**   container, sum total.

118–26 **Sir, his definement. . .nothing more**   in this speech, Hamlet parodies Osric's elaborate and artificial way of speaking. This makes the detail of the speech hard to understand.

118 **perdition**   loss.

119 **divide him inventorially**   divide up and list his good qualities.

120 **dozy th' arithmatic of memory**   bewilder the ability of memory to organise the information.

yaw   wander aimlessly. A ship is said to yaw when it fails to keep a straight course.

121 **neither in respect of**   in comparison with.

123 **article**   an item on a list (looking back to the 'inventory' of line 119).

infusion   temperament.

dearth   rareness.

124 **make true diction**   speak the truth.

124–5 **his semblable is his mirror**   the only thing that can be compared to him is his own reflection.

125 **who**   whoever.

trace   copy.

126 **umbrage**   shadow.

OSRIC

It is indifferent cold, my lord, indeed.

HAMLET

But yet methinks it is very sultry and hot for my
complexion.   105

OSRIC

Exceedingly, my lord; it is very sultry, as 'twere
– I cannot tell how. But, my lord, his Majesty bade
me signify to you that 'a has laid a great wager on
your head. Sir, this is the matter –

HAMLET

I beseech you, remember.   110

HAMLET *moves him to put on his hat.*

OSRIC

Nay, good my lord; for my ease, in good faith. Sir,
here is newly come to court Laertes; believe me,
an absolute gentleman, full of most excellent differences, of very soft society and great showing.
Indeed, to speak feelingly of him, he is the card or 115
calendar of gentry, for you shall find in him the
continent of what part a gentleman would see.

HAMLET

Sir, his definement suffers no perdition in you;
though, I know, to divide him inventorially would
dozy th' arithmetic of memory, and yet but yaw 120
neither in respect of his quick sail. But, in the
verity of extolment, I take him to be a soul of great
article, and his infusion of such dearth and rareness as, to make true diction of him, his semblable
is his mirror, and who else would trace him, his 125
umbrage, nothing more.

128 **The concernancy, sir?**   why are we talking about him?

129 **rawer**   less perfect and refined.

131–2 **Is't not possible. . .tongue?**   is it not possible that he would understand if you spoke in a different (i.e. simpler) language?

132 **You will to't, sir, really**   you will surely have a go at it.

133 **What imports the nomination of**   what is the significance of your mentioning.

140 **approve**   commend.

OSRIC

Your lordship speaks most infallibly of him.

HAMLET

The concernancy, sir? Why do we wrap the
gentleman in our more rawer breath?

OSRIC

Sir?   130

HORATIO

(*Aside to* HAMLET) Is't not possible to understand in
another tongue? You will to't, sir, really.

HAMLET

What imports the nomination of this gentleman?

OSRIC

Of Laertes?

HORATIO

(*Aside*) His purse is empty already; all's golden 135
words are spent.

HAMLET

Of him, sir.

OSRIC

I know you are not ignorant −

HAMLET

I would you did, sir; yet, in faith, if you did, it
would not much approve me. Well, sir.   140

OSRIC

You are not ignorant of what excellence Laertes is −

HAMLET

I dare not confess that, lest I should compare with

361

145 **for his weapon**   i.e. for his abilities in sword-fighting.

     imputation   reputation.

146 **in his meed he's unfellowed**   in his ability he is unrivalled.

150 **Barbary**   North African.

151 **he has impon'd**   Laertes has wagered in return.

152 **poniards**   daggers.

153 **assigns**   accessories.

     girdle   belt.

     hangers   straps.

154 **carriages**   another term for the straps ('hangers') referred to in the previous line.

     dear to fancy   desirable.

155 **responsive**   in keeping with.

156 **of very liberal conceit**   lavishly ingenious.

158–9 **edified by the margent**   literally, improved by marginal notes in a book. Hamlet requires a footnote to Osric's affected speech.

161 **germane**   relevant.

162 **if we could carry a cannon**   Hamlet associates 'carriages' (line 160) with gun-carriages, which support cannon.

362

him in excellence; but to know a man well were
to know himself.

OSRIC

I mean, sir, for his weapon; but in the imputation 145
laid on him by them, in his meed he's unfellowed.

HAMLET

What's his weapon?

OSRIC

Rapier and dagger.

HAMLET

That's two of his weapons – but well.

OSRIC

The King, sir, hath wager'd with him six Barbary 150
horses; against the which he has impon'd, as I take
it, six French rapiers and poniards, with their
assigns, as girdle, hangers, and so – three of the
carriages, in faith, are very dear to fancy, very
responsive to the hilts, most delicate carriages, and 155
of very liberal conceit.

HAMLET

What call you the carriages?

HORATIO

(*Aside to* HAMLET) I knew you must be edified by the
margent ere you had done.

OSRIC

The carriages, sir, are the hangers. 160

HAMLET

The phrase would be more germane to the matter
if we could carry a cannon by our sides. I would

168   *laid*   bet.

      passes   bouts.

169–70   *exceed you three hits*   be more than three hits ahead of you.

  170   *he hath laid on twelve for nine*   unclear, but perhaps Laertes has bet on nine hits out of twelve.

  171   *come to immediate trial*   i.e. the fight could go straight ahead.

  177   *breathing time of day*   time for exercise.

  182   *redeliver*   deliver the message.

it might be hangers till then. But on: six Barbary
horses against six French swords, their assigns,
and three liberal conceited carriages; that's the 165
French bet against the Danish. Why is this all
impon'd, as you call it?

OSRIC

The King, sir, hath laid, sir, that in a dozen passes
between yourself and him he shall not exceed you
three hits; he hath laid on twelve for nine, and it 170
would come to immediate trial if your lordship
would vouchsafe the answer.

HAMLET

How if I answer no?

OSRIC

I mean, my lord, the opposition of your person in
trial.   175

HAMLET

Sir, I will walk here in the hall. If it please his
Majesty, it is the breathing time of day with me;
let the foils be brought, the gentleman willing, and
the King hold his purpose, I will win for him an
I can; if not, I will gain nothing but my shame and 180
the odd hits.

OSRIC

Shall I redeliver you e'en so?

HAMLET

To this effect, sir, after what flourish your nature
will.

OSRIC

I commend my duty to your lordship.   185

187 **there are no tongues else for's turn**   i.e. nobody else will praise his duty for him.

188 **This lapwing runs. . .head**   i.e. he is very inexperienced but also precocious (like a lapwing chick, which can walk within hours of hatching).

189 **comply**   speak ceremoniously to.

    dug   mother's breast.

190 **bevy**   type, generation.

191 **drossy**   corrupt.

192 **tune of the time**   fashionable speech of the period.

    outward habit of encounter   superficial manners of polite society.

193 **yesty**   yeasty, and therefore frothy.

193–5 **carries them. . .winnowed opinions**   enables them to hold their own with people with firm and well-substantiated views.

195–6 **and do but blow. . .are out**   but if you put them to the test, they burst like bubbles.

203 **if his fitness speaks**   if he says that he is ready.

HAMLET

Yours, yours. (*Exit* OSRIC) He does well to commend it himself; there are no tongues else for's turn.

HORATIO

This lapwing runs away with the shell on his head.

HAMLET

'A did comply, sir, with his dug before 'a suck'd it. Thus has he, and many more of the same bevy, 190 that I know the drossy age dotes on, only got the tune of the time and outward habit of encounter – a kind of yesty collection, which carries them through and through the most fann'd and winnowed opinions; and do but blow them to their 195 trial, the bubbles are out.

Enter a Lord.

LORD

My lord, his Majesty commended him to you by young Osric, who brings back to him that you attend him in the hall. He sends to know if your pleasure hold to play with Laertes, or that you will 200 take longer time.

HAMLET

I am constant to my purposes; they follow the king's pleasure: if his fitness speaks, mine is ready now – or whensoever, provided I be so able as now.   205

LORD

The King and Queen and all are coming down.

HAMLET

In happy time.

208–9 **use some gentle entertainment**   i.e. behave politely towards.

217 **gain-giving**   misgiving, premonition.

219–20 **forestall their repair**   prevent their coming.

221 **Not a whit**   not at all.

   we defy augury   we reject the art of foretelling the future.

221–2 **there is a special. . .sparrow**   God's care for his creation even extends to the death of sparrows (and He will therefore surely care for me). The reference is to the Bible (Matthew 10: 29–31).

225 **of aught he leaves**   anything about what he leaves behind him.

226 **betimes**   early.

LORD

The Queen desires you to use some gentle entertainment to Laertes before you fall to play.

HAMLET

She well instructs me.   210

Exit Lord

HORATIO

You will lose this wager, my lord.

HAMLET

I do not think so; since he went into France I have
been in continual practice. I shall win at the odds.
But thou wouldst not think how ill all's here about
my heart; but it is no matter.   215

HORATIO

Nay, good my lord –

HAMLET

It is but foolery; but it is such a kind of gain-giving
as would perhaps trouble a woman.

HORATIO

If your mind dislike anything, obey it. I will forestall their repair hither, and say you are not fit.   220

HAMLET

Not a whit, we defy augury: there is a special providence in the fall of a sparrow. If it be now, 'tis not
to come; if it be not to come, it will be now; if it
be not now, yet it will come – the readiness is all.
Since no man knows of aught he leaves, what is't 225
to leave betimes? Let be.

A table prepared. Trumpets, Drums, *and* Officers *with*

369

s.d. *State*   nobles of the court.

230 *presence*   company.

232 *sore distraction*   grievous madness.

233 *exception*   dislike.

243 *disclaiming from a purpos'd evil*   disassociating myself from an evil purpose.

247 *nature*   natural feelings (of loyalty to my father).

250 *will no*   will accept no.

cushions, foils and daggers. Enter KING, QUEEN, LAERTES, *and
all the* State

KING

    Come, Hamlet, come, and take this hand from me.
    (*The* KING *puts* LAERTES's *hand into* HAMLET's.)

HAMLET

    Give me your pardon, sir. I have done you wrong;
    But pardon't, as you are a gentleman.
    This presence knows,   230
    And you must needs have heard how I am
      punish'd
    With a sore distraction. What I have done
    That might your nature, honour, and exception
    Roughly awake, I here proclaim was madness.
    Was't Hamlet wrong'd Laertes? Never Hamlet.   235
    If Hamlet from himself be ta'en away,
    And when he's not himself does wrong Laertes,
    Then Hamlet does it not, Hamlet denies it.
    Who does it, then? His madness. If't be so,
    Hamlet is of the faction that is wrong'd;   240
    His madness is poor Hamlet's enemy.
    Sir, in this audience,
    Let my disclaiming from a purpos'd evil
    Free me so far in your most generous thoughts
    That I have shot my arrow o'er the house   245
    And hurt my brother.

LAERTES

    I am satisfied in nature,
    Whose motive in this case should stir me most
    To my revenge; but in my terms of honour
    I stand aloof, and will no reconcilement   250
    Till by some elder masters of known honour

371

252 **voice**   opinion.

253 **name ungor'd**   reputation undamaged.

260 **I'll be your foil**   I will act as a background to show off your skill.

262 **Stick fiery off**   be shown sparkling.

270 **better'd**   improved.

I have a voice and precedent of peace
To keep my name ungor'd – but till that time
I do receive your offer'd love like love,
And will not wrong it.   255

HAMLET

I embrace it freely;
And will this brother's wager frankly play.
Give us the foils. Come on.

LAERTES

Come, one for me,

HAMLET

I'll be your foil, Laertes; in mine ignorance   260
Your skill shall, like a star i' th' darkest night,
Stick fiery off indeed.

LAERTES

You mock me, sir.

HAMLET

No, by this hand.

KING

Give them the foils, young Osric. Cousin Hamlet, 265
You know the wager?

HAMLET

Very well, my lord;
Your Grace has laid the odds a' th' weaker side.

KING

I do not fear it: I have seen you both;
But since he's better'd, we have therefore odds.   270

LAERTES

This is too heavy; let me see another.

272 *have all a length?*   are of equal lengths?

276 *quit in answer of the third exchange*   repays Laertes' first two hits by winning
     the third.

279 *union*   pearl.

282 *kettle*   kettle drum.

289 *One*   Hamlet claims a hit.

HAMLET

This likes me well. These foils have all a length?

They prepare to play.

OSRIC

Ay, my good lord.

KING

Set me the stoups of wine upon that table.
If Hamlet give the first or second hit,   275
Or quit in answer of the third exchange,
Let all the battlements their ordnance fire;
The King shall drink to Hamlet's better breath
And in the cup an union shall he throw,
Richer than that which four successive kings   280
In Denmark's crown have worn. Give me the cups;
And let the kettle to the trumpet speak,
The trumpet to the cannoneer without,
The cannons to the heavens, the heaven to earth,
'Now the King drinks to Hamlet'. Come, begin – 285
And you, the judges, bear a wary eye.

HAMLET

Come on sir,

LAERTES

Come, my lord.

They play.

HAMLET

One.

LAERTES

No.   290

HAMLET

Judgment?

292   *palpable*   obvious, evident.

OSRIC

A hit, a very palpable hit.

LAERTES

Well, again.

KING

Stay, give me drink. Hamlet, this pearl is thine;
Here's to thy health.   295

Drum, trumpets, and shot.

Give him the cup.

HAMLET

I'll play this bout first; set it by awhile.
Come.

They play.

Another hit; what say you?

LAERTES

A touch, a touch, I do confess't.   300

KING

Our son shall win.

QUEEN

He's fat, and scant of breath.
Here, Hamlet, take my napkin, rub thy brows.
The Queen carouses to thy fortune, Hamlet.

HAMLET

Good madam!   305

KING

Gertrude, do not drink.

316 **make a wanton of me**   treat me as if I were a child (by not trying his best).

QUEEN

I will, my lord; I pray you pardon me.

KING

(*Aside*) It is the poison'd cup; it is too late.

HAMLET

I dare not drink yet, madam; by and by.

QUEEN

Come, let me wipe thy face.   310

LAERTES

My lord, I'll hit him now.

KING

I do not think't.

LAERTES

(*Aside*) And yet it is almost against my conscience.

HAMLET

Come, for the third. Laertes, you do but dally;
I pray you pass with your best violence;   315
I am afeard you make a wanton of me.

LAERTES

Say you so? Come on.

They play.

OSRIC

Nothing, neither way.

LAERTES

Have at you now!

LAERTES *wounds* HAMLET: *then, in scuffling, they change rapiers, and* HAMLET *wounds* LAERTES.

379

325 **springe** trap.

KING

Part them; they are incens'd. 320

HAMLET

Nay, come again.

The QUEEN *falls.*

OSRIC

Look to the Queen there, ho!

HORATIO

They bleed on both sides. How is it, my lord?

OSRIC

How is't, Laertes?

LAERTES

Why, as a woodcock, to mine own springe,
    Osric; 325
I am justly kill'd with mine own treachery.

HAMLET

How does the Queen?

KING

She swoons to see them bleed.

QUEEN

No, no, the drink, the drink! O my dear Hamlet!
The drink, the drink! I am poison'd. 330

Dies.

HAMLET

O, villainy! Ho! let the door be lock'd.
Treachery! seek it out.

LAERTES *falls.*

337 *foul practice*   deceitful trick.

346 *union*   pearl, and also union in death with Gertrude.

349 *temper'd*   prepared.

351 *come not upon thee*   be blamed on you.

LAERTES

It is here, Hamlet. Hamlet, thou art slain;
No med'cine in the world can do thee good;
In thee there is not half an hour's life;   335
The treacherous instrument is in thy hand,
Unbated and envenom'd. The foul practice
Hath turn'd itself on me; lo, here I lie,
Never to rise again. Thy mother's poison'd.
I can no more. The King, the King's to blame.   340

HAMLET

The point envenom'd too!
Then, venom, to thy work.

Stabs the KING.

ALL

Treason! treason!

KING

O, yet defend me, friends; I am but hurt.

HAMLET

Here, thou incestuous, murd'rous, damned Dane, 345
Drink off this potion. Is thy union here?
Follow my mother.

KING *dies*.

LAERTES

He is justly serv'd:
It is a poison temper'd by himself.
Exchange forgiveness with me, noble Hamlet.   350
Mine and my father's death come not upon thee,
Nor thine on me!

Dies.

356 **mutes**   actors without speaking parts.

363 **antique Roman**   an ancient Roman, whose stoic philosophy saw suicide as
     an honourable action.

370 **felicity**   the happiness of death.

HAMLET

Heaven make thee free of it! I follow thee.
I am dead, Horatio. Wretched queen adieu!
You that look pale and tremble at this chance,   355
That are but mutes or audience to this act,
Had I but time, as this fell sergeant Death
Is strict in his arrest, O, I could tell you –
But let it be. Horatio, I am dead:
Thou livest; report me and my cause aright   360
To the unsatisfied.

HORATIO

Never believe it.
I am more an antique Roman than a Dane;
Here's yet some liquor left.

HAMLET

As th'art a man,   365
Give me the cup. Let go. By heaven, I'll ha't.
O God! Horatio, what a wounded name,
Things standing thus unknown, shall live behind
   me!
If thou didst ever hold me in thy heart,
Absent thee from felicity awhile,   370
And in this harsh world draw thy breath in pain,
To tell my story.

March afar off, and shot within.

What warlike noise is this?

OSRIC

Young Fortinbras, with conquest come from
   Poland,
To th' ambassadors of England gives   375
This warlike volley.

385

378 **o'er-crows**   crows over in triumph.

380 **election**   i.e. the election for the next King of Denmark.

381 **voice**   vote.

382 **occurrents, more and less**   things which have happened, both important and less important.

383 **solicited**   urged (me to give my vote to Fortinbras). The sentence is incomplete.

390 **This quarry cries on havoc**   these corpses show that indiscriminate slaughter has occurred.

391 **toward**   in preparation.

394 **dismal**   dreadful (a much stronger word in Shakespeare's time).

HAMLET

O, I die, Horatio!
The potent poison quite o'er-crows my spirit.
I cannot live to hear the news from England,
But I do prophesy th' election lights   380
On Fortinbras; he has my dying voice.
So tell him, with th' occurrents, more and less,
Which have solicited – the rest is silence.

Dies.

HORATIO

Now cracks a noble heart. Good night, sweet
    prince,
And flights of angels sing thee to thy rest!   385

March within.

Why does the drum come hither?

Enter FORTINBRAS *and* English Ambassadors, *with drum,
colours, and* Attendants.

FORTINBRAS

Where is this sight?

HORATIO

What is it you would see?
If aught of woe or wonder, cease your search.

FORTINBRAS

This quarry cries on havoc. O proud death,   390
What feast is toward in thine eternal cell
That thou so many princes at a shot
So bloodily hast struck?

1 AMBASSADOR

The sight is dismal;

396 **The ears**   i.e. Claudius' ears.

399 **Where**   from whom.

403 **jump**   exactly.

411 **put on**   brought about.

forc'd cause   necessary reason.

418 **rights of memory**   ancient, unforgotten rights.

421 **his mouth**   i.e. Hamlet's, whose vote will persuade others to support Fortinbras as the next king.

422 **this same**   i.e. that the bodies be placed on a stage and Horatio recount the events.

And our affairs from England come too late: 395
The ears are senseless that should give us hearing
To tell him his commandment is fulfill'd,
That Rosencrantz and Guildenstern are dead.
Where should we have our thanks?

HORATIO

Not from his mouth,   400
Had it th' ability of life to thank you:
He never gave commandment for their death.
But since, so jump upon this bloody question,
You from the Polack wars, and you from England,
Are here arrived, give order that these bodies   405
High on a stage be placed to the view;
And let me speak to th' yet unknowing world
How these things came about. So shall you hear
Of carnal, bloody, and unnatural acts;
Of accidental judgments, casual slaughters;   410
Of deaths put on by cunning and forc'd cause;
And, in this upshot, purposes mistook
Fall'n on th' inventors' heads – all this can I
Truly deliver.

FORTINBRAS

Let us haste to hear it,   415
And call the noblest to the audience.
For me, with sorrow I embrace my fortune;
I have some rights of memory in this kingdom,
Which now to claim my vantage doth invite me.

HORATIO

Of that I shall have also cause to speak,   420
And from his mouth whose voice will draw on
    more.
But let this same be presently perform'd,

389

423 **wild**   disturbed.

427 **put on**   put to the test of being king.

Why does Hamlet wants
that Fortinbras becomes king?

Fortinbras does what he wants,
he's courageous and Hamlet
hasn't got family anymore.

Even while men's minds are wild, lest more
   mischance
On plots and errors happen.

FORTINBRAS
   Let four captains   425
Bear Hamlet like a soldier to the stage;
For he was likely, had he been put on,
To have prov'd most royal; and for his passage
The soldier's music and the rite of war
Speak loudly for him.   430
Take up the bodies. Such a sight as this
Becomes the field, but here shows much amiss.
Go, bid the soldiers shoot.

        Exeunt marching. A peal of ordnance shot off.

Study programme

Before reading the play

Plot

1. Read the act summaries to yourself. Then, as a group (preferably in a circle), build up the story of the play, contributing a line each.

2. Having read the act summaries what do you think may be some of the moments of greatest tension in the play? Discuss your thoughts with a partner or in a small group.

3. Can you see any parallels between any of the characters' situations? Jot down your ideas in note form. Then for each parallel situation give the names to a partner and see if they can guess the parallels that you have drawn between them.

Themes

Revenge

In Shakespeare's time there were conflicting attitudes towards revenge. There was more sympathy than there might be nowadays for people who took private vengeance against serious criminals such as murderers. This attitude was left over from the days when taking personal revenge was seen as defending one's honour. However, the laws of the courts and the church were quite clear in condemning this. You can imagine the complication which would arise if the originator of the law and the head of the church, the sovereign, had committed the crime. The mantle of the avenger might well not sit easily on the person chosen to bring about revenge on such a criminal. . .

Interest in the theme of revenge was widespread and led playwrights of this time to develop a genre of plays known as Revenge Tragedies. This type of play is described in the following lines of Horatio:

> . . . So shall you hear
> Of carnal, bloody, and unnatural acts;
> Of accidental judgments, casual slaughters;
> Of deaths put on by cunning and forc'd cause;
> And, in this upshot, purposes mistook
> Fall'n on th' inventors' heads . . .

(Act 5, scene 2, lines 408–13)

Revenge Tragedies have many features of the plays of Lucius Seneca, a Roman playwright who lived in the first century A.D. His plays often included bloodthirsty details, ghosts and magic within a plot centring on the revenge of a murder. Often characters not directly involved in the plot were drawn into the general mayhem.

1 Find out the titles of some of Seneca's plays and look for summaries of their plots to give you an idea of the stories they presented.

2 Below is a list of a few of the popular Elizabethan Revenge Tragedies:

The Spanish Tragedy
The Revenger's Tragedy
The White Devil
The Duchess of Malfi

In groups of four, divide the titles between you. Each of you should then find a synopsis of your play and present it to the group.

When you have done this, discuss any similarities you have found between the plots, characters and settings of the four plays

3 Look at the typical elements of the Revenge Tragedy:

- violent crimes with plenty of blood and murder;
- a fascination with the means by which these were committed;
- a ghost;

393

- madness;
- a play within the play;
- characters of noble birth.

How many of these features do the plays in assignment 2 above have?

Now you have read the plot summary, how many of these features do you think **Hamlet** appears to have?

4 Here is a description of the five-part structure of the Senecan tragedy, which Elizabethan Revenge Tragedy often used as its model:

- the crime requiring revenge is described, often by a ghost;
- the revenger starts to plan his revenge;
- the revenger confronts the criminal;
- the revenge is partly completed, but not fully;
- the revenge is finally completed.

How far does **Hamlet** follow this pattern?

Within this pattern, and using a mixture of the typical elements of Revenge Tragedy listed in assignment 3, playwrights might choose to explore certain areas with more emphasis. Having read the act summaries, what areas do you think Shakespeare chose to explore?

5 In our society, the law exists to punish those who have committed crimes. Individuals who have been wronged do not have the responsibility or the right to take revenge for themselves. This position is not always accepted or clear-cut, however. Can you think of occasions, perhaps those mentioned in the media, perhaps in your own surroundings, where individuals have decided to take their own revenge?

- What was your opinion of their actions?
- What factors made you more or less sympathetic to the revengers?
- What did your opinions reflect about your values?

Corruption

 Something is rotten in the state of Denmark.

(Act 1, scene 4, line 99)

The power centre at the court at Elsinore from which Denmark is ruled is corrupt. This corruption enfolds an increasing number of people, many as pawns of others, and most with little understanding of what is really going on.

Can you find examples in recent history of cases where the search for power has led to corruption becoming rife? Perhaps there were attempted murders and spying, relationships collapsing as trust was corroded and the exile of people whose presence was inconvenient for the power-holder. Language may have become abused, functioning not as a tool for communication but for manipulation and deception. Why, for example, were the deaths of Iraqi civilians due to American bombing in 1991 described as 'collateral damage' by the American government?

Exchange descriptions and opinions of what went on in these cases in a small group. You will find them all present – and much more – in **Hamlet**. If you can't think of examples reported by the media, try novels or films as sources.

Kingship

 There's such divinity doth hedge a king
That treason can but peep to what it would,
Acts little of his will.

(Act 4, scene 5, lines 130–2)

Most holy and religious fear it is
To keep those many many bodies safe
That live and feed upon your Majesty.

(Act 3, scene 3, lines 9–11)

With a partner or in a small group, find out as much as you can about the position of the sovereign in Shakespeare's time. Compare your findings as a class.

How has the position of the sovereign changed since then?

Family relations

[8] Imagine the following situation: a young girl is going out with the son and heir of a powerful businessman. Her father is a senior executive who works for the businessman. Neither her father nor her brother approve of this relationship because they don't think he's serious about her, and they intend to make this very clear to her.

Your task, in groups of three, is to role-play three short discussions between brother and sister, brother and father and father and sister on this matter.

When you have finished compare the outcome of your discussions with the other groups. Who emerged as the more powerful figures in your role-plays and why was this? When you are reading **Hamlet** you can compare these outcomes to what is going on in Act 1, scene 3.

Public relations

[9] Imagine you are a man who has just become head of a powerful business empire, succeeding your brother who has recently died. You have also married your brother's wife, and you know that some suspect you and your new wife of having had an affair before your brother's death. You have to deliver your first public speech to your workforce. It obviously needs to present you in a positive light and instil confidence in your employees. What would you say? Deliver your speech to two others, then swap over.

When you have all finished, discuss what you were aiming to do in your own speech in detail and how far you managed to achieve it. Did your audience feel it succeeded?

If you would rather write than role-play, you could write the diary entry of the man on the evening after he has delivered the speech. How would he describe and assess his own performance?

Satire

10 Look up the word 'satire' in a dictionary. What is the difference between satire and comedy?

Think of modem-day comedians who succeed in satirising people's behaviour while acting in a way that many might describe as mad. What are their targets and how do they set about ridiculing them? Discuss your thoughts in a small group, and then as a class.

11 Characters who have a primarily satirical role crop up in several plays by Shakespeare. Sometimes they may be employed as 'fools' by wealthy nobles to provide amusement by their wit. Look at the following characters in the scenes listed and discuss how the satirist makes his point:

- Feste in *Twelfth Night*, Act 1, scene 5, lines 1–137;
- Thersites in *Troilus and Cressida*, Act 2, scene 3, line 1–80;
- The Fool in *King Lear*, Act I, scene 4, lines 93–185;
- Touchstone in *As You Like It*, Act 3, scene 2, lines 11–122.

There is no official Fool in *Hamlet*. However, Hamlet's assumed madness gives him a chance to act as a satirist. As you read *Hamlet* consider where and how Hamlet satirises the world around him.

Acting

12 Have you ever found yourself in a situation where you are acting in a way that you don't really feel is in keeping with your true character? Perhaps a situation has been created in which you are playing a part but it's a part of which you don't feel fully in control. You may be 'acting' in the sense of consciously playing an assumed role as well. Discuss or write about this sort of personal experience. It is a situation which you will find in *Hamlet*.

What's it all about?

13 Have you ever wondered, on a day when all seems to be going wrong, what it is that keeps you going? Try to share thoughts of this area of experience with a partner. It is a question you will find Hamlet asking himself in the play. As you read it, you can ask yourself whether Shakespeare provides him with any answers.

During reading

Act I

Check your knowledge of Act I

- Where and when is the first scene set?
- Who has seen the Ghost before Hamlet?
- What do we learn of the Danish political situation from scene 1?
- What information does Claudius detail in his opening speech?
- What is Hamlet's reaction to Horatio's news of the Ghost?
- What advice does:
  - Laertes give to Ophelia?
  - Polonius give to Laertes?
  - Polonius give to Ophelia?
- How does Hamlet describe the condition of Denmark?
- Does Hamlet show any reluctance to follow the Ghost?
- What do we learn from the Ghost, and what does the Ghost want Hamlet to do?
- What does Hamlet say to his friends that he may do if he thinks it necessary?

Questioning the text in Act I

Do the first thirty lines of the play provide a successful opening for you? Discuss why or why not with a partner.

In groups of four, act out these lines, trying to capture the mood that is created.

2 Imagine the soldiers on guard were discussing Horatio. How would they describe him?

Horatio is used to provide important descriptions of others and to advance the plot. Look closely together at the text to see where and how he does this.

3 If you were an attendant at the court in Elsinore, knowing nothing of Claudius' crime, how would you describe him after hearing his first speech in scene 2 and his speech to Hamlet in lines 89–119 that follows soon after? Imagine you are writing down your thoughts at the end of the day or talking to a friend.

Now write down the thoughts of Claudius and Gertrude before each enters in scene 2 and at the end of scene 2. Think carefully about what their main concerns are and how they perceive their public image.

4 Imagine Polonius, Laertes and Ophelia each make a diary entry after their conversations in scene 3. Write the entry you think one or more of them would make. Now look at the questions below.

Do any of the following adjectives reflect what you have read of Polonius?

sensible	caring	self-seeking	banal
protective	pompous	wise	long-winded

Compare your diary with a partner's, and see if your readings are similar. Discuss as a class whether the text supports the different readings these adjectives suggest.

Now do the same for Laertes using the following adjectives:

arrogant	kind	protective	close
perceptive	helpful	self-seeking	patronising

and for Ophelia:

innocent	respectful	obedient	spirited
independent	ironic	meek	immature

5 The first three scenes apparently offer different settings, characters, subjects to be discussed, themes and moods. Fill in a chart like the one below to see if you can establish ways in which they may be seen as interrelated and what effects could be created for an audience:

	Scene 1	Scene 2	Scene 3	Relationship between 3 scenes
Setting	The castle front. Outside the centre of power.	Inside the castle. The heart of political power in formal public display.	In Polonius' house. Domestic family meeting.	A world at Elsinore in Denmark being created, on a political and domestic level, inside and outside the court.
Characters	Soldiers (common people as opposed to nobles) and Horatio. The Ghost.			
Subjects discussed	Political situation between Denmark and Norway: preparation for war. Perspectives on Fortinbras, Old Hamlet and Hamlet. The Ghost.			
Mood	Fear and tension openly expressed. Lack of trust.			
Themes	Father/son relationship. Attitudes to revenge. Leadership. The effect of power struggles on the country as a whole.			

Having completed this chart, and answered the first three questions in 'Check your knowledge of Act 1', discuss what the effect could be if, as some directors have chosen to do, scene 1 is left out. What might be possible reasons for cutting it?

Now either give a talk to a small group or write an essay on 'The impact I would choose to create by the first three scenes of **Hamlet** were I to direct it'.

6   It is clear that the soldiers are fearful of the Ghost in Act 1. Find out more about what ghosts might signify to an Elizabethan audience, and compare your findings with others. How do scenes 4 and 5 in this Act reflect these views of ghosts?

7   Re-read scene 5 and discuss the following in groups:

- How does the Ghost see Hamlet's duty?
- How does Hamlet see his duty after he has received his instructions from the Ghost?
- How are we invited to see the Ghost's instructions and Hamlet's duty?

8   Collect information other characters give us about old Hamlet and Claudius (as opposed to what they say themselves) in scenes 1, 2 and 4. Now look at who offers this information, and how far their assessments of the characters can be seen as objective. Do you think Hamlet's view of the simple and total contrast between them is the one which Shakespeare invites his audience to share?

Why do you think Shakespeare gives such a long description of the murder of one by the other? Is it to heighten the horror of the crime, or does it reflect less positively on old Hamlet?

9   The Ghost has been portrayed in a variety of ways on stage. In many productions he is dressed as he is described by Horatio in Act 1, scene 1, line 72 and Act 1, scene 2, lines 206 and 236–56. However,

he has also been represented as a strong light, which shines off the faces of the other characters on stage and, on another occasion, as a voice which issues forth from Hamlet, appearing to possess him.

Think about the three approaches described above and discuss why they might or might not be effective. Consider also whether they would require a change in any of the rest of the play. Then suggest (and draw if you can) any alternative presentations of the Ghost that you think might walk on stage. Give reasons for your ideas.

10 What are your first impressions of Hamlet himself? Jot down adjectives to describe him as you reach the following points, together with reasons for your choices:

- after scene 1 (as he is mentioned);
- after his first soliloquy;
- at the end of scene 2;
- after scene 3 (as he is discussed);
- after scene 4;
- after scene 5.

Have you had to find new words for different aspects of his character with each new section? Compare your words with a partner and as a class.

11 It is thought that an Elizabethan audience may have seen characters less in terms of psychological coherence and more as fulfilling conventional roles found in contemporary theatre. Some critics have seen Hamlet as taking on a range of roles including the Avenger, keen to take his revenge for a crime, the Malcontent, who draws out general denunciations of the world at large from his particular observations, and the Madman, who can be both the Fool and the Satirist, exposing folly and corruption around him.

Make a chart with three columns and then go through this Act writing down references where Hamlet can be seen as fulfilling these roles. Keep your chart and continue to fill it in as you read the rest of the play.

402

12 What function does a soliloquy have? Discuss this question as a group.

It is thought that in Shakespeare's time the soliloquy was performed to contemporary audiences as if they were being directly addressed by the speaker. This would mean that the speaker was presenting his thoughts for the audience to respond to rather than simply thinking aloud as if he were alone, which is how most modern productions present soliloquy.

Discuss how Hamlet's first soliloquy (Act 1, scene 2, lines 131–61) might be directed differently if you were taking each of these two approaches to its presentation. Think carefully about how the character of Hamlet might be built up differently in each approach and how our impression of what he describes and its accuracy might change. How might position, gesture and voice vary?

Now write a director's letter to an actor about to play Hamlet outlining your suggestions for either method of performance, giving the reasons behind your advice.

13 Make a chart with four columns headed **Laertes**, **Ophelia**, **Hamlet** and **Fortinbras**. Write down as many different comparisons and contrasts as you can find between these characters in their relations with their parents. For each point, note where you would draw your evidence from in the text.

When you have done this discuss whether it is useful to consider these characters as a group in this way.

14 Different threads of imagery have been used in this Act and are developed as the play continues. The main ones could be seen as:

- images which concentrate on the gap between appearance and reality. They are often centred on clothes or paint. They are first introduced in the play by Hamlet in his speech to his mother (Act 1, scene 2, lines 78–88). Here he combines the image and the idea when he says that his mourning clothes are not simply an affectation:

> But I have that within which passes show –
> These but the trappings and the suits of woe.

- images which concentrate on something which is healthy becoming diseased and decaying. This links up with the creeping corruption in the court of Elsinore. These are first introduced by Hamlet as he describes how his world seems to him (more accurately than he realises at this point):

> 'tis an unweeded garden,
> That grows to seed; things rank and gross in nature
> Possess it merely.

(Act 1, scene 2, 137–9)

- images which concentrate on the theatre and performance. These are often used to reflect Hamlet's perception of his role(s). In particular they emphasise the interplay between acting in the sense of performing and acting in the sense of doing, not just in relation to Hamlet, but to all the characters in the play. The words 'act', 'play' and 'perform' recur throughout **Hamlet** and link up different situations. Watch out for them! An example from Act 1 is when Hamlet is telling his mother that his grief for his fathers death is deeper than the mere outwardly visible signs of it:

> These, indeed, seem;
> For they are actions that a man might play;

(Act 1, scene 2, lines 85–6)

- images which concentrate on ears and hearing. Although these are less frequent than those mentioned above, they are important in contributing to the exploration of language as an instrument of power. The series of images is closely fused with the plot at the outset when we are given a detailed description of how old Hamlet is poisoned in the ear. The Ghost itself makes the link with the way language can be abused when it says:

> . . . so the whole ear of Denmark
> Is by a forged process of my death
> Rankly abus'd.
>
> (Act I, scene 5, lines 41–3)

By repeating these images in different contexts throughout the play, connected themes are emphasised and developed. Remember however, that the fact that one thing is being compared to another may say as much about the person making the comparison as the things compared.

Go through the Act again, noting down images that fit into these categories. As you discover each new one, think about how its meaning is enriched by the previous uses of this thread of imagery. Keep your list to add to and discuss as the play develops.

Are there any other images that seemed particularly powerful to you in this Act?

Act 2

Check your knowledge of Act 2

- What is Polonius asking Reynaldo to do in the first part of scene 1?
- How does Ophelia describe Hamlet to her father, and what does Polonius decide to do?
- What do Claudius and Gertrude ask Rosencrantz and Guildenstern to do in the first thirty-nine lines of scene 2?
- What do we learn of the political situation between Denmark and Norway?
- What letter does Polonius read to Gertrude and Claudius?
- Does Hamlet find out that Rosencrantz and Guildenstern have been sent by the king?
- What is described in the speech that Hamlet asks the First Player to perform and what does Hamlet then ask the players to do?
- On what course of action does Hamlet say he has decided at the end of his soliloquy?

Questioning the text in Act 2

1 Discuss with a partner your reactions to hearing of Polonius's plans and the methods he uses to carry out his spying in scene 1, lines 1–79. Then look at the readings of his speech below.

Polonius is acting as:

- a concerned father whose methods are quite justifiable;
- a well-meaning but confused and misguided father;
- a repressive and untrusting father, who is intruding on his son's privacy;
- the first example in this Act and the next of widespread spying. This shows the extent of the breakdown of trust on a domestic and political level at Elsinore.

With careful reference to the text, consider which of the readings could be seen as valid. (There could be more than one.) Then in groups of three (two to take parts and one to direct) present these lines according to a reading you have chosen as a group.

2 'By indirections find directions out' (Act 2, scene 1, line 69).

Elsinore is full of people spying and reporting on other people. There are several examples throughout this Act. Write down as many examples as you can find, and discuss what overall effect is built up.

3 Shakespeare chose not to dramatise two important events in Hamlet's relationship with Ophelia:

- his visit to her room, described by her in scene 1, lines 83–108;
- the writing and presentation of Hamlet's love-letter to Ophelia, read out by Polonius in scene 2, lines 116–31.

Think about why Shakespeare chose to present Hamlet's behaviour in this way. Consider in particular how our view of Ophelia, Polonius and Hamlet could be affected by the manner in which these events are reported.

4. Look back at Rosencrantz and Guildenstern's conversations with Hamlet, Claudius and Gertrude. How would you assess their motives for spying? Were they acting in:

- Hamlet's best interest?
- their own self-interest?
- their roles as unquestioning loyal servants of the king?

Could each of these three readings be validly constructed from the text? Are there any other possible motives for their actions?

Imagine Rosencrantz and Guildenstern are talking about their meeting with Hamlet in Act 2, scene 2, lines 233–386. In pairs, role-play their conversation.

5. With what characters and situations in **Hamlet** are the following in the First Player's speech (Act 2, scene 2, lines 473–539) linked?

- Pyrrhus and his revenge;
- the killing of Priam;
- Hecuba and her reaction.

Either as a simple discussion, or as a short interview with a reincarnated Shakespeare, discuss:

- why the playwright gives Hamlet rather than the Player the first lines describing Pyrrhus;
- whether we are invited to pass any moral judgement on the characters in the mythical story, in particular Pyrrhus and his revenge.

6. 'Though this be madness, yet there is method in't' (Act 2, scene 2, lines 220–1).

Hamlet said in Act I, scene 5, lines 189–90 that he might 'think meet To put an antic disposition on'. Identify those passages in Act 2, scene 2 where he could be described as mad. In each case, with close reference to the text, discuss what could be seen as going on by considering the following possibilities:

- Hamlet is genuinely mad;

- Hamlet (and Shakespeare through him) is using the cover of madness to make satirical comments about the corrupt world about him. In this scene he is fulfilling one of the roles of the Fool often used by Shakespeare (see 'Before reading the play', assignment 11).

- Hamlet's madness acts as a cover for the emotional disturbance he is feeling, and it gives him time to explore and express his changing views of the world.

Is there a difference between what is going on here in Act 2, scene 2, and the madness in the scene described by Ophelia in scene 1, lines 83–108?

7 Re-read Hamlet's soliloquy (Act 2, scene 2, lines 569–628) closely. Then, in the form of a box plan, show how the thoughts in it could be seen as developing. You might begin like this:

A denunciation of himself contrasting the First Player's attitude to revenge with his own	lines 570–92

Creates a critical audience who express the contempt that he feels for his own cowardice, reinforcing the image of himself as an actor unable to act	lines 592–7

As the soliloquy develops, the focus of Hamlet's thoughts changes quickly; some of your boxes may only describe a line or two.

When you have completed this, cut up your boxes and mix them up. Now see if a partner can re-assemble them into the right order and identify which lines are explained by which box. Stick your boxes back onto a piece of paper in the correct order for later reference.

8 Here are some questions on acting to unpick in groups.

- Think about the verb 'to act'. What different meanings does it have?

- Where can you see these meanings interacting in Hamlet's soliloquy at the end of the act (Act 2, scene 2, lines 569–628). How are other theatrical metaphors such as 'act', 'perform' and 'stage' used in this speech?
- In what sense does the Player act but not act?
- In what senses does Hamlet act but not act?
- What roles has Hamlet felt the pressure of so far in the play?
- In what sense is his madness an act?
- Who else is acting (in the sense of pretending) in the play?
- Who else could be seen as having to play a role imposed on them?

9 Continue to note down images that develop the threads of imagery that you established and discussed whilst doing assignment 14 on Act 1.

10 A mixture of verse and prose is used in this Act. Can you explain why Shakespeare changed where he did?

Act 3

Check your knowledge of Act 3

- Is Rosencrantz and Guildenstern's account of their conversation with Hamlet accurate?
- Who spies on Ophelia and Hamlet, and what is their reaction to the conversation they overhear?
- What does the dumb-show represent?
- What happens in the main part of 'The Murder of Gonzago'?
- At what point does Claudius ask for light?
- What message do Rosencrantz and Guildenstern and then Polonius bring to Hamlet?
- What does Claudius do when left alone in scene 3?

● What does Hamlet decide to do when he sees him praying?

● What happens to Polonius in scene 4?

● Why does the Ghost say he appears in this scene?

Questioning the text in Act 3

☐ Discuss in what ways the opening of this Act can be compared to the opening of the two scenes in Act 2. Look back at your answer to assignment 2 in 'Questioning the text in Act 2' to help you.

☐ Below are some general descriptions that might be used for Hamlet's soliloquies in Acts 1 and 2 and 'To be or not to be . . . ' in Act 3, scene 1. Put a tick by the descriptions you feel apply to 'To be or not to be . . . .

- an explosion of feelings suppressed when with others;
- Hamlet's views on another character;
- an invitation to a debate with the audience;
- a decision-making process which carries the plot forward;
- a process of self-questioning;
- a means of building Hamlet's character for the audience;
- an exploration of ideas;
- a means of conveying information about events in the play;
- a reaction to immediately preceding events;
- a reflection arising from his predicament, but more general in its expression and application;
- a pursuit of one subject rather than a number;
- a reflection uninterrupted by exclamations or rhetorical outbursts;
- a mixture of sentence length and overall pace, suggesting a confused and disturbed state of mind;
- a reflection from Hamlet the Malcontent;
- Hamlet trying on the role of Revenger.

Now choose a diagrammatic form to represent the development of ideas in the soliloquy.

Alternatively, write a series of questions with a partner designed to guide another pair in looking at the important ideas in the 'To be or not to be . . .' soliloquy. Exchange your questions and then see if the pair you swapped with have answered in the way you had expected.

Write an essay on the differences between this soliloquy and one of those which have preceded it.

3 Remind yourself of the scenes in which Ophelia has appeared in the play so far with Laertes and Polonius. Now look again at Act 3, scene 1, lines 95–161 and Act 3, scene 2, lines 115–58 and 252–7.

Make three columns alongside the list below, headed **Hamlet**, **Laertes** and **Polonius**. For each statement put a tick or cross in each column depending on whether you think it applies to each man's treatment of Ophelia.

- he tells her what she should think;
- he tells her what she must do;
- he does not consider her feelings as they talk;
- he does consider her feelings as they talk;
- he is acting in her best interest;
- he thinks he is acting in her best interest;
- he assumes her opinions are of little value;
- he thinks all young women are in danger from men;
- he uses his position of authority to force her into submission;
- he is merely responding to her treatment of him;
- if asked, he would say he loved her.

Now give a talk or write a essay on the grounds for comparison and contrast that can be found between the three men's treatment of Ophelia.

4 Imagine Ophelia kept a diary in which she wrote in great detail of the events in scene 1, lines 95–161 . What would she write about her own and Hamlet's behaviour? After you have written your diary

entry, annotate it giving line numbers alongside showing from where you have drawn the evidence for your writing.

Now compare your diaries in small groups to see how similar your readings of the scene are. Are there a range of interpretations available which affect the way we see Hamlet and Ophelia?

5 Read the following interpretations of Claudius in Act 3, scene 3, line 39–101 and discuss whether both could be seen as valid:

- Claudius invites some sympathy, along with our condemnation of his crime, as a man trying to pray out of a sincere wish to repent. He has already shown in the previous scene that his conscience is 'lashed'. He can't pray, because he is aware of the magnitude of his crime. He has shown good qualities as an effective leader. The fact that he is defenceless before Hamlet also adds to the picture of a man who is not entirely the 'Remorseless, treacherous, lecherous, kindless villain' condemned by Hamlet in Act 2, scene 2, line 603.

- Claudius is trying to pray out of fear for himself. He fails, as he admits in the final rhyming couplet of the scene, because he is not prepared to renounce what he has acquired through his crime. He is only spared from death because of Hamlet's moral dilemmas. Any qualities of kingship seen earlier are always undercut by his hypocrisy and manipulation of others.

In 'Questioning the text in Act 1', assignment 8, you compared Claudius and old Hamlet. Now you have seen more of Claudius, how does the contrast Hamlet drew in Act 1, scene 2, and goes on to reinforce in Act 3, scene 4, appear? Is it a judgement that Shakespeare is inviting us to share without question?

Consider in this light why Shakespeare chooses to include Rosencrantz and Guildenstern's remarks on the importance of the king (in Act 3, scene 3, lines 9–11 and 14–24) at this particular point. Is this passage simply an ironic comment on Claudius, or is Shakespeare posing questions about the importance of kingship and what makes a good king?

[6] In Hamlet's final speech in scene 3, he may be seen as the ruthless Revenger held back only by the thought of finding a fuller vengeance when the king is not at prayer. Other critics have suggested Hamlet is unwittingly revealing his wish not to play this role by fabricating excuses. Discuss whether both readings are equally valid.

[7] Imagine Gertrude kept a diary in which she wrote in great detail of the events in scene 4. What would she write about her own and Hamlet's behaviour? After you have written your diary entry, annotate it giving line numbers alongside showing from where you have drawn the evidence for your writing.

Now compare your diaries in small groups to see how similar your readings of the scene are. Are there a range of interpretations available which affect the way we see Hamlet and Gertrude?

[8] Read through the Act again to examine the imagery used. In what way are the threads established in 'Questioning the text in Act 1', assignment 14 continued? Remember that the use of images reflects on the speaker as well as the situation described. For example, in scene 4, does the imagery used by Hamlet to describe his mother's behaviour tell us more about Hamlet's perception of his parents than offering us a trustworthy description and assessment of them?

Act 4

Check your knowledge of Act 4

- What is Claudius's first thought on hearing of Polonius's death?
- What does he decide to do?
- What is Fortinbras doing in Denmark?
- What has changed about Ophelia's behaviour?
- Why has Laertes returned to Denmark?
- What is the mob with Laertes demanding?

- What does Hamlet's letter to Horatio describe?
- What plan does Claudius unfold to Laertes to gain revenge on Hamlet?
- How did Ophelia die?

Questioning the text in Act 4

1 Gertrude simply describes Hamlet as 'Mad' and 'lawless' at the beginning of the first scene of this Act. Why do you think Shakespeare did not give Gertrude more space to describe the reality of the closet scene and its effect on her either to Claudius or on her own? Consider the responses to this question below.

- Gertrude's interpretation of events has changed: she no longer sees what she has done as a problem, and there is no need to discuss it;
- Gertrude wishes to protect her son although she may not agree with him;
- Gertrude has been very affected by the scene and wishes to protect herself in her confusion;
- Gertrude wishes to protect Claudius from Hamlet's attitude to him;
- Gertrude's feelings and thoughts were not valued in the society of this play;
- Gertrude's feelings and thoughts were not valued in the society of Shakespeare's time.

Discuss on what basis you would decide which of these interpretations you would choose.

Does the Queen's comment in scene 5 of this Act (lines 18–21) and her wish not to see Ophelia (scene 5, line 1) make any difference to possible readings of this earlier interlude?

2 Read scene 4 in this Act again and:
- note down as many parallels as you can between Fortinbras and Hamlet;

- consider whether we are invited to see Fortinbras in the same way that Hamlet does;

- compare Hamlet's soliloquy (lines 34–68) to the one in Act 2, scene 2, lines 570–628. Think about the ideas and Hamlet's attitude to his situation as you do so.

A number of productions of **Hamlet** have cut Fortinbras from the script. Write a letter to a director who is proposing to do this defending his inclusion (using your knowledge of the play so far). Outline clearly the reasons for your argument. You could also write the director's reply in which he or she justifies their proposals.

3 Below are some questions for discussion as a whole class after reading scene 4 in which Hamlet describes his revenge as 'dull' and that he has 'let all sleep'.

- What reasons has he put forward in the play so far for his delay? Look at Act 2, scene 2, lines 621–6 and Act 3, scene 3, lines 76–82. In this a complete explanation for his lack of action?

- Is there any evidence that he has faced practical difficulties in attempting to kill Claudius?

- What elements in his character might account for his inaction?

4 Critics disagree in their interpretations of how Ophelia's madness reflects on her character and her relationship with Hamlet. Read what she says and sings in scene 5, and consider the possibilities below.

- Ophelia is an innocent young girl. Her madness is the tragic breakdown of a fragile personality faced by a situation with which she is unable to cope.

- Ophelia's identity, including her sexuality, has been repressed by the pressures of her father and the male-dominated society she lives in to be 'pure'. This leads to and is revealed in her madness.

- Ophelia's madness shows her in her true nature: a sexually-aware and experienced woman who has been unable to express her true feelings.

Write two contrasting medical reports on Ophelia's condition using her songs and chatter as evidence.

5 Look at Claudius's reaction to seeing Ophelia mad in scene 5 and the speech in which he expresses his feelings to Gertrude (lines 76–97). Look also at his description of his concern for Gertrude in scene 7, lines 13–18. Now discuss the following question.

How can these speeches, and consequently Claudius's character, be read in different ways, depending on the different level of sincerity one attaches to them?

Imagine you are an actor playing Claudius. You are explaining to a friend how you are going to deliver these speeches. What would you say?

6 Look back at the comparisons you made between Laertes and Hamlet in 'Questioning the text in Act 1', assignment 13. What would you add to them after reading Act 4?

7 Discuss the claim that Ophelia's entrance in scene 5 and the description of her death in scene 7 are very carefully timed for maximum dramatic effectiveness.

8 Re-read Gertrude's description of the death of Ophelia (scene 7, lines 184–201). Below are some questions to think about, discuss and report back on.

- Why is Gertrude given this speech?
- Why is it written in this descriptive and vivid way?
- Why do its sentence lengths and rhythm suggest little emotion in its delivery? How could we read the effect of Ophelia's death on Gertrude?

Act 5

Check your knowledge of Act 5

- Are the gravediggers aware whose grave is being dug and the manner of her death?
- Which occupations does Hamlet suggest for the first two skulls that are thrown up?
- Who was Yorick?
- Where do Hamlet and Laertes fight until they are separated?
- What does Hamlet tell Horatio of Rosencrantz and Guildenstern's fate?
- What information does Osric bring?
- What exchange takes place between Hamlet and Laertes before they fence?
- How do each of the four main characters die?
- What role does Hamlet assign to Horatio at the end?
- What role does Fortinbras assume at the end?

Questioning the text in Act 5

What do you think was Shakespeare's intention behind the inclusion of the gravediggers' scene? Imagine you could conduct an interview with the playwright to find some answers to this question. Before going ahead with your role-play in pairs, discuss the possibilities below.

- They provide comic relief.
- They build up suspense before the final tragedy unfolds, so tension is held and increased.
- We see Ophelia's death and Hamlet's departure for England through the eyes of outsiders to the court.
- The gravediggers emphasise in their profession and their comments on it the universality of death and its levelling of all, whatever one's station in life. This prepares us for the final climax.

- The gravediggers show Hamlet's increased awareness and acceptance of this.
- As part of the world outside the court, the gravediggers provide a different perspective on Elsinore. It is beginning to be seen from a distance; we will move on beyond it by the end of the play.
- We learn that one of the gravediggers began work on the day Hamlet was born. This gives us a sense of Hamlet being overshadowed and enveloped by death.
- Time for scene shifting and costume changes.

Are there any other functions to this scene?

2   'I lov'd Ophelia ... I'll rant as well as thou.' Discuss how we should read this claim of Hamlet's by considering the possible readings below.

- It is a realisation for the first time of the truth for Hamlet.
- It is a public declaration of something he has always known that he felt.
- It is an expression of commitment to something, a reaction against the gravediggers' concentration on death and decay.
- It is less to do with his feelings for Ophelia than his desire not to be outfaced by Laertes.
- It shows once again Hamlet's preoccupation with words and acting. It is the manner in which Laertes' grief is expressed that prompts Hamlet's reaction and it is this that he wishes to rival.
- Its sincerity provides a contrast to Laertes' 'ranting'.

3 Discuss with a small group what your first reactions were to Hamlet's treatment of Rosencrantz and Guildenstern. Then read through these possible interpretations and discuss how near they were to your own.

- Hamlet showed a new commitment to action and an ability to think quickly when needed.

- Rosencrantz and Guildenstern deserved their fate. Therefore Hamlet's action can be excused.
- Hamlet's behaviour was arrogant and ruthless.
- It shows how subordinates can be swallowed up in a power struggle beyond their understanding or control.
- It shows how evil spreads. Hamlet has been unable to remain untainted.

[4] After Hamlet talks of the fate of Rosencrantz and Guildenstern to Horatio he mentions Laertes and says he is sorry for his earlier behaviour:

> For by the image of my cause I see
> The portraiture of his. I'll court his favours.
>
> (Act 5, scene 2, lines 82–3)

Later, Hamlet asks for Laertes' pardon (Act 5, scene I lines 228–46). Imagine you are Hamlet. Write down all the thoughts going through your mind as the court enters before you speak. Think carefully before you start whether you see the speech as sincere or manipulative. Are both readings possible, and on what basis might you chose one rather than the other?

[5] Imagine that a director is considering cutting Osric at the last moment from her production of the play. You are the actor who is ready to play him. Role-play a conversation with the director in which you try to defend his indispensability while the director states her case for dropping the character.

Before you start, discuss the following questions in relation to Osric:

- Does he advance the plot?
- Does he provide comic relief?
- Does he provide an extreme example of the way language is used to misrepresent and confuse?
- Does he build up tension as we approach the climax of the play?

- Does he show us that Hamlet's wit and enjoyment of ideas remain unaffected by his other preoccupations?

6 Hamlet's attitude seems to have undergone a change in this Act. In small groups, discuss where you would point to for evidence of this change and how you would describe it. Look at the following lines in particular:

- Act 5, scene 2, lines 10–11
- Act 5, scene 2, lines 221–6

Discuss what you think Hamlet means by 'divinity' and 'special providence' and whether this attitude can be seen as a strength or a weakness. Here are some positions that critics in the past have adopted which you can debate in your discussion:

- Hamlet has adopted a new-found Christianity, patience and humility.
- Hamlet is now deferring to a higher controlling power, but it is vague and not specifically religious.
- Hamlet has given up responsibility for his actions, and this leads to his destruction.
- Hamlet is recognising that the moral dilemma he has – that to avenge a murder, he must become a murderer – is insoluble, and he has decided simply to accept whatever hand fate deals him.

Do you think it matters for the dramatic impact of the final build-up that there is little explanation of the reasons for any change in Hamlet?

7 With a partner, take the short exchange between Claudius and Gertrude in Act 5, scene 2, lines 306–8 and try acting it out in different ways depending on whether you want to emphasise Claudius's concern primarily for Gertrude or himself.

Then look at what Claudius has to say between Gertrude taking the drink and actually dying. Does his behaviour affect your choice of readings?

8 All the deaths involve poison. How could this be seen as particularly appropriate, given the threads of imagery you have been following throughout the play? Discuss this as a class.

9 Two critics have written about the final moments of the play like this. Would you agree with one rather than the other or did you have a different response altogether?

> *The scene in which Hamlet, Laertes, Gertrude and Claudius die is in itself almost a play-within-a-play . . . But far from being inevitable, far from us having the sense of a fated event working its way out, it is a shambles. It is a mess. It is all about 'purposes mistook fall'n on th' inventors' heads'. Hamlet cannot even kill Claudius cleanly and singly. He has to, as it were, kill him twice, with poison and with stabbing. The single act which should balance out everything becomes double. Nothing will work out as it should, nothing will stick to its place in the script.*
>
> *Even with his death, Hamlet has achieved nothing. We are in a truly tragic world, left with only the straw man, the man who will die for a straw and is puffed up with ambition, who will countenance 'The imminent death of twenty thousand men' for the sake of 'a fantasy and trick of fame'. Fortinbras, the man who sends thousands to their slaughter for no good reason, is hardly someone to make a single, individual death meaningful. He is the ultimate image of Hamlet's failure.*
>
> Fintan O'Toole, **No More Heroes**

> *The sudden huddle of violent events is in itself effective after the long delays of plot and counterplot . . .*
>
> *For finally he has not failed. The wrong to be righted led him to no such gallant adventure as his father or this hero (Fortinbras), whose prowess he so envied, would have confidently taken in hand. It was a cancerous wrong – 'carnal, bloody and unnatural . . . ' – eating into the sanctities of life and his faith in them. But at the cost of his life he has righted it at last; and Fortinbras comes to a heritage purged of evil.*
>
> Harley Granville-Barker, **Prefaces to Shakespeare**

Consider what sort of different stagings might be used to reflect the different values these two approaches choose to emphasise. You will need to think about delivery of words, movement, costume and setting. In groups try staging the ending in different ways according to different readings.

After reading

Plot

1. Write a series of true and false statements about the situations in the play. Test a partner as to which is which.

2. In groups, take one act each and try to present it in a short series of silent tableaux. See if the other groups agree with your choice of tableaux as a fair representation of the act.

3. The plot of **Hamlet** was developed from a Danish legend which Saxo Grammaticus first wrote down as **Amleth** in the thirteenth century and which was retold by Belleforest in his **Histoires Tragiques** in the sixteenth century. Find a summary of the plot of **Amleth** and discuss or write about what has been changed, added or omitted by Shakespeare.

4. How would the plot of the play be affected if one of the following characters were omitted: Polonius, Laertes, Fortinbras, Rosencrantz and Guildenstern (as a pair).

5. As you read or watched the play what did you find were the moments of greatest tension? Discuss your thoughts with a partner or group. Were these moments different from those you expected when looking at assignment 2 on plot, in 'Before reading the play', page 392.

Character

Below are sequences of work for each of the major characters in the play. At the end of this section there is a Character assignment which can be completed in relation to any of the characters after you have carried out the more specific tasks outlined below.

Hamlet

🗓 If you find problems in sorting out Hamlet's character, don't worry – you are not the first! Many critics have disagreed in their estimation of the man. Here are a few examples:

> *A beautiful, pure, noble and most moral nature, without the strength of nerve which makes the hero, sinks beneath a burden which it can neither bear nor throw off.*
>
> Goethe

> *I despise Hamlet. He is a slob, a talker, an analyser, a rationaliser. Like the parlour liberal or the paralysed intellectual, he can describe every facet of a problem, yet never pull his finger out. Is Hamlet a coward, as he himself suggests, or simply a poseur, a frustrated actor who plays the scholar, the courtier and the soldier as an actor (a very bad actor) assumes a variety of different roles?*
>
> Charles Marowitz

> *. . . he is also a childish creature full of tantrums and resentments who, in a purely Freudian way, is reluctant to kill the object he seems to hate because by keeping Claudius, the object of his hatred, alive he can ignore the person he might have loathed even more – his father . . . Hamlet can then indulge in self deluding fantasies of affection for the dead father.*
>
> Jonathan Miller

> *Hamlet is a man of painful sensitivity, tortured by the crassness of the world he sees and by the crudities of the action demanded of him.*
>
> F. Richmond

> *Hamlet gives dignity to the human race by showing of what*
> *feats it is capable: he extends the bounds of experience for others*
> *and enhances their appreciation of life by the example of his*
> *abundant vitality.*
>
> C. M. Bowra

> *I prefer the youth, deeply involved in politics, rid of illusions,*
> *sarcastic, passionate and brutal . . . Action, not reflection, is his*
> *forte. He is wild and drunk with indignation . . . 'To be' means for*
> *him to revenge his father and assassinate the King; while 'not to be'*
> *means – give up the fight.*
>
> Jan Kott

How can they differ so much? Hamlet does exhibit a range of behaviour as the descriptions below suggest by their arrangement in contradictory pairs. Can you find episodes in the text which could be used to support these descriptions? You may find some episodes which could be used to support both sides of the contradictory pair, depending on your reading of the text at this point.

- decisive / indecisive
- uses words to get at the truth / uses words to hide the truth
- obsessed with death / convinced of the importance of acting
- cynical / idealistic
- thinks clearly and logically / thinks in a confused and contorted way
- philosopher / man of action
- admires vengeful characters / uneasy with the role of the revenger
- a good friend / a betrayer of friends
- perceptive to others' situations / insensitive to others' situations
- a man unwilling to take the roles offered to him / a man searching for a role
- self-centred / generous
- brave / cowardly
- only acts after much deliberation / impetuous

Given these different aspects, how does one arrive at a coherent reading of the character? Discuss the possibilities below:

- Instead of trying to build a unified picture of Hamlet through character analysis, one can see him as embodying certain situations and conflicts Shakespeare wished to explore.
- Like all human beings, Hamlet is a complex personality with many contradictory elements in his character.
- Shakespeare has offered us the raw material for many different characterisations of Hamlet.

2 Now in pairs, choose two of the critics' quotations from assignment I above. Try to imagine how each critic would have interpreted the following aspects and episodes in the play to lead to the opinions they express.

- Hamlet's killing of Polonius;
- the 'closet' scene with Gertrude;
- Hamlet's treatment of Ophelia;
- his decision not to kill the praying Claudius;
- his relationship with the Ghost;
- his death;
- Hamlet compared and contrasted to Laertes and Fortinbras.

Claudius

1 Look at the possible descriptions of Claudius below:

evil	a very skilful speech-maker
ambitious	perceptive
quick-thinking and decisive	remorseless
pitiful	manipulative
conscience-ridden	caring towards Gertrude
an ineffective king	an efficient, diplomatic king

Which of the quotations below would you use to illustrate the descriptions above? Remember to consider who is the speaker and the context in which the words are spoken.

The King doth wake to-night and takes his rouse,
Keeps wassail, and the swagg'ring up-spring reels,

(Act I, scene 4, lines 9–10)

Though yet of Hamlet . . .
        . . . For all, our thanks.

(Act I, scene 2, lines I–16)

O villain, villain, smiling, damned villain!

(Act I, scene 5, line 112)

She is so conjunctive to my life and soul
That, as the star moves not but in his sphere,
I could not but by her.

(Act 4, scene 7, lines 16–18)

I have in quick determination
Thus set it down: he shall with speed to England

(Act 3, scene 1, lines 180–1)

My crown, mine own ambition, and my queen.

(Act 3, scene 3, line 58)

Love! His affections do not that way tend;
Nor what he spake, though it lack'd form a little,
Was not like madness.

(Act 3, scene 1, lines 174–6)

HAMLET
    How does the Queen?

CLAUDIUS
    She swoons to see them bleed.

(Act 5, scene 2, lines 327–8)

O, my offence is rank, it smells to heaven;

(Act 3, scene 3, line 39)

                . . .I will work him
To an exploit now ripe in my device,
Under the which he shall not choose but fall;

(Act 4, scene 7, lines 71–4)

O Gertrude, Gertrude!
When sorrows come, they come not single spies,
But in battalions!

(Act 4, scene 5, lines 78–80)

This business is well ended.

(Act 2, scene 2, line 91)

Did you differ in your opinions in matching any of these? If so, discuss your differences and the reasons for them.

Ophelia

1. Make a list by brainstorming for all the words that come into your mind when you think of Ophelia. Share your list with a partner and discuss any areas of difference.

2. Make a list of what other people say about Ophelia, particularly in Act 1, scene 3; Act 3, scene 1; Act 4, scene 7; and Act 5, scene 2.

   For each comment consider who is speaking about her and in what context. Are we as the audience invited to share their assessments?

3. Below is a list of the scenes in which Ophelia appears. In pairs, read out each set of lines twice: the first time one partner should read Ophelia in the interpretation offered by one of the descriptions; the second time the other partner takes their turn to read Ophelia in the light of the alternative approach. After each set of lines discuss:

   - whether one reading seemed more appropriate than the other and if so why;
   - what other readings there might be;
   - how the presentation of the other characters had to change.

   Act 1, scene 3, lines 1–55: meek / spirited

   Act 1, scene 3, lines 93–141: submissive / independent and simply pretending to obey at the end

   Act 2, scene 1, lines 80–108: too distraught to be able to reflect

427

on the situation for herself / calm, but concerned and anxious to discuss the matter with her father

Act 3, scene 1, lines 95–173: confused and subservient / saddened but forthright and independent in her answers

Act 3, scene 2, lines 117-33: shocked and upset / trying to hold her own.

4 Finally look at Act 4, scene 5, lines 22–74 and 177–211. What does Ophelia's madness reveal about Hamlet and Polonius? (See 'Questioning the text in Act 4', assignment 4.)

Gertrude

1 For the most part, Gertrude is only described by Hamlet and the Ghost while Claudius offers a few comments. Go through these scenes looking at how she is described by these three characters.

- Act 1, scenes 2 and 5
- Act 3, scene 4
- Act 4, scene 7

Now discuss whether we are invited to share Hamlet's and the Ghost's condemnation of her behaviour.

2 What can we learn about her from her own words? Discuss the questions below, which should help you to construct some readings of her behaviour.

- In Act 1, scene 2, are lines 73–4 considerate or insensitive and trite?

- Why does she not refer to her own bereavement in Act 1, scene 2?

- In Act 2, scene 2, do lines 59–60 suggest an innocence or a knowledge of Claudius's crime?

- In Act 3, scene 1, are lines 43–7 said with real concern, or a certain superficial sentimentality?

- In Act 3, scene 2, is line 237 simply a comment on the play's style, or does it imply pangs of conscience?

- In the light of your discussions so far, what readings would you offer of Act 3, scene 4?
- In Act 4, scene 5, lines 18–21, do Gertrude's lines represent a development in her character?
- In Act 4, scene 7, lines 184–201, what contribution does this speech make to the construction of a reading of her character?
- In Act 5, scene 1, in lines 293–7, is Gertrude trying to protect Hamlet, or is she speaking as a less involved observer?
- In Act 5, scene 2, how could her last words be seen as contributing to different readings of her?

3. Gertrude is often left silent by Shakespeare, for example, after Claudius's speech in Act 4, scene 5, lines 76–97. Why do you think this is?

4. Having discussed these questions, conduct a group role-play in which you put Gertrude 'in the psychiatrist's chair' in order to look at what might lie behind her words, actions and silences on stage.

Gertrude and Ophelia

1. It is interesting that Gertrude and Ophelia are placed together as we hear Gertrude's guilty aside in Act 4, scene 5, lines 18–21. Ophelia enters and it is Gertrude who is the first person on stage to witness her madness. Do you think that as the only two women in the play they are set up to be compared?

- Is their combined presence here the linking up for the audience of two women who have both been scarred by their involvement in the action of the play or are they to be contrasted one as guilty, one as innocent?
- Is it in fact more important to see Gertrude as others saw her? Perhaps she is deliberately not given a rounded personality because she, like Ophelia, functions in other people's minds as a stereotypical image? Hamlet's 'Frailty, thy name is woman!'

(Act 1, scene 2, line 148) might invite our thoughts to take this direction.

Polonius

🔲 Below are a series of quotations and questions which point up some of the different approaches critics and actors have taken towards Polonius.

Remind yourselves of the context in which these lines are spoken and then discuss the questions below each extract. Remember texts can support a number of interpretations and they may ask questions rather than offer clear-cut character studies.

> The head is not more native to the heart,
> The hand more instrumental to the mouth,
> Than is the throne of Denmark to thy father.
>
> (Act I, scene 2, lines 47–9)

Is Claudius's comment to be taken as a true statement of how highly he values Polonius or simply a reflection of Claudius's wish to be popular and to set up Laertes as a sort of model for Hamlet, to whom he turns next?

> This above all – to thine own self be true,
> And it must follow, as the night the day,
> Thou canst not then be false to any man.
>
> (Act I, scene 3, lines 82–4)

Does this show banality, hypocrisy, grasping selfishness, or wisdom and kindness?

> Tender yourself more dearly;
> Or – not to crack the wind of the poor phrase,
> Running it thus – you'll tender me a fool.
>
> (Act I, scene 3, lines 112–14)

Are these the words of a repressive father who is worried primarily for his own position, a father whose main concern is his daughter's well-being or a father who is considering his family's position as a whole, which could be furthered if Ophelia plays her cards right with Hamlet?

Does his choice of imagery in these lines and the longer speech that follows influence possible readings?

> More matter with less art.
>
> (Act 2, scene 2, line 102)

Can you find examples where Polonius's use of language draws attention to itself? Consider how they could be described in a way which contributed to a more or less sympathetic reading of Polonius.

2   . . . a foolish prating knave.

> (Act 3, scene 4, line 234)

> The unseen good old man.
>
> (Act 4, scene 1, line 12)

These comments, although not necessarily the last words that their speakers would have to say about Polonius, summarise two interpretations of him. In pairs or small groups, using your discussion ideas, can you think of others?

Character assignment

1   Choose an interpretation of one of the central characters in **Hamlet**. Describe how, as director of a forthcoming production, you would want your actor to dress, move and speak to support your reading. You will need to make detailed reference to a number of scenes to give your actor a clear idea of what you would like. You may also need to indicate briefly how you are hoping to portray other characters with whom they interact, because the reading of one character will affect the others. Include in your answer what it is in the play as a whole that you want to emphasise which has lead to this interpretation.

Themes and ideas

1 Write down everything you can think of that *Hamlet* is about.

Compare and join your list with a partner's, then with another pair, then with a foursome and so on until the class as a whole has a collective list.

Looking at your list, is it possible to place the items in order of importance? As you have probably found, it is not easy!

2 Re-read Act 3, scene 1, lines 63–161. Which themes would you suggest are being explored? Discuss your thoughts with a partner and with the class. You should find that this section provides a good example of how the play can invite a wide variety of readings.

3 In small groups, choose different episodes from the play. Each group should see which themes could be read into their section of the text, and then report back to the class as a whole.

4 Certain emphases will be developed throughout the play. If a director wants to stress, for example, that the play is about the constantly war-like nature of power politics she or he might emphasise King Hamlet's war-like qualities, Fortinbras as a military leader, the nature of Laertes' return to Denmark or even the imagery of Hamlet's 'To be or not to be . . .' soliloquy.

What would a director emphasise if he or she wanted to see *Hamlet* as a play about:

- a man growing up?
- good and evil?
- a psychologically disturbed personality?
- politics and power?

5 Imagine you were directing the play. Explain to your assembled cast what you would like to emphasise and then how certain scenes would be performed to support this reading.

In performance

1 The play is too long to be performed in its entirety and what is cut will depend very much on what a director wishes to emphasise in the play. If, for example, Rosencrantz and Guildenstern were cut it might be more difficult to explore the themes of corruption in politics and the relationship of authority and obedience.

If, for practical reasons to do with the running length of the play, you were forced to cut about ten to twenty per cent of the text, where would you start to wield your axe? Having come up with a list of suggestions, compare your cuts with a partner's or share your ideas as a group.

2 The play is set throughout at Elsinore and almost entirely in the castle. What might the effect be of this concentration in the setting?

We are given no descriptive information about Elsinore. Take on the role of designer of a new production of the play. How would you choose to portray the inside of the castle? Would you choose a detailed set, which attempted to look like a specific place, or would you opt for a relatively bare stage? Would you set the play in the Dark Ages, the Renaissance, the present day or another time? Draw a plan of the stage and show what you would put on it, where, and why.

Give an example of how one or two specific scenes could exploit this set to reinforce the dramatic effect created by the actors. You might include in your description the lighting and props you would like to see.

3 In small groups, choose a scene or episode from the play and prepare a workshop performance of it to be presented to the rest of the class. Set, props and costume can be very simple or non-existent. The words should, if possible, be learned.

Before you start, jot down what are the main aspects of the scene that you want to communicate to the rest of the class. After the performance compare these notes with the impressions your audience gained. Did you succeed in your aims?

4 Write a review of a production of **Hamlet** you have seen either at the theatre, cinema or on video.

In your review you will need to tell your readers how the production approached the central concerns of the play and give your opinion on how far it succeeded. You will also need to comment on the set, costume, lighting, music and so on.

5 Imagine you have been commissioned to design a programme for a forthcoming production of **Hamlet**. It will need to provide information about the play and the actors at the same time as being visually appealing. Prepare this programme using the list below to help you plan its contents:

- cover design;
- brief plot summary;
- pictures / photographs of actors;
- some approaches to the themes of the play;
- photographs of this production.

Try to find copies of programmes from past productions of **Hamlet** and other plays, especially by the Royal Shakespeare Company or the Royal National Theatre, to inspire you.

Language

1 Below each question in this assignment is a question for discussion.

Suit the action to the word, the word to the action.

(Act 3, scene 2, lines 18–19)

- Where does Hamlet talk about the gap between speaking and doing?

. . . the candied tongue . . .

(Act 3, scene 2, line 65)

- Where do we see a gap between speaking and doing or thinking as a result of hypocrisy?

  > More matter with less art.
  >
  > (Act 2, scene 2, line 102)

- Can you find examples of how Osric, and to a lesser extent Polonius, parody the way the simple use of language as a tool of communication has become complicated and distorted?

  > The harlot's cheek, beautied with plast'ring art,
  > Is not more ugly to the thing that helps it
  > Than is my deed to my most painted word.
  >
  > (Act 3, scene 1, lines 58–60)

- Can you find other examples of imagery that is used to explore this manipulation of language? You should find that if you have completed the assignments on imagery in 'Questioning the text', your notes will help you here.

Finally, look at how important it is to the dying Hamlet that people are told the truth (as he sees it), and words are once again used honestly. Look at how this emerges in Hamlet's words to Horatio after Laertes' death.

Now write an essay exploring the following:

'Words, words, words': in what sense could language be seen as one of the principal areas of exploration in **Hamlet**?

2 In pairs, find different scenes in which both prose and blank verse are used. Suggest why Shakespeare changed where he did. Can you find examples where Hamlet speaks to the same person in prose and blank verse on different occasions? Suggest some reasons why. Share your thoughts with other pairs in the class.

In 'The Murder of Gonzago', a different sort of verse, made up of rhyming couplets is used. There is a heavy, rhetorical style of speech, the metre becomes much more regular and a single idea is often repeated a number of times in different ways. Look at Act 3, scene 2, lines 159–64 for a quick example.

Shakespeare may have used this style deliberately to encapsulate particular ideas that relate to the whole play's action and themes. Look particularly at the Player King's speech in lines 192–221 and discuss what these ideas are and the effect of them being expressed in this way.

3 Divide yourselves into four groups. Each group should take one of the four main threads of imagery that run through the play: these are images relating to disease and corruption, to appearance as opposed to reality, to ears and hearing and to the theatre and acting. (See 'Questioning the text in Act 1', assignment 14.)

Each group should prepare a presentation to the rest of the class. This should include:

- a list of all the places where these images occur which can be distributed to each member of the class for reference;
- an explanation of how the image is used in at least three places (remember to consider what it tells us about the speaker as well as the thing described);
- an explanation, using at least three examples, of how Shakespeare can deepen his meaning by using repeated images.

Now write an essay on Shakespeare's use of imagery in the play.

4 Re-read the following lines spoken by Hamlet:

- Act 3, scene 1, lines 63–72
- Act 3, scene 2, lines 369–78
- Act 3, scene 2, lines 393–405
- Act 5, scene 2, lines 221–6

Now choose one of these and turn it into modern English. The glossary will help you. Try to end with a version that still contains all the sense, and is understandable without notes.

Read through the two versions and decide what has been lost in your 'translation'. What is it that makes Shakespeare's use of language so skilful? Think carefully about sound, rhythm and choice of words.

Study questions

Many of the activities you have already completed in the Study programme will help you to answer the questions which come at the end of this section and many others that you might meet in examinations or as titles for coursework assignments. Before you begin work on them, consider these points about essay writing:

- The length and detail needed for your essay will depend to some extent upon the conditions under which it is written. These might be:

  a) as an assignment for coursework;

  b) as an answer in an open book examination;

  c) as an answer in an examination where texts are not permitted.

- In the case of a), you will usually be expected to write at a reasonable length (although there will almost always be a word limit) and you will have sufficient time to research your points and explore them in considerable detail within your essay. Drafting, re-drafting and proof-reading are all possible within the time given, and are desirable. Dictionaries, thesauruses and other reference works will all be of use to you.

- In the case of b), your time for writing will be restricted (work out how long you will have for each question *before* you go into the examination), but you will be able to take in a copy of the text. According to your board's regulations this might either be un-marked or annotated by yourself – *check the regulations.* It may seem a boon to have a text with you, but beware. Spending time flicking desperately through the text in search of quotations or references will always reduce the time available for writing (and thinking). You must make sure that you are *very* familiar with the text to take advantage of the book on your desk. Do not be tempted to put in quotations for quotations' sake: ask yourself whether each is necessary and relevant first.

- In the case of c), again your writing time is restricted and you will need to rely entirely on your memory of the text. For both c) and b) it is essential to use time effectively, but do *not* miss out the planning stage, and keep a piece of scrap paper handy to jot down ideas as they occur to you. Do not overrun your allocated time – it is often better to write less on, say, all four questions, than to write well on three but lose all marks for the fourth by not attempting it. If this means ending some questions in note form, this is usually acceptable to examiners, provided that your notes are clear and conclusive. Again, *check the regulations* and ask your teacher or tutor's advice before the exam.

- In all cases you should read the question carefully. If it includes a quotation, do not ignore it – use it in some way. Remember that you do not have to agree with statements in titles; you may have a strong argument against it and this will help you. If a title falls into several parts, break it up and deal with each part separately.

- Planning – note down the ideas you wish to develop and any references or quotations also relevant to the answer.

- Decide on a structure – it may be useful to think of a shape for your argument, perhaps in flow-chart form.

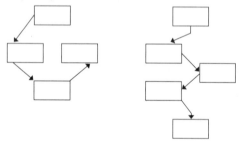

- Organise your notes and references into relevant sections (perhaps keeping to these for your paragraph divisions as you write) and consider how you will link each section to the next.

- Write, starting with a clear introduction setting out your approach or how you intend to tackle the question. Place the bulk of your arguments in the middle of the essay. The conclusion is vital – add any further brief comments and refer back to the title. This will act as a check as to whether you have actually done what you set out to do.

The questions below may be used as coursework assignment titles or serve as revision essays.

1.
>   So shall you hear
>   Of carnal, bloody, and unnatural acts;
>   Of accidental judgments, casual slaughters;
>   Of deaths put on by cunning and forc'd cause;
>   And, in this upshot, purposes mistook
>   Fall'n on th' inventors' heads. . .

(Act 5, scene 2, lines 408–14)

How adequate a summary of the play is this?

2. '*Hamlet* is a political play before a psychological study.' Do you agree?

3. Do you find the plot of *Hamlet* a carefully constructed one?

4. How effectively do you think Shakespeare develops the theme of revenge in *Hamlet*?

5. 'If the dramas of Shakespeare were to be characterised, each by the particular excellence which distinguishes it from the rest, we must allow to the tragedy of *Hamlet* the praise of variety.' Do you agree with Johnson's assessment of *Hamlet*?

6. Do you think *Hamlet* is an exciting play?

7. 'Essentially the play is about the conflict between good and evil.' How fair is this statement as an assessment of *Hamlet*?

8. 'Elsinore is a blueprint for the corrupt political state.' How does Shakespeare construct a sense of the way in which Elsinore functions?

9. If you were an actor or a director, what particular problems do you think you would face in interpreting the role of Hamlet, and how

would you go about overcoming them?

10 Far from holding up the play's action, the soliloquies in **Hamlet** contribute to it: they are in the fullest sense dramatic. Discuss with close reference to the text.

11
> For he was likely, had he been put on,
> To have prov'd most royal;

(Act 5, scene 2, lines 427–8)

Does the play offer evidence to support this claim?

12 How does Hamlet's humour contribute to the interest of the play?

13 'It is difficult to construct a rounded character in Claudius. He seems to operate simply as a symbol of evil and a counter in the plot.' Do you agree?

14 'Thou wretched rash intruding fool' . . . 'The unseen good old man.' Consider these views of Polonius and outline his dramatic importance in the play.

15 What does Laertes contribute to the plot and themes of **Hamlet**?

16 'Hamlet's relationship with Gertrude is central to our understanding of his behaviour.' Discuss this statement.

17 In what ways do you feel Ophelia adds to the dramatic interest **Hamlet**?

18 Is it useful to compare Shakespeare's presentation of Gertrude and Ophelia as the only two women in the play?

19 Choose one scene from the play that you find particularly effective from the dramatic standpoint and explain why.

20 How would you assess **Hamlet**'s relevance to the audiences of today?

Pearson Education Limited
Edinburgh Gate, Harlow,
Essex CM20 2JE, England
and Associated Companies throughout the world.

First published 1993
Ninth impression 2000

Editorial material set in 10/12 point Gill Sans Light
Printed in Singapore (KKP)

ISBN 0 582 09720 7

The Publisher's policy is to use paper manufactured
from sustainable forests.

Acknowledgements

We are grateful to the following for permission to reproduce
photographs:
Donald Cooper (Photostage), pages 4, 160, 248 and 316;
Christopher Pearce (The Panic Pictures Library), page 90.

New Century Readers
Post-1914 Contemporary Fiction

Nina Bawden   *Granny the Pag*   0 582 32847 0
                    The Real Plato Jones   0 582 29254 9
Marjorie Darke   *A Question of Courage*   0 582 25395 0
Berlie Doherty   *Daughter of the Sea*   0 582 32845 4
                    The Snake-stone   0 582 31764 9
Josephine Feeney   *My Family and other Natural Disasters*   0 582 29262 X
Anne Fine   *The Tulip Touch*   0 582 31941 2
             Flour Babies   0 582 29259 X
             A Pack of Liars   0 582 29257 3
             The Book of the Banshee   0 582 29258 1
             Madame Doubtfire   0 582 29261 1
             Step by Wicked Step   0 582 29251 4
             Goggle Eyes   0 582 29260 3
Lesley Howarth   *Maphead*   0 582 29255 7
George Layton   *A Northern Childhood*   0 582 25404 3
Joan Lingard   *Lizzie's Leaving*   0 582 32846 2
                Night Fires   0 582 31967 6
Michelle Magorian   *Goodnight Mister Tom*   0 582 31965 X
Beverley Naidoo   *Journey to Jo'burg*   0 582 25402 7
Andrew Norriss   *Aquila*   0 582 36419 1
Catherine Sefton   *Along a Lonely Road*   0 582 29256 5
Robert Swindells   *A Serpent's Tooth*   0 582 31966 8
                    Follow a Shadow   0 582 31968 4
Robert Westall   *Urn Burial*   0 582 31964 1

Post-1914 Poetry

edited by Celeste Flower   *Poems 1*   0 582 25400 0
collected by John Agard   *Poems in my Earphone*   0 582 22587 6

Post-1914 Plays

Ad de Bont   *Mirad, a Boy from Bosnia*   0 582 24949 X
Anne Fine   *Bill's New Frock*   0 582 09556 5
Nigel Hinton   *Collision Course*   0 582 09555 7
Tony Robinson   *Maid Marian and her Merry Men*   0 582 09554 9
Kaye Umansky   *The Fwog Prince*   0 582 10156 5

Pre-1914

Charles Dickens   *Oliver Twist*   0 582 28729 4
varoius writers   *Twisters:stories from other centuries*   0 582 29253 0

New Longman Literature
Post-1914 Fiction

Susan Hill   *I'm the King of the Castle*   0 582 22173 0
   The Woman in Black   0 582 02660 1
   The Mist in the Mirror   0 582 25399 3
Aldous Huxley   *Brave New World*   0 582 06016 8
Robin Jenks   *The Cone-Gatherers*   0 582 06017 6
Doris Lessing   *The Fifth Child*   0 582 06021 4
Joan Lindsay   *Picnic at Hanging Rock*   0 582 08174 2
Bernard MacLaverty   *Lamb*   0 582 06557 7
Brian Moore   *Lies of Silence*   0 582 08170 X
George Orwell   *Animal Farm*   0 582 06010 9
F Scott Fitzgerald   *The Great Gatsby*   0 582 06023 0
Robert Swindells   *Daz 4 Zoe*   0 582 30243 9
Anne Tyler   *A Slipping-Down Life*   0 582 29247 6
Virginia Woolf   *To the Lighthouse*   0 582 09714 2

Post-1914 Short Stories

Angelou, Goodison, Senior & Walker   *Quartet of Stories*   0 582 28730 8
Stan Barstow   *The Human Element and Other Stories*   0 582 23369 0
Roald Dahl   *A Roald Dahl Selection*   0 582 22281 8
selected by Geoff Barton   *Stories Old and New*   0 582 28931 9
selected by Madhu Bhinda   *Stories from Africa*   0 582 25393 4
   Stories from Asia   0 582 03922 3
selected by Celeste Flower   *Mystery and Horror*   0 582 28928 9
selected by Jane Christopher   *War Stories*   0 582 28927 0
selected by Susan Hill   *Ghost Stories*   0 582 02661 X
selected by Beverley Naidoo,   *Global Tales*   0 582 28929 7
Christine Donovan & Alun Hicks
selected by Andrew Whittle &   *Ten D H Lawrence Short Stories*   0 582 29249 2
Roy Blatchford

Post-1914 Poetry

collected & edited by Roy Blatchford   *Voices of the Great War*   0 582 29248 4
edited by George MacBeth   *Poetry 1900-1975*   0 582 35149 9
edited by Julia Markus & Paul Jordan   *Poems 2*   0 582 25401 9

Post-1914 Plays

Alan Ayckbourn   *Absent Friends*   0 582 30242 0
Terrence Rattigan   *The Winslow Boy*   0 582 06019 2
Jack Rosenthal   *P'Tang, Yang Kipperbang and other TV Plays*
   0 582 22389 X
Willy Russell   *Educating Rita*   0 582 06013 3
   Shirley Valentine   0 582 08173 4
selected by Geoff Barton   *Ten Short Plays*   0 582 25383 7
selected by Michael Marland   *Scenes from Plays*   0 582 25394 2
Peter Shaffer   *The Royal Hunt of the Sun*   0 582 06014 1
   Equus   0 582 09712 6
Bernard Shaw   *Pygmalion*   0 582 06015 X
   Saint Joan   0 582 07786 9
Sheridan, Richard Brinsley   *The Rivals/The School for Scandal*   0 582 25396 9